DK

POCKET
ENCYCLOPEDIA

MICROWAVE
COOKERY

DK

POCKET
ENCYCLOPEDIA

MICROWAVE COOKERY

Contributing editor
Sarah Brown

DORLING KINDERSLEY • LONDON

Sarah Brown has contributed only the vegetarian recipes
and information about vegetarian cookery in
The Pocket Encyclopedia of Microwave Cookery.
She is not responsible for any of the recipes or information
concerning meat or fish or their by-products.

First published in Great Britain in 1989
by Dorling Kindersley Limited,
9 Henrietta Street, London WC2E 8PS

Designed and edited by Swallow Books,
260 Pentonville Road, London N1 9JY

British Library Cataloguing in Publication Data

DK pocket encyclopedia, microwave
cookery
1. Brown, Sarah
1. Food: Dishes prepared using
microwave ovens – Recipes
641.5′882
ISBN 0-86318-344-1

Printed in Singapore by Kyodo-Shing Loong Printing
Industries Pte Ltd.

CONTENTS

Introduction 6

COOKING TIMES AND TECHNIQUES

Brassicas and leaves 8   Shoots and bulbs 11   Fruit vegetables 14
Pods and seeds 17   Roots and tubers 20   Fruit 23   Dried fruit 26
Nuts and seeds 27   Pulses 28   Mushrooms and seaweeds 29
Grains and cereals 30   Pasta 31   Flat fish 32   Round fish 34
Shellfish 37   Beef 38   Pork 40   Lamb 42
Poultry and game 44   Offal 46   Veal 48

RECIPES

Recipe guidelines 50   Soups and starters 51
Main courses
Fish and shellfish 71   Meat, poultry and game 84
Vegetable dishes 99
Vegetable accompaniments 115   Desserts 131
Sauces and preserves 147   Breads, cakes and biscuits 159

GETTING TO KNOW YOUR MICROWAVE

Converting recipes for the microwave 168
Cooking for one 170
Menu-planning 171
Microwave troubleshooting guide 172
Choosing a microwave oven 176
Understanding microwave ovens 181
Cleaning and maintaining your microwave oven 184
Microwave tools and equipment 186
Factors that affect microwave cooking 193
Microwave cooking techniques 196
The microwave and the freezer 204
Blanching fruit and vegetables for the freezer 210
Hints and tips 212   Glossary 215

Index 217

INTRODUCTION

To those new to microwaves, cooking without any source of direct heat is a strange concept which seems to entail a whole new set of rules. With a gadget like a food processor, for example, it's obvious what it will and will not do. With a microwave oven, however, you not only have to get used to a new piece of equipment, but also to an entirely new method of cooking.

In reality there is absolutely nothing difficult about it, but it does take some time to adjust initially. Techniques such as stirring, arranging and covering foods are all far more crucial in the microwave than in conventional cookery. For this reason this book includes a section on these techniques, on pages 196-203.

Timing is essential in microwave cookery. With some dishes it is vital to watch the seconds pass, while others can be left to stand and finish cooking until you are ready. This book starts with a comprehensive ingredients section which describes just how long you need to cook standard quantities of each. As in the recipes that follow, cooking times are given for the three standard power ratings.

Once you have become familiar with microwaves, you will find that they are excellent for most types of cooking. They are marvellous for vegetables, preserving the maximum number of nutrients because so little water is used. The flavours are fresh, and the colours remain rich, while the texture can be firm and tender. They are just as good for most varieties of fish, as they cook them quickly with less chance of them drying out or breaking up. The only disadvantage with cooking meat in a microwave is that, though it is cooked through, it is not browned; but for appearance sake it can be finished in a conventional oven or browning agents can be added.

There is a particular emphasis on healthy cooking in this book, in keeping with modern thinking about diet and nutrition. This might mean that very occasionally there is an ingredient that you are not familiar with, but if that is the case it will be available from larger supermarkets or from a health food shop. Microwaves are good for production of healthy food as shorter cooking times can mean less destruction of vitamins.

Finally, although it is hoped that this book will provide new straightforward recipes to tempt your tastebuds, using a microwave does not mean abandoning old, tried and tested favourites, and advice on converting recipes is given on pages 168-170.

COOKING
TIMES AND
TECHNIQUES

This section gives you all the information necessary to cook meat, poultry and game, fish and vegetarian ingredients in the microwave. Cooking times have been given, where appropriate, for fresh, frozen and dried products in 500W, 600W and 700W ovens. With large amounts of food, increase the timings by a third to a half. Look at foods often when they are in the microwave and check after the minimum cooking time.

All meat and poultry can be cooked in the microwave, but some types are more successful than others. Chops, sausages and beefburgers, for example, will look more attractive if they are cooked in a browning dish. Fish only needs to be cooked for a short time in the microwave and remains tender and flavoursome.

The shortest cooking time has been given for vegetables so that they remain crunchy; if you prefer a softer texture, just increase the cooking time slightly. To reheat canned foods, place in a dish and cook on FULL for 2-4 mins. 600W (1-3 mins. 700W, 3-5 mins. 500W) stirring once or twice. Other ingredients like pasta and pulses cook well in the microwave and create less mess, although often no real cooking time is saved.

Brassicas and leaves

It is very easy to overcook these types of vegetables, making them soggy and tasteless in the process. To enjoy them with a fresh flavour and crisp texture, cook for a short time in the microwave with a little water.

BRUSSELS SPROUTS

Fresh

Quantity	Cooking time on FULL in minutes		
	500W	600W	700W
225g (8oz)	5-6	4-5	3-4
450g (1lb)	8-10	7-8	6-7

Cooking technique Wash and trim. Cut a cross in each base then place in a dish. Add 30ml (2 tbsp) water. Cover and cook, stirring once or twice. Allow to stand for 2-3 mins.

Frozen

Quantity	Cooking time on FULL in minutes		
	500W	600W	700W
225g (8oz)	8-9	6-7	5-6

Cooking technique Place in a dish and cover. Stir 2 or 3 times. Allow to stand for 3-5 mins.

CAULIFLOWER

Fresh

Quantity	Cooking time on FULL in minutes		
	500W	600W	700W
225g (8oz)	6-8	4-6	3-5
450g (1lb)	10-12	8-10	6-8

Cooking technique Wash and break into small, even-sized florets. Place in a dish with 30-45ml (2-3 tbsp) water and cover. Stir during cooking. Stand for 2-3 mins. To cook whole, trim off outer leaves and stem. Cut a cross in the base. Place in a plastic bag, secure loosely and put on a plate, base up. Turn over halfway through and half turn the plate every 30 secs. Stand for at least 3 mins.

Frozen

Quantity	Cooking time on FULL in minutes		
	500W	600W	700W
225g (8oz)	6-10	5-8	4-6

Cooking technique Cook covered but stir or shake twice. Allow to stand for 3-5 mins.

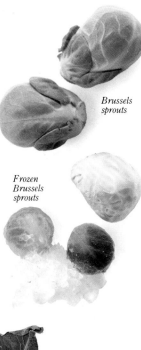

Brussels sprouts

Frozen Brussels sprouts

Fresh green cauliflower

Frozen cauliflower

Chinese leaves

CHINESE LEAVES

Fresh

Quantity	Cooking time on FULL in minutes		
	500W	**600W**	700W
225g (8oz)	3-5	**2-4**	2-4
450g (1lb)	8-10	**6-8**	5-7

Cooking technique Wash and remove any damaged leaves. Trim the stalk and shred the leaves. Place in a dish and add 30ml (2 tbsp) water. Cook covered, stirring once or twice. Allow to stand for 2-3 mins.

BROCCOLI

Fresh

Quantity	Cooking time on FULL in minutes		
	500W	**600W**	700W
225g (8oz)	5-6	**4-5**	3-4
450g (1lb)	6-10	**5-8**	4-7

Cooking technique Wash, remove any tough stalks and cut a slit in mature stalks. Arrange in a dish with the heads toward the centre. Add 30ml (2 tbsp) water and cover. Rearrange slightly halfway through the cooking time. Allow to stand for 2-3 mins.

Frozen

Quantity	Cooking time on FULL in minutes		
	500W	**600W**	700W
225g (8oz)	8-11	**6-9**	5-8

Cooking technique Leave in the bag, pierced, or place in a dish and cover. Stir or shake once or twice during the cooking time. Allow to stand for 3-5 mins.

Fresh broccoli

Frozen broccoli

CABBAGE (All varieties)

Fresh

Quantity	Cooking time on FULL in minutes		
	500W	**600W**	700W
225g (8oz)	3-5	**2-4**	2-4
450g (1lb)	8-10	**6-8**	5-7

Cooking technique Discard any damaged leaves. Wash and shred. Place in a dish with 30ml (2 tbsp) water. Omit the water when cooking young, green cabbage and reduce to 15ml (1 tbsp) when cooking Chinese cabbage. Stir once during cooking. Allow to stand for 2-4 mins. Alternatively, cook in a little sunflower margarine in a covered dish. Stir once during cooking and stand for 2 mins. When stewing red cabbage, extend the cooking time by about 2 mins.

Fresh spinach

Frozen spinach

SPINACH

Fresh

Quantity	Cooking time on FULL in minutes		
	500W	**600W**	700W
225g (8oz)	2-5	**2-4**	2-3
450g (1lb)	4-8	**3-6**	2-5

Cooking technique Wash and rinse well, discarding any damaged leaves. Cook covered without adding any water. Stir halfway through. Allow to stand for 2-3 mins.

Frozen

Quantity	Cooking time on FULL in minutes		
	500W	**600W**	700W
225g (8oz)	6-9	**5-7**	4-6
450g (1lb)	9-11	**7-9**	6-8

Cooking technique Place in a dish and cover. Do not add water. Stir once during cooking.

Fresh Savoy cabbage

Fresh white cabbage

Fresh red cabbage

Shoots and bulbs

Always buy fresh looking vegetables and avoid any that are wilting or yellowing. Cook shoots and bulbs in the microwave with some water or fat. Stir or rearrange the vegetables once or twice during cooking.

Asparagus

ASPARAGUS

Fresh

Quantity	Cooking time on FULL in minutes		
	500W	**600W**	700W
225g (8oz)	6-10	**5-8**	4-6
450g (1lb)	8-12	**7-10**	6-8

Cooking technique Trim off woody stems and arrange on a dish with the tender tips pointing toward the centre. Sprinkle with 15ml (1 tbsp) water. Cover and cook. Rearrange the spears, keeping the tips to the centre of the dish, halfway through the cooking time. Thicker ends should be tender when pierced with a knife. Allow to stand for 3 mins.

Frozen

Quantity	Cooking time on FULL in minutes		
	500W	**600W**	700W
275g (10oz)	8-11	**6-9**	5-8

Cooking technique Place in a dish and cover. Separate and rearrange during the cooking time, keeping the tips in the centre. Allow to stand for 5 mins.

Chicory

Kohlrabi

KOHLRABI

Fresh

Quantity	Cooking time on FULL in minutes		
	500W	**600W**	700W
450g (1lb)	10-12	**8-10**	6-8

Cooking technique Peel and chop into even-sized pieces. Add 60ml (4 tbsp) water and cook covered. Stir once during the cooking time. Stand for 3 mins.

CHICORY

Fresh

Quantity	Cooking time on FULL in minutes		
	500W	**600W**	700W
4 heads	7-10	**6-8**	5-7

Cooking technique Trim the heads, discarding any damaged leaves. Slice in two lengthways and arrange in a casserole dish, narrower parts to the centre. Add 15ml (1 tbsp) lemon juice and 15ml (1 tbsp) water. Cover and cook. Rearrange halfway through cooking, moving heads from the edge to the centre of the dish. Allow to stand for 3 mins.

Celery

*Sliced
celery*

LEEKS
Fresh

Quantity	Cooking time on FULL in minutes		
	500W	**600W**	700W
225g (8oz)	3-6	**3-5**	2-4
450g (1lb)	6-8	**5-7**	4-6

Cooking technique Wash, trim and slice evenly. Add 30ml (2 tbsp) water, cover and cook. Stir once during cooking. Allow to stand for 3-5 mins. before serving.

Leek

*Sliced
leek*

CELERY
Fresh

Quantity	Cooking time on FULL in minutes		
	500W	**600W**	700W
225g (8oz)	6-8	**5-7**	4-6
450g (1lb)	10-12	**8-10**	6-8

Cooking technique Separate the stems. Wash, trim and cut into 1cm (½ in) slices. Add 60ml (4 tbsp) water and cover. Stir halfway through the cooking time. Allow to stand for 3 mins.

FENNEL
Fresh

Quantity	Cooking time on FULL in minutes		
	500W	600W	700W
225g (8oz)	5-7	**4-6**	3-5
450g (1lb)	7-10	**6-8**	5-6

Cooking technique Trim and wash leaves. Slice in half lengthways. Place in a dish or bag with 30ml (2 tbsp) water. Cover and cook, stirring twice. Leave to stand for 3 mins. This method results in a crisp vegetable. Cook for 1 or 2 mins. longer for a softer texture.

Onions

Frozen onion slices

Fennel

ONIONS
Fresh

Quantity	Cooking time on FULL in minutes		
	500W	600W	700W
225g (8oz)	4-6	**3-5**	2-4

Cooking technique Peel and slice. Add 30ml (2 tbsp) water or cook in 15ml (1 tbsp) of oil, preheated for 1 min. Cover and stir once during cooking. Extend the cooking time by a few minutes when cooking larger quantities or if stewing until soft. To bake whole with a stuffing, cook uncovered for double the time and stand for 3 mins.

Frozen

Quantity	Cooking time on FULL in minutes		
	500W	600W	700W
225g (8oz)	5-7	**4-6**	3-5

Cooking technique Pierce the pack or place in a dish and cover. Shake or stir once. Leave to stand for 3 mins.

GLOBE ARTICHOKE
Fresh

Quantity	Cooking time on FULL in minutes		
	500W	600W	700W
1 head	6-7	**5-6**	4-5
2 heads	9-10	**7-8**	6-7

Cooking technique Wash, cut off stalk and lower leaves. Snip leaf tips. Place in a large roasting bag or covered dish with 60ml (4 tbsp) water and 30ml (2 tbsp) lemon juice. Turn once during the cooking time. Test if ready by removing one of the leaves—it should come away easily. Drain and stand for 3-5 mins. before serving with butter.

Globe artichoke

Fruit vegetables

Fruit vegetables, like aubergines, can be
cooked whole in the microwave but pierce
the skins to let steam escape. These
vegetables have moist flesh which cooks in its
own juices, and absorbs other flavours.

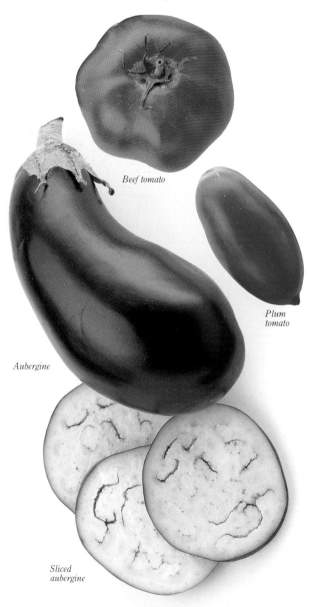

Beef tomato

*Plum
tomato*

Aubergine

*Sliced
aubergine*

TOMATOES

Fresh

Quantity	Cooking time on FULL in minutes		
	500W	**600W**	700W
225g (8oz)	3-6	**3-5**	2-4
450g (1lb)	6-8	**5-7**	4-6

Cooking technique Cut in half or into
slices. Flavour with black pepper
and basil, marjoram, thyme or
oregano. Cover and stir once
during cooking. The large beef
tomatoes make excellent containers
for savoury stuffings.

AUBERGINE

Fresh

Quantity	Cooking time on FULL in minutes		
	500W	**600W**	700W
225g (8oz)	3-6	**3-5**	2-4
450g (1lb)	6-10	**5-8**	4-6

Cooking technique To bake whole,
trim, then pierce skin. Wrap in
absorbent paper. Turn over and
rearrange once during cooking.
Allow to stand for 4 mins. Serve
whole, sliced or mashed with lemon
juice. For stuffed aubergines, cook
for minimum time and stand. Scoop
out the flesh and mix with a cooked
grain and vegetable or minced beef
filling before replacing in the shell.
Reheat for 2-4 mins. before serving.
To stew sliced aubergines, cover
and cook in 15ml (1 tbsp) heated oil
or water, following above timings.
Stir once during cooking. Season
with salt, pepper and fresh herbs.
Allow to stand for 4 mins.

Courgettes

Frozen courgette slices

Red pepper

Green pepper

Yellow pepper

COURGETTES

Fresh

Quantity	Cooking time on FULL in minutes		
	500W	**600W**	700W
225g (8oz)	5-7	**4-6**	3-5
450g (1lb)	7-10	**6-8**	5-7

Cooking technique Cut into strips or rings. Dot with sunflower margarine or allow to stew in own juices. Add herbs and ground black pepper for extra flavour. Cover and stir once during cooking. Simply cut the ends off baby courgettes and cook whole. Allow to stand for 3 mins.

Frozen

Quantity	Cooking time on FULL in minutes		
	500W	**600W**	700W
225g (8oz)	8-11	**7-9**	6-7
450g (1lb)	11-14	**9-11**	7-9

Cooking technique Pierce the bag. Shake during cooking. Allow to stand for 3 mins.

PEPPERS

Fresh

Quantity	Cooking time on FULL in minutes		
	500W	**600W**	700W
225g (8oz)	2-3	**2-3**	1-2
450g (1lb)	5-7	**4-6**	3-5

Cooking technique Remove the central stalk and seeds. Cut into rings, slices or halves. Cook, covered, in 15ml (1 tbsp) water or hot oil. Stir or rearrange once during cooking.

MARROW

Fresh

Quantity	Cooking time on FULL in minutes		
	500W	**600W**	700W
225g (8oz)	5-7	**4-6**	3-5
450g (1lb)	7-10	**6-8**	5-7

Cooking technique Peel if the skin is tough. Slice in half and remove seeds and fibrous flesh. Cut into cubes. Add herbs and ground black pepper to enhance the flavour. Cover and allow to stew in own juices. Stir once during cooking. Stand for 3 mins.

Marrow

PUMPKIN

Fresh

Quantity	Cooking time on FULL in minutes		
	500W	**600W**	700W
450g (1lb)	7-10	**6-8**	5-6

Cooking technique Halve and remove stem and base so each half can sit on a plate. Cover with greaseproof paper and cook one half at a time. Test for tenderness as timing will depend on age and size. Allow to stand for 2 mins. before scooping out the seeds and pith. Purée the flesh with coriander and garlic.

Pumpkin

Pods and seeds

Beans and peas are best spread out and cooked in a shallow dish. When fresh, add only a little water to cook, and none at all if frozen. The timings given are the minimum and ideal for crunchy vegetables.

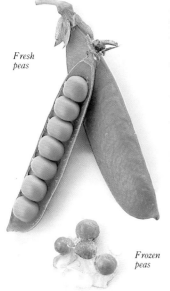

Fresh peas

RUNNER BEANS

Fresh

Quantity	Cooking time on FULL in minutes		
	500W	**600W**	700W
225g (8oz)	6-8	**5-7**	4-6
450g (1lb)	8-11	**7-9**	6-8

Cooking technique String and slice. Add 30ml (2 tbsp) water and cover. Stir 2-3 times during cooking. Leave to stand for 2 mins. Allow more time for larger beans.

Frozen peas

Fresh runner beans

GARDEN PEAS

Fresh

Quantity	Cooking time on FULL in minutes		
	500W	**600W**	700W
225g (8oz)	6-8	**5-7**	4-6
450g (1lb)	10-12	**8-10**	7-8

Cooking technique Shell. Add 30ml (2 tbsp) water. Cover and stir during cooking. Allow to stand for 3-5 mins.

Frozen

Quantity	Cooking time on FULL in minutes		
	500W	**600W**	700W
225g (8oz)	5-6	**4-5**	3-4
450g (1lb)	9-10	**7-8**	6-7

Cooking technique Add a knob of butter and cover. Stir during cooking. Allow to stand for 2-3 mins.

PETIT POIS

Frozen

Quantity	Cooking time on FULL in minutes		
	500W	**600W**	700W
225g (8oz)	4-6	**3-5**	2-4
450g (1lb)	7-10	**6-8**	5-7

Cooking technique Add a knob of butter and cover. Stir once during cooking. Allow to stand for 2 mins.

Frozen petit pois

MANGETOUT

Fresh

Quantity	Cooking time on FULL in minutes		
	500W	**600W**	700W
225g (8oz)	7-9	**6-7**	5-6
450g (1lb)	10-11	**8-9**	6-7

Cooking technique Wash and trim. Add 30ml (2 tbsp) water and cover. Stir during cooking. Allow to stand for 2-3 mins.

Fresh mangetout

FRENCH BEANS

Fresh

Quantity	Cooking time on FULL in minutes		
	500W	**600W**	700W
225g (8oz)	6-9	**5-7**	4-6
450g (1lb)	9-11	**7-9**	6-8

Cooking technique Wash and trim. Add 45ml (3 tbsp) water and cover. Stir once during cooking. Allow to stand for 3 mins.

BROAD BEANS

Fresh

Quantity	Cooking time on FULL in minutes		
	500W	**600W**	700W
225g (8oz)	8-10	**6-8**	5-7
450g (1lb)	11-12	**9-10**	8-9

Cooking technique Add 45ml (3 tbsp) water and cover. Stir after 3 mins. and test after 5 mins. Dot with butter and allow to stand for 5 mins.

Frozen

Quantity	Cooking time on FULL in minutes		
	500W	**600W**	700W
225g (8oz)	9-10	**7-8**	6-7
450g (1lb)	12-15	**10-12**	8-10

Cooking technique Add a knob of butter or 30-60ml (2-4 tbsp) water and cover. Stir once or twice during cooking. Allow to stand for 5 mins.

Fresh French beans

Fresh broad beans

Frozen broad beans

GREEN BEANS

Frozen

Quantity	Cooking time on FULL in minutes		
	500W	**600W**	700W
225g (8oz)	8-10	**7-8**	6-7
450g (1lb)	10-12	**9-10**	8-9

Cooking technique Add a knob of butter or 45-60ml (3-4 tbsp) water. Cover. Stir once during cooking. Allow to stand for 5 mins.

Frozen green beans

Fresh bobby beans

BOBBY BEANS

Fresh

Quantity	Cooking time on FULL in minutes		
	500W	**600W**	700W
225g (8oz)	5-6	**4-5**	3-4
450g (1lb)	6-9	**5-7**	4-6

Cooking technique Wash and trim. Add 30ml (2 tbsp) water and cover. Stir during cooking. Allow to stand for 2-3 mins.

Fresh okra

CORN-ON-THE-COB

Fresh

Quantity	Cooking time on FULL in minutes		
	500W	**600W**	700W
1×225g/8oz	5-6	**4-5**	3-4
2×450g/1lb	8-10	**6-8**	5-7
4×900g/2lb	10-12	**8-10**	7-9

Cooking technique Trim and wash. Add 15ml (1 tbsp) water per cob and cover. Turn over during cooking. Leave to stand 2-3 mins. Serve with butter. Alternatively, wrap in greased, greaseproof paper. Turn over and rearrange halfway through the cooking time. For baby cobs, cook by weight and reduce the time by 2 mins.

Frozen

Quantity	Cooking time on FULL in minutes		
	500W	**600W**	700W
1 cob	4-5	**3-4**	2-3
2 cobs	8-9	**6-7**	5-6

Cooking technique Dot with butter and wrap in greaseproof paper. Turn over and rearrange halfway through cooking. Leave to stand for 3-5 mins.

Frozen sweetcorn

SWEETCORN

Frozen

Quantity	Cooking time on FULL in minutes		
	500W	**600W**	700W
225g (8oz)	5-8	**4-6**	3-5
450g (1lb)	9-10	**7-8**	6-7

Cooking technique Add 30ml (2 tbsp) water or a knob of butter. Cover and stir during cooking. Allow to stand for 3 mins.

OKRA

Fresh

Quantity	Cooking time on FULL in minutes		
	500W	**600W**	700W
225g (8oz)	8-9	**6-7**	5-6
450g (1lb)	10-11	**8-9**	7-8

Cooking technique Trim and wash. Cook whole or cut into 2.5cm (1 in) lengths. Add 60ml (4 tbsp) water or 15ml (1 tbsp) preheated oil. Cover. Turn the bowl halfway through the cooking time. Stand for 3 mins.

Frozen corn-on-the-cob

Fresh baby corn-on-the-cob

Fresh corn-on-the-cob

Roots and tubers

Fresh sweet potatoes

These vegetables are particularly good cooked in the microwave as they keep their flavour and texture well. Potatoes, young beetroots and baby carrots are best cooked whole and then sliced to serve.

Fresh, raw beetroot

BEETROOTS
Fresh

Quantity	Cooking time on FULL in minutes		
	500W	**600W**	700W
450g (1lb)	12-15	**10-12**	8-10

Cooking technique Scrub small ones and remove their stems and bases. Pierce well on all sides then cook in a plastic bag. Turn over and rearrange halfway through the cooking time. Allow to stand for 3-5 mins. then scrape off skins. Serve whole or diced. If cooking large beetroots, peel and cut into even-sized chunks. Cook covered for about half the length of time. Delicious served as a hot vegetable or chilled in salads.

SWEET POTATOES
Fresh

Quantity	Cooking time on FULL in minutes		
	500W	**600W**	700W
450g (1lb)	8-10	**6-8**	5-7

Cooking technique Select small, even-shaped potatoes. Scrub and remove any long tail parts. Pierce all over and space around the edge of a plate. Cover and cook, turning over and rearranging halfway through the cooking time. Allow to stand for 2-3 mins. then dot with butter and fresh chopped parsley or mint. Serve whole or sliced.

POTATOES
Fresh

Quantity	Cooking time on FULL in minutes		
	500W	**600W**	700W
225g (8oz)	5-6	**4-5**	3-4
450g (1lb)	10-15	**8-10**	6-8

Cooking technique Choose even-sized potatoes and scrub well before cooking. Pierce all over and wrap in absorbent paper. Arrange in an evenly spaced circle on a plate and cook. Turn over and rearrange halfway through the cooking time. Allow to stand for 5 mins. Serve whole or sliced thinly as required.

Fresh potatoes

CARROTS

Fresh

Quantity	Cooking time on FULL in minutes		
	500W	**600W**	700W
225g (8oz)	5-8	**4-6**	3-5
450g (1lb)	8-10	**6-8**	5-7

Cooking technique Wash and prepare as usual. Leave baby carrots whole but slice larger ones into julienne strips or rings. Place in a dish and add 30-45ml (2-3 tbsp) water. Cover and cook, stirring once or twice. Allow to stand for 2-3 mins.

Frozen

Quantity	Cooking time on FULL in minutes		
	500W	**600W**	700W
225g (8oz)	6-8	**5-7**	4-6

Cooking technique Pierce the bag or pour the carrots into a dish and cover. Cook, stirring once or twice during the time. Allow to stand for 2-3 mins.

TURNIPS

Fresh

Quantity	Cooking time on FULL in minutes		
	500W	**600W**	700W
450g (1lb)	10-12	**8-10**	6-8

Cooking technique Peel and slice evenly, but leave baby turnips whole. Add 30ml (2 tbsp) water and cook covered until tender, stirring twice. Leave to stand for 3-5 mins. Drain well.

PARSNIPS

Fresh

Quantity	Cooking time on FULL in minutes		
	500W	**600W**	700W
450g (1lb)	6-10	**5-8**	4-7

Cooking technique Peel, cut in half or slice into even-sized chunks or julienne strips and place in a dish. If cooking halves, arrange with the thinner ends toward the centre. Add 30ml (2 tbsp) water and a few drops of lemon juice. Cook covered and stir or rearrange halfway through cooking. Allow to stand for 2-3 mins. then drain. Toss in butter and season.

Fresh parsnips

Fresh baby carrots

Fresh carrot rings

Fresh carrot julienne strips

Frozen carrots

Fresh turnips

*Frozen
swede*

*Fresh
swede*

CELERIAC

Fresh

Quantity	Cooking time on FULL in minutes		
	500W	**600W**	700W
450g (1lb)	8-10	**6-8**	4-6

Cooking technique Scrub, trim and peel. Cut into julienne strips and place in a dish with 45ml (3 tbsp) water. Cover and cook, stirring once or twice during cooking. Drain well and toss in lemon juice. To blanch celeriac for salads, cook for half the length of time, stirring every minute. Then drain and toss in lemon juice and serve with a dressing.

SWEDE

Fresh

Quantity	Cooking time on FULL in minutes		
	500W	**600W**	700W
450g (1lb)	10-12	**8-10**	7-9

Cooking technique Peel and dice. Place in a dish with 30ml (2 tbsp) water. Cover and cook until tender, stirring once or twice. Drain well. Serve sprinkled with black pepper and chopped parsley. Swede is also delicious mashed with some butter or margarine, yogurt and ground black pepper.

Frozen

Quantity	Cooking time on FULL in minutes		
	500W	**600W**	700W
225g (8oz)	12-15	**10-12**	8-10

Cooking technique Place in a dish and add 60ml (4 tbsp) water. Cover and cook, stirring halfway through the time. Stand for 2 mins, then drain. See serving ideas above.

Fresh celeriac

Fruit

Fruits cook extremely well in the microwave. They can be cooked quickly to retain their colour, flavour and texture. If a recipe calls for a soft purée, just cook the fruits for a few minutes longer.

Frozen apple slices

Fresh cooking apple

Fresh blueberries

Frozen blueberries

Fresh apple

APPLES

Fresh

Quantity	Cooking time on FULL in minutes		
	500W	600W	700W
225g (8oz)	3-5	3-4	2-3
450g (1lb)	7-10	6-8	5-7

Cooking technique Peel, core and slice. Sprinkle with lemon juice and a little honey, if preferred. Cover and stir once during cooking. Allow to stand for 3 mins. To bake whole apples, use the same cooking times, but remember that they will vary according to the size of the apples. Core and fill with a mixture of dried fruit, chopped nuts and a little margarine. Score round the centre to prevent bursting. Arrange in a circle and rearrange halfway through the cooking time. Allow to stand for 2 mins. Cook for a further 2 mins. if required.

Frozen

Quantity	Cooking time on FULL in minutes		
	500W	600W	700W
225g (8oz)	2-5	2-4	2-3
450g (1lb)	6-10	4-8	5-7

Cooking technique Add a knob of butter and cover. Stir or shake the apples during cooking. Leave to stand for 5 mins.

Frozen blackberries

Fresh blackberries

BLACKBERRIES

Fresh

Quantity	Cooking time on FULL in minutes		
	500W	600W	700W
225g (8oz)	2-5	2-4	2-3
450g (1lb)	3-6	2-5	2-4

Cooking technique Hull and wash. Cover. Stir the berries once. Allow to stand for 3 mins.

Frozen

Quantity	Cooking time on FULL in minutes		
	500W	600W	700W
225g (8oz)	3-6	3-5	2-4
450g (1lb)	4-7	4-6	3-5

Cooking technique Cover. Stir or shake the fruit once. Allow to stand for 5 mins.

BLUEBERRIES AND BLACKCURRANTS

Fresh

Quantity	Cooking time on FULL in minutes		
	500W	600W	700W
225g (8oz)	2-5	2-4	2-3
450g (1lb)	3-6	3-5	2-4

Cooking technique Top and tail, then wash the fruit. Add 15ml (1 tbsp) honey if preferred. Cover the fruit and stir once. Allow to stand for 3 mins.

Frozen

Quantity	Cooking time on FULL in minutes		
	500W	600W	700W
225g (8oz)	3-6	3-5	2-4
450g (1lb)	4-7	4-6	3-5

Cooking technique Pierce freezer bag or place frozen fruit in a covered container. Stir once during cooking. Stand for 5 mins.

Frozen blackcurrants

Fresh blackcurrants

REDCURRANTS

Fresh

Quantity	Cooking time on FULL in minutes		
	500W	600W	700W
225g (8oz)	2-5	**2-4**	2-3
450g (1lb)	3-6	**2-5**	2-3

Cooking technique Top and tail, then wash. Cover and stir once during cooking time. Redcurrants add colour to poached fruit; or try them with pears or peaches, in mixed fruit compotes or crumbles.

Frozen

Quantity	Cooking time on FULL in minutes		
	500W	600W	700W
225g (8oz)	3-6	**3-5**	2-4
450g (1lb)	4-7	**4-6**	3-5

Cooking technique Cover and stir or shake once during cooking. Stand for 5 mins.

Fresh nectarines

Fresh peach

Frozen redcurrants

Fresh redcurrants

GREENGAGES

Fresh

Quantity	Cooking time on FULL in minutes		
	500W	600W	700W
225g (8oz)	3-6	**3-5**	2-4
450g (1lb)	5-7	**4-6**	3-5

Cooking technique Wash, cut in half and remove stones. Add 15ml (1 tbsp) water, or orange juice for a different flavour. Cover and cook, stirring once during the cooking time. Allow to stand for 3 mins.

Fresh greengages

Fresh plums

NECTARINES

Fresh

Quantity	Cooking time on FULL in minutes		
	500W	600W	700W
225g (8oz)	3-6	**3-5**	2-4
450g (1lb)	5-7	**4-6**	3-5

Cooking technique Wash, cut in half and remove stones. Slice, quarter or leave as halves. Add 30ml (2 tbsp) water or fruit juice. Cover. Stir or rearrange once during cooking. Allow to stand for 3 mins.

PEACHES

Fresh

Quantity	Cooking time on FULL in minutes		
	500W	600W	700W
225g (8oz)	3-6	**3-5**	2-4
450g (1lb)	5-7	**4-6**	3-5

Cooking technique Wash, cut in half and remove stones. Slice, quarter or leave as halves. Add 30ml (2 tbsp) water or fruit juice. Cover. Stir or rearrange once during cooking. Allow to stand for 3 mins.

PLUMS

Fresh

Quantity	Cooking time on FULL in minutes		
	500W	600W	700W
225g (8oz)	3-6	**3-5**	2-4
450g (1lb)	5-7	**4-6**	3-5

Cooking technique Wash, then slice each fruit in half and remove stone. Add a touch of cinnamon and grated lemon rind for extra flavour, or cook in 15-30ml (1-2 tbsp) red wine. Cover and stir the plums once during cooking. Allow to stand for 5 mins.

Fresh
apricots

PEARS

Fresh

Quantity	Cooking time on FULL in minutes		
	500W	**600W**	700W
225g (8oz)	3-5	**3-4**	2-3
450g (1lb)	6-8	**5-7**	4-6

Cooking technique Peel, then cut in half lengthways and remove the cores. Arrange in a circular dish with the broadest ends at the outer edge. Pour over 30ml (2 tbsp) orange juice and sprinkle in some ground ginger. Cover and cook until tender, rearranging halfway through. Allow to stand for 3 mins.

BANANAS

Fresh

Quantity	Cooking time on FULL in minutes		
	500W	**600W**	700W
2	2-3	**2-3**	1-2
4	3-5	**3-4**	2-3

Cooking technique Use firm bananas. Peel and place in a dish. Mix together the juice of 1 lemon and 15-30ml (1-2 tbsp) honey. Pour over the bananas. Cook uncovered and leave to stand for 2 mins. Serve with yogurt or flambé with rum. Heating spirits in the microwave can be dangerous as it may ignite, so flambé conventionally.

Fresh
pears

APRICOTS

Fresh

Quantity	Cooking time on FULL in minutes		
	500W	**600W**	700W
225g (8oz)	5-7	**4-6**	3-5
450g (1lb)	7-10	**6-8**	5-7

Cooking technique Wash, halve and remove stones. Leave halved or cut into slices. Add 15ml (1 tbsp) apple juice and some grated lemon peel if wished. Cover and stir once. Allow to stand for 3 mins.

RHUBARB

Fresh

Quantity	Cooking time on FULL in minutes		
	500W	**600W**	700W
225g (8oz)	5-7	**4-6**	3-5
450g (1lb)	7-11	**6-9**	5-8

Cooking technique Trim, wash and cut into even 2.5cm (1 in) lengths. Place in a dish and sprinkle with grated orange peel or some ground ginger. Cover. Stir twice during cooking. Allow to stand for 3 mins.

Fresh
banana

Fresh
rhubarb

Dried fruit

Dried apricots

Dried fruit are ideal for microwave cooking as they quickly plump and soften, taking away the need for long hours of pre-soaking. The longer you leave the fruit to stand after cooking, the richer the flavours.

Dried figs

Hunza apricot

DRIED APRICOTS

Quantity	Cooking time on FULL in minutes		
	500W	**600W**	700W
100g (4oz)	6-10	**5-8**	5-8

Cooking technique Place in a bowl and cover with 600ml (1 pint) boiling water. Cover and cook, stirring once. Allow to stand for 10-30 mins.

HUNZA APRICOTS

Quantity	Cooking time on FULL in minutes		
	500W	**600W**	700W
225g (8oz)	6-10	**5-8**	5-8

Cooking technique Place in a dish and cover with 900ml (1½ pints) of boiling water. Cover and cook, stirring once. Allow to stand for 10-30 mins.

Prunes

PRUNES

Quantity	Cooking time on FULL in minutes		
	500W	**600W**	700W
225g (8oz)	10-12	**10-12**	10-12

Cooking technique Place in a dish with 600ml (1 pint) of boiling water. Cover and cook, stirring once or twice. Leave to stand for 15-30 mins.

DRIED BANANAS

Quantity	Cooking time on FULL in minutes		
	500W	**600W**	700W
225g (8oz)	10-12	**10-12**	10-12

Cooking technique To make an interesting purée or spread, chop the bananas finely then place in a dish with 600ml (1 pint) boiling water. Cover and cook, stirring once or twice. Stand until cool, then drain and purée with orange or lemon juice added to taste.

Dried dates

DRIED DATES

Quantity	Cooking time on FULL in minutes		
	500W	**600W**	700W
225g (8oz)	4-6	**3-5**	3-5

Cooking technique Place in a dish with 150ml (¼ pint) of boiling water. Cover and cook, stirring once. Leave to stand for 10-15 mins. Cook with fresh fruit to add sweetness, for example, try cooking with rhubarb or some cooking apples.

DRIED PEACHES

Quantity	Cooking time on FULL in minutes		
	500W	**600W**	700W
100g (4oz)	6-10	**5-8**	5-8

Cooking technique Place in a dish with 600ml (1 pint) of boiling water. Cover and cook, stirring once. Allow the peaches to stand for 10-30 mins.

DRIED FIGS

Quantity	Cooking time on FULL in minutes		
	500W	**600W**	700W
225g (8oz)	8-10	**8-10**	8-10

Cooking technique Place in a dish and cover with boiling water. Cover and cook, stirring once or twice. Leave the figs to stand for 30 mins. to soften.

Dried pear

Dried apple ring

DRIED PEARS AND APPLE SLICES

Quantity	Cooking time on FULL in minutes		
	500W	**600W**	700W
100g (4oz)	5-8	**5-8**	5-8

Cooking technique Place in a large dish and add 900ml (1½ pints) of boiling water. Cover and cook, stirring once. Leave to stand for 10-30 mins. Avoid doing more than 100g (4oz) at one time as they swell during cooking.

Nuts and seeds

Dried chestnuts

Fresh chestnut

The microwave can help you to toast nuts and seeds in a few minutes. They can then be used for toppings, fillings and to garnish other dishes. Adding spices and seasonings to the nuts will make them into tasty snacks.

Sunflower seeds

Sesame seeds

NUTS (GENERAL)

Quantity	Cooking time on FULL in minutes		
	500W	**600W**	700W
100g (4oz)	3-5	**2-3**	2-3

Cooking technique To roast nuts for garnishes and toppings, simply shell, chop and spread out on a small plate. Cook uncovered and shake or stir the nuts 2 or 3 times to prevent any scorching. Whole nuts and large pieces will take a little longer; try doubling the times. To make savoury nuts, roast as described then add 15-30ml (1-2 tbsp) shoyu. Stir well, then cook for another minute. Cool and serve as a snack or as an addition to salads.

DRIED CHESTNUTS

Quantity	Cooking time on FULL and MEDIUM DEFROST in minutes		
	500W	**600W**	700W
50g (2oz)	6/22	**5/15**	4/12

Cooking technique Steep the chestnuts in boiling water for 1 hour. Cover and cook on FULL for 5 mins. then reduce power and simmer for 15 mins. or until soft.

FRESH CHESTNUTS

Quantity	Cooking time on FULL in minutes		
	500W	**600W**	700W
50g (2oz)	1-2	**1-2**	½-1

Cooking technique To shell fresh chestnuts, score the outer case of each nut (or they are liable to explode). Place on a flat dish and shake halfway through. If they don't peel easily, cook for a further 10-15 secs.

HAZELNUTS AND PEANUTS

Quantity	Cooking time on FULL in minutes		
	500W	**600W**	700W
50g (2oz)	6-10	**5-8**	3-6

Cooking technique To toast and skin, shell the nuts and put on a small plate. Cook uncovered and stir 3 or 4 times during the cooking period. Leave to cool, then place the nuts in a clean tea-towel and rub off the skins.

SEEDS (GENERAL)

Quantity	Cooking time on FULL in minutes		
	500W	**600W**	700W
50g (2oz)	2-4	**2-3**	1-2

Cooking technique Sunflower and pumpkin seeds are delicious plainly toasted or mixed with 15ml (1 tbsp) shoyu and cooked for a further minute to make a savoury snack. Stir frequently during the cooking period to avoid scorching. You can make gomasio (a nutty condiment from the Far East) by toasting sesame seeds and then grinding them with sea salt in a ratio of 10:1. Sprinkle over foods as a seasoning. Try toasting other seeds too when required in recipes as it always brings out their flavour. Cumin and coriander are particularly good toasted, then mixed with yogurt and served as an accompaniment to rice dishes.

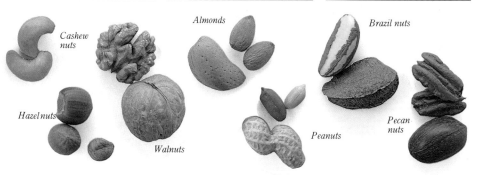

Cashew nuts

Almonds

Brazil nuts

Hazel nuts

Walnuts

Peanuts

Pecan nuts

Pulses

All pulses, except for split peas and lentils,
need to be soaked for 8 hours and then rinsed
before being cooked in the microwave.
Always use a large container as the beans will
swell and often need more water during cooking.

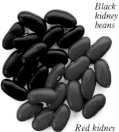

*Black
kidney
beans*

WHOLE LENTILS

Quantity	Cooking time on FULL in minutes		
	500W	**600W**	700W
225g (8oz)	15-20	**15-20**	15-20

Cooking technique Sieve through for
grit and stones, rinse and place in a
large dish. Cover with fresh boiling
water. Cook covered, stirring 2 or
3 times. Leave to stand for 10-15
mins. If they are still hard, cook for
longer and test again.

Mung beans

MUNG BEANS

Quantity	Cooking time on FULL in minutes		
	500W	**600W**	700W
225g (8oz)	20-25	**20-25**	20-25

Cooking technique Soak the mung
beans overnight. Rinse then drain.
Put in a large dish and cover with
fresh boiling water. Cook covered,
stirring 2 or 3 times. Leave to
stand for about 10 mins.

*Red kidney
beans*

These *must* boil for the first 10 mins.

Aduki beans

ADUKI BEANS

Quantity	Cooking time on FULL in minutes		
	500W	**600W**	700W
225g (8oz)	25-30	**25-30**	25-30

Cooking technique After soaking,
rinse the beans and place them in a
large dish. Fill with fresh boiling
water and then cook covered. Stir 2
or 3 times during cooking then
leave to stand for 15-20 mins. If
they are not completely soft, cook
for a further 5 mins. and test again.

SPLIT PEAS AND RED LENTILS

Quantity	Cooking time on FULL in minutes		
	500W	**600W**	700W
225g (8oz)	12-15	**10-12**	8-10

Cooking technique Put in a large
dish and cover with boiling water.
Stand the dish on a plate in case the
liquid boils over. Cook covered
then allow to stand for 5-10 mins.

Black-eyed beans

Chick peas

Pinto beans

WHOLE GREEN PEAS

Quantity	Cooking time on FULL in minutes		
	500W	**600W**	700W
225g (8oz)	25-30	**25-30**	25-30

Cooking technique Presoak then
rinse and drain. Put in a large dish
and cover with fresh boiling water.
Cook covered, stirring 2 or 3 times.
Leave to stand for 5-10 mins. Test,
and extend the cooking time by a
further 5 mins. if still hard, then
test again.

Split red lentils

Split green peas

Split yellow peas

ALL LARGER PULSES

Quantity	Cooking time on FULL in minutes		
	500W	**600W**	700W
225g (8oz)	20-30	**20-30**	20-30

Cooking technique Presoak, rinse
and drain. Put in a large dish and
cover with fresh boiling water.
Cook covered but ensure the beans
are boiling hard for the first
10 mins. Stir 2 or 3 times. Leave
to stand for 5-10 mins. Cook for
a further 5-10 mins. if hard.

Mushrooms and seaweeds

Wakame

Dried mushrooms and seaweeds quickly reconstitute in the microwave, keeping their flavour and nutritional value. The mushrooms can add flavour to soups and vegetable dishes; the seaweed is best used as a seasoning.

Kombu

Fresh button mushrooms

Shitake (Dried Chinese mushrooms)

Fresh oyster mushrooms

DRIED WAKAME, KOMBU AND ARAME

Quantity	Cooking time on FULL in minutes		
	500W	**600W**	700W
10g (½oz)	1-2	**1-2**	1-2

Cooking technique To reconstitute, rinse and then cook, covered, in about 200ml (7 fl oz) of boiling water. Drain and mix with vegetables or allow to cool for use in salads. Alternatively, add uncooked to soups, stews and stocks or use as a seasoning for sprinkling over dishes by toasting for 1 min. then grinding with toasted sesame seeds.

SHITAKE (DRIED CHINESE MUSHROOMS)

Quantity	Cooking time on FULL in minutes		
	500W	**600W**	700W
25g (1oz)	2-4	**2-3**	1-2

Cooking technique Place in a bowl and cover with boiling water. Cook covered then leave to stand for 10-15 mins. Chop and use in soups, stews and stocks. Save the rich soaking liquid as it provides extra flavour in stocks and sauces.

Arame

FRESH MUSHROOMS

Quantity	Cooking time on FULL in minutes		
	500W	**600W**	700W
100g (4oz)	3-5	**3-5**	2-4

Cooking technique Select dry, firm mushrooms for use in the microwave and avoid any that are wet, shrivelled or limp. Wipe carefully, then slice or leave whole. Place in a bowl, sprinkle with lemon juice, or dot with butter, and cook. To yield more juice for use in sauces and stocks, cover and cook for 1-2 mins. longer.

DULSE

Quantity	Cooking time on FULL in minutes		
	500W	**600W**	700W
10g (½oz)	2-3	**2-3**	2-3

Cooking technique Rinse. Cook, covered, in 200ml (7 fl oz) water and 15ml (1 tbsp) shoyu.

Dulse

Grains and cereals

Cooking grains in the microwave won't save
you time, but they will stay separate and have
a light, fluffy texture. Cook them in large
containers as they increase greatly in size.
Cover loosely to let steam escape.

Pot barley

POT BARLEY

Quantity	Cooking time on FULL in minutes		
	500W	**600W**	700W
100g (4oz)	20-25	**20-25**	20-25

Cooking technique Place in a large
dish and pour over 600ml (1 pint)
boiling water. Soak for 1 hour then
cook as above, stirring 2 or 3
times. Stand for 10 mins. then
drain. For a stronger flavour, roast
the grains for 1-2 mins. before
adding the water.

BULGAR WHEAT

Quantity	Cooking time on FULL in minutes		
	500W	**600W**	700W
100g (4oz)	2-3	**2-3**	2-3

Cooking technique Place in a bowl
with 300ml (½ pint) boiling water,
stir well. Cover and cook, stirring
once. Allow to stand for 5 mins.
then drain and fork through. Season
well. Use the same method for
COUSCOUS.

POLENTA

Quantity	Cooking time on FULL in minutes		
	500W	**600W**	700W
100g (4oz)	12-15	**10-12**	8-10

Cooking technique Add 600ml (1
pint) boiling water to the polenta in
a bowl and stir until smooth. Mix in
25g (1 oz) margarine. Cover and
cook, stirring 4 times. Spoon into a
greased shallow dish. Stand for
10-15 mins.

BROWN RICE

Quantity	Cooking time on FULL in minutes		
	500W	**600W**	700W
225g (8oz)	16-20	**16-20**	16-20

Cooking technique Place in a large
bowl. Fill with double the quantity
of boiling water. Cover and stir the
rice halfway through. Allow to
stand for 5-10 mins. then drain.

Brown rice (long grain)

Oatflakes

OATFLAKES

Quantity	Cooking time on FULL in minutes		
	500W	**600W**	700W
50g (2oz)	4-6	**3-5**	2-4

Cooking technique To make
porridge for 1 person and serve it in
the same container, put the oatflakes
into a bowl and fill with 2-3 times
their volume of cold water or milk.
Stir in well then cover and cook.
Stir once or twice during cooking.
Leave to stand for 3 mins. Stir
again then serve. Follow the same
method to make porridge from
other flaked grains or a richer,
muesli-based mixture.

BUCKWHEAT

Quantity	Cooking time on FULL in minutes		
	500W	**600W**	700W
225g (8oz)	8-10	**8-10**	8-10

Cooking technique Place grains in a
large bowl. Add 900ml (1½ pints)
boiling water and stir well. Cover
and cook, stirring once or twice.
Leave to stand for 4-5 mins.
Excess water should be absorbed,
but drain if necessary.

WHOLE WHEAT

Quantity	Cooking time on FULL in minutes		
	500W	**600W**	700W
225g (8oz)	25-30	**25-30**	25-30

Cooking technique Place in a bowl,
fill with boiling water and soak for
1 hour. Drain and add 900ml (1½
pints) of boiling water. Cover and
cook, stirring frequently. Stand for
15-20 mins. then drain. If hard, cook
for a further 5 mins. and test again.

MILLET

Quantity	Cooking time on FULL in minutes		
	500W	**600W**	700W
50g (2oz)	12-15	**12-15**	12-15

Cooking technique Place grains in a
bowl. Add 300ml (½ pint) boiling
water. Cover and stir 2 or 3 times.
Stand for 4 mins. to cook through
and drain if necessary.

Millet

Pasta

Fresh pasta shapes

Cooking pasta in the microwave will not save time from normal cooking, but you will be spared messy saucepans. You can also cook accompanying sauces in the microwave while the pasta is standing and still cooking.

Dried spaghetti

Fresh spaghetti

Dried pasta shapes

PASTA SHAPES

Dried

Quantity	Cooking time on FULL in minutes		
	500W	600W	700W
225g (8oz)	6-8	6-8	6-8

Cooking technique Pour enough boiling water into a dish to immerse pasta completely. Add a little salt and 15ml (1 tbsp) oil. Stir to separate the pasta pieces. Cook uncovered. Allow to stand for 3 mins. then drain and toss well in some olive oil or butter.

Fresh

Quantity	Cooking time on FULL in minutes		
	500W	600W	700W
225g (8oz)	1-3	1-3	1-3

Cooking technique Immerse in boiling water and stir. Cook uncovered. Allow to stand for 2 mins. then drain.

EGG AND SPINACH NOODLES

Dried

Quantity	Cooking time on FULL in minutes		
	500W	600W	700W
225g (8oz)	2-5	2-4	2-4

Cooking technique Place in a bowl of boiling water and completely immerse. Stir, then cook. Stir once during cooking. Allow to stand for 3 mins. then drain.

MACARONI

Dried

Quantity	Cooking time on FULL in minutes		
	500W	600W	700W
225g (8oz)	6-8	6-8	6-8

Cooking technique Immerse in a bowl of boiling water. Stir, then cook and stir once during cooking. Allow to stand for 3 mins. Drain then toss in some oil or butter.

LASAGNE

Dried

Quantity	Cooking time on FULL in minutes		
	500W	600W	700W
225g (8oz)	8-10	8-10	8-10

Cooking technique Place lasagne in a large bowl of boiling water so it is completely immersed. Cook uncovered, stirring once to prevent pieces sticking together. Leave to stand for 5-10 mins. then drain. Fresh and precooked lasagne can be used as they are in pasta dishes as they will soften in the sauce.

Dried egg noodles

SPAGHETTI

Dried

Quantity	Cooking time on FULL in minutes		
	500W	600W	700W
225g (8oz)	6-8	6-8	6-8

Cooking technique Immerse in boiling water, ensuring that every strand is covered. Add 15ml (1 tbsp) oil and stir. Cook, stirring once, then stand for 5 mins. Drain and toss in some olive oil or butter.

Fresh

Quantity	Cooking time on FULL in minutes		
	500W	600W	700W
225g (8oz)	1-4	1-3	1-3

Cooking technique Immerse in boiling water, separate strands and ensure that none are protruding. Cook uncovered then stand for 3 mins. Drain and then toss in some olive oil or butter before serving.

Flat fish

Because these fish are so thin they don't
need to be turned over during the fast
cooking time. They have such a good fresh
taste that there is no need to make elaborate
sauces to accompany them.

PLAICE

Fresh and defrosted

Quantity	Cooking time on FULL in minutes		
	500W	**600W**	700W
225g (8oz)	5-6	**3-4**	2-3
450g (1lb)	8-9	**5-6**	4-5

Cooking technique Plaice is sold
whole or in fillets, and has soft
white flesh which cooks quickly.
The fillets can be poached like
flounder or cooked in a browning
dish preheated for 5 mins. with
some butter. Place them skinned
side up in the hot butter and press
down, then turn over before
cooking. Cover. Add some lemon
juice and parsley and serve.

TURBOT

Fresh and defrosted

Quantity	Cooking time on FULL in minutes		
	500W	**600W**	700W
per 450g (1lb)	5-7	**4-6**	3-4

Cooking technique Turbot is
thought to be the finest flat fish and
is certainly one of the largest and
most expensive. It is often huge
and is usually divided into fillets or
steaks, but there are small ones
known as chicken turbot which can
be cooked whole like sole. Place
steaks in a dish on top of cooked
onion, sprinkle with dry vermouth
and cover. Stand for 3 mins.

BRILL

Fresh and defrosted

Quantity	Cooking time on FULL in minutes		
	500W	**600W**	700W
per 450g (1lb)	5-7	**4-6**	3-4

Cooking technique Brill is smaller
than turbot, but is still too big to
cook whole so is cut into steaks.
Place in a greased dish with some
white wine and herbs. Cover. Turn
and rearrange the steaks after half
the cooking time. Stand for 5 mins.
The flavour of brill goes very well
with mussels and they can be
combined to good effect in fish pies
and sauces.

FLOUNDER

Fresh and defrosted

Quantity	Cooking time on FULL in minutes		
	500W	**600W**	700W
per 450g (1lb)	5-7	**4-6**	3-4

Cooking technique This fish is
similar to plaice, but does not have
such a good flavour. It can be
cooked whole or as fillets. Place in
a greased dish with some lemon
juice and butter and cover. Stand
for 3 mins. It is delicious served
with a well-flavoured sauce such as
béarnaise.

Plaice

Turbot

Flounder

Halibut

Lemon sole   Dover sole

LEMON SOLE

Fresh and defrosted

Quantity	Cooking time on FULL in minutes		
	500W	**600W**	700W
225g (8oz)	5-6	**3-4**	2-3

Cooking technique Lemon sole fillets can be made into paupiettes. Make a moist stuffing from fresh breadcrumbs, chopped mushrooms, butter and minced fish. Spread over the skinned side of the fish and roll up. Place in a circle in a greased dish with some white wine. Cover. Stand for 3 mins. Mix the juices with cream to make a sauce.

HALIBUT

Fresh and defrosted

Quantity	Cooking time on FULL in minutes		
	500W	**600W**	700W
per 450g (1lb)	5-7	**4-6**	3-4

Cooking technique This is a very large flat fish which is divided into steaks. The flesh is firm and white, but can be dry. To keep moist, wrap steaks individually in greaseproof paper with butter and herbs. Place the packages on a plate to cook. Stand for 3 mins. Top each steak with an extra pat of savoury butter to serve.

DOVER SOLE

Fresh and defrosted

Quantity	Cooking time on FULL in minutes		
	500W	**600W**	700W
per 450g (1lb)	5-7	**4-6**	3-4

Cooking technique Dover sole is firm textured and white and has a lovely flavour. It can be filleted and cooked like lemon sole or left whole. For whole fish skin and remove heads. Place in a buttered dish. Dot with butter, sprinkle with lemon juice and chopped herbs. Cover. Stand for 3 mins. Serve with the cooking juices.

Dab

DAB

Fresh and defrosted

Quantity	Cooking time on FULL in minutes		
	500W	**600W**	700W
225g (8oz)	5-6	**3-4**	2-3
450g (1lb)	8-9	**5-6**	4-5

Cooking technique Dab is similar to plaice, but smaller. It is sold whole or in fillets. The fillets can be poached in a greased dish with some wine and herbs. Cover. Stand for 3 mins.

Skate wing

SKATE

Fresh and defrosted

Quantity	Cooking time on FULL in minutes		
	500W	**600W**	700W
450g (1lb)	4-5	**3½-4**	2½-3

Cooking technique Generally it's only skate wings that are for sale, although occasionally skate nobs – small chunks from the tail – can be found. Choose small tender wings weighing about 225g (8 oz) each. Cook two at a time in a browning dish preheated for 5 mins. Add 25g (1 oz) of butter and press down the skate wings. Turn over after half the cooking time. Stand for 3 mins.

Round fish

Fish cooks very fast by microwave. To stop
overcooking, score whole fish both sides,
placing head to tail in a dish, overlap thin
ends of fillets and arrange thin parts of steaks
towards the centre.

Trout

TROUT

Fresh and defrosted

Quantity	Cooking time on FULL in minutes		
	500W	**600W**	700W
2 × 225g (8oz)			
	10-12	**6-8**	5-6
4 × 225g (8oz)			
	11-15	**8-10**	6-7

Cooking technique The most
common fish are rainbow trout, but
river or brown trout have a superior
flavour. Score and place in a
buttered dish, add some lemon
juice and cover. Turn over after half
the cooking time and add 50g (2 oz)
flaked almonds. Stand for 5 mins.

RED MULLET

Fresh and defrosted

Quantity	Cooking time on FULL in minutes		
	500W	**600W**	700W
2 × 175g (6oz)			
	7-9	**5-6**	4-5

Cooking technique Red mullet has a
firm white flesh. The liver is usually
left inside because it gives the fish a
delicious flavour. Score and place
on a buttered plate and tuck in a
few sprigs of fennel, cover. Turn
over after half the cooking time.
Stand for 5 mins.

GREY MULLET

Fresh and defrosted

Quantity	Cooking time on FULL in minutes		
	500W	**600W**	700W
2 × 900g (2lb)			
	18-19	**16-17**	14-15

Cooking technique This fish is no
relation to red mullet, has rather
coarse fatty flesh, but is still good
to eat. Place in a buttered dish with
some white wine, lemon rind and
chopped sage and cover. Turn over
after half the cooking time. Stand
for 5 mins.

SALMON

Fresh and defrosted

Quantity	Cooking time on FULL in minutes		
	500W	**600W**	700W
per 450g (1lb), whole fish			
	5-7	**4-6**	3-4
steaks			
225g (8oz)	5-6	**3-4**	2-3

Cooking technique Cook whole
salmon as salmon trout. Sprinkle
steaks with lemon juice, wrap in
greased greaseproof paper with
tarragon sprigs. Turn once during
cooking time. Stand for 3 mins.

Red mullet

Salmon

COD

Fresh and defrosted

Quantity	Cooking time on FULL in minutes		
	500W	600W	700W
225g (8oz)	5-6	3-4	2-3

Cooking technique Cod has firm white flesh. Cook with a little butter, sliced mushrooms and crushed garlic. Arrange steaks with the thin ends towards the centre and overlap thin parts of fillets, cover. Turn over after half the cooking time. Stand for 3 mins.

Cod

CARP

Fresh and defrosted

Quantity	Cooking time on FULL in minutes		
	500W	600W	700W
per 450g (1lb), whole fish	5-7	4-6	3-4

Cooking technique Soak fish-pond carp in vinegary water to remove the muddy taste before cooking. Place in a greased dish, dot with butter and cover. Turn after half the cooking time, stand for 5 mins.

KIPPER

Fresh and defrosted

Quantity	Cooking time on FULL in minutes		
	500W	600W	700W
2 × 175g (6oz)	8-10	6-7	5-6

Cooking technique Smoked kippers are the mildest type of cured herring. Place in a buttered dish, skin side down, dot with butter and cover. Turn over halfway through cooking time and add more butter. Stand for 3 mins.

Kipper

SALMON TROUT

Fresh and defrosted

Quantity	Cooking time on FULL in minutes		
	500W	600W	700W
per 450g (1lb), whole fish	5-7	4-6	3-4

Cooking technique A freshwater fish similar to salmon with a delicate flavour. Score and cut large fish in half crossways. Place in a dish with 75ml (5 tbsp) each of water and white wine, a few peppercorns and herbs, cover. Stand for 5 mins. Serve hot.

HERRING

Fresh and defrosted

Quantity	Cooking time on FULL in minutes		
	500W	600W	700W
2 × 175g (6oz)	7-9	5-6	4-5

Cooking technique Cook in a browning dish preheated for 5 mins., add a little butter or bacon fat and press the scored herring into the fat. Turn over after half the cooking time. Cover and stand for 3 mins. Serve with a mustard sauce.

HAKE

Fresh and defrosted

Quantity	Cooking time on FULL in minutes		
	500W	600W	700W
225g (8oz)	5-6	3-4	2-3

Cooking technique Hake is a member of the cod family and usually sold as cutlets. The flesh has little flavour so is good cooked with lemon, garlic and herbs. Place in a buttered dish and cover. Turn during cooking. Stand for 3 mins.

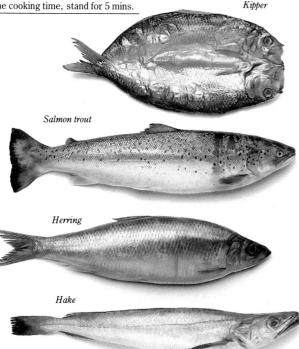

Salmon trout

Herring

Hake

Mackerel

MONKFISH

Fresh and defrosted

Quantity	Cooking time on FULL in minutes		
	500W	**600W**	700W
225g (8oz)	5-6	**3-4**	2-3

Cooking technique A large-headed ugly fish that is usually sold without the head. The tail has white, firm flesh similar to lobster or scampi and can be cut into steaks or even-size pieces for kebabs. Arrange on a plate, brush with butter and cover, turn during cooking. Stand for 5 mins.

RED BREAM

Fresh and defrosted

Quantity	Cooking time on FULL in minutes		
	500W	**600W**	700W
per 450g (1lb), whole fish	5-7	**4-6**	3-4

Cooking technique This is a fine fish that is best baked whole. Score and place in a dish with 75ml (5 tbsp) each olive oil and lemon juice, add chopped chives and marinate for half an hour. Cover. Turn after half the cooking time. Stand for 5 mins.

WHITING

Fresh and defrosted

Quantity	Cooking time on FULL in minutes		
	500W	**600W**	700W
225g (8oz)	5-6	**3-4**	2-3

Cooking technique Usually sold filleted, whiting has flaky, flavoursome white flesh. Cook simply, place in a dish overlapping thin ends. Add 30-45ml (2-3 tbsp) of cider and some chopped herbs and cover. Stand for 5 mins.

SARDINE

Fresh and defrosted

Quantity	Cooking time on FULL in minutes		
	500W	**600W**	700W
4 × 75g (3oz)	8-10	**6-7**	5-6

Cooking technique These young pilchards are delicious fresh, gutted and cooked whole. Heat a browning dish for 5 mins., add 30ml (2 tbsp) olive oil, put in the scored sardines and cover. Turn over after a third of the cooking time. Stand for 3 mins. Serve with herb butter and lemon.

MACKEREL

Fresh and defrosted

Quantity	Cooking time on FULL in minutes		
	500W	**600W**	700W
2 × 450g (1lb)	18-19	**16-17**	14-15

Cooking technique This oily fish has rich pink flesh which needs to be cooked very fresh. Place in a greased dish with 30ml (2 tbsp) water and cover. Turn over after half the cooking time. Stand for 5 mins. Serve with a tangy sauce such as tomato or gooseberry.

HADDOCK

Fresh and defrosted

Quantity	Cooking time on FULL in minutes		
	500W	**600W**	700W
225g (8oz)	5-6	**3-4**	2-3

Cooking technique Fillets of fresh haddock are cooked in the same way as cod or whiting. Smoked haddock has a lovely pale lemon colour and delicate flavour. Place in a dish overlapping thin ends. Add 30-45ml (2-3 tbsp) of milk and cover. Allow to stand for 5 mins.

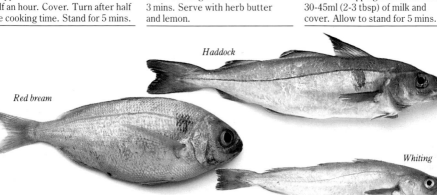

Haddock

Red bream

Whiting

Shellfish

Large shellfish like crab and lobster must be cooked conventionally, but small shellfish, like mussels, work very well in the microwave. Watch timings carefully as they lose moisture easily.

Prawn

Shrimp

Crayfish

SCALLOPS

Fresh and defrosted

Quantity	Cooking time on MEDIUM in minutes		
	500W	**600W**	700W
12	14-16	**12-14**	10-12

Cooking technique Scallops are normally sold opened and cleaned. Separate the orange roes and slice the white flesh. Place the whites in a dish with lemon juice and herbs. Cover. Stir during cooking. Add roes for the last 4-6 minutes. Stir in 60-90ml (4-6 tbsp) of cream if liked and stand for 3 mins.

MUSSELS

Fresh

Quantity	Cooking time on FULL in minutes		
	500W	**600W**	700W
675g (1½lb)	5-7	**4-6**	3-4

Cooking technique Cook mussels live on the day of buying, and wash under cold running water, scraping the shells clean. Pull off beards and discard mussels that are broken or do not close when tapped. Place in a bowl with some white wine. Cover. Stir once. Stand for 3 mins. Discard any closed mussels.

CRAYFISH AND DUBLIN BAY PRAWNS

Fresh

Quantity	Cooking time on FULL in minutes		
	500W	**600W**	700W
per 250g (8oz)	1-1½	¾-1	½-¾

Cooking technique These are both mini lobsters, despite their names. Crayfish is a freshwater shellfish and Dublin Bay prawns (also known as Norwegian Lobsters and scampi) are seawater. They are sold both cooked or raw, with or without heads. To heat up or cook, place in a dish and cover. Allow to stand for 3 mins.

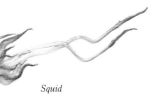

Squid

SQUID

Fresh

Quantity	Cooking time on FULL in minutes		
	500W	**600W**	700W
450g (1lb)	9-11	**8-10**	6-7

Cooking technique Cleaned, prepared squid are available from supermarkets and fishmongers. For microwave cooking, stuff with a mixture of cooked onion, breadcrumbs and herbs. Close the ends with wooden cocktail sticks. Place in a dish with 300ml (½ pint) fresh tomato sauce. Cover. Stand for 3 mins.

PRAWNS AND SHRIMP

Fresh and defrosted

Quantity	Cooking time on FULL in minutes		
	500W	**600W**	700W
per 450g (1lb)	3-6	**2-4**	1-3

Cooking technique To heat cooked prawns in a microwave, put on a plate and cover. Add some garlic butter and herbs before heating, if liked. To cook raw prawns or shrimps, place in a bowl and cover. Toss two or three times until they change colour. Stand for 3 mins.

KING OR MEDITERRANEAN PRAWNS

Fresh

Quantity	Cooking time on FULL in minutes		
	500W	**600W**	700W
per 450g (1lb)	1½-2	**1-1½**	¾-1

Cooking technique These large prawns, also called crevettes, are usually sold cooked, but are available raw whole or without heads. To cook them, place in a dish and cover. Stand for 3 mins.

CLAMS

Fresh

Quantity	Cooking time on FULL in minutes		
	500W	**600W**	700W
675g (1½lb)	5-7	**4-6**	3-4

Cooking technique Large clams are ideal for chowder, but can be cooked as mussels. Wash under cold water and place in a large bowl. Cover. Stir often during cooking. Stand for 3 mins. Remove top shell, serve with garlic butter.

Beef

Microwaved beef, when properly cooked, is tender and moist. Turn joints once, for even cooking. Test with a meat thermometer: 50°C/120°F for rare, 65°C/135°F for medium and 65°C/150°F for well done.

Silverside

Top rump

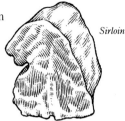

Sirloin

SILVERSIDE

Fresh and defrosted

Quantity	Cooking time on FULL and MEDIUM in minutes		
	500W	**600W**	700W
1.4kg (3lb)	55-60	**50-55**	45-50

Cooking technique Place joint in a large bowl with a sliced onion, a sliced celery stalk, a bouquet garni, 150ml (¼ pint) wine and pepper. Marinate overnight. Cover and cook on FULL for first 6-8 mins. then MEDIUM. Stand for 20 mins.

TOP RUMP

Fresh and defrosted

Quantity	Cooking time on FULL and MEDIUM in minutes		
	500W	**600W**	700W
450g (1lb)	40-45	**35-40**	30-35

Cooking technique Pot-roast like silverside or slice and braise by placing in a dish with 150ml (½ pint) beef stock, 15ml (1 tbsp) gravy granules, 75g (3 oz) sliced celery and 1 sliced onion. Cover and cook on FULL for first 6-8 mins. then MEDIUM. Stir during cooking. Stand for 10 mins.

SIRLOIN

Fresh and defrosted

Quantity	Cooking time on FULL in minutes		
	500W	**600W**	700W
per 450g (1lb), boned and rolled			
rare	9-11	**5-6**	5-5½
medium	11-12	**7-8**	6-6½
well done	14-15	**8-10**	7-8

Cooking technique Place fat side down on a roasting rack and dish and cook on FULL. Drain off any liquid halfway through the cooking time. Cover and stand for 15 mins.

Rump steak

Entrecote steak

Topside

RUMP STEAK

Fresh and defrosted

Quantity	Cooking time on FULL in minutes		
	500W	**600W**	700W
2 × 450g (1lb)			
rare	4	**2½-3**	2-2½
med-rare	5-5½	**3½-4**	2½-3
medium	6½	**5**	3½
well done	8-9	**7-7½**	4½-5

Cooking technique Cook in the same way as entrecôte steak. To add a creamy pepper sauce, put 45ml (3 tbsp) soured cream, 15ml (1 tbsp) brandy, 5ml (1 tsp) black pepper in a bowl with juices from steaks. Cook on FULL for 1-1½ mins. Serve poured on steaks.

ENTRECOTE STEAK

Fresh and defrosted

Quantity	Cooking time on FULL in minutes		
	500W	**600W**	700W
4 × 225g (8oz)			
rare	4	**3**	2-2½
medium	6½	**5**	3½
well done	8-9	**6½-7**	4½-5

Cooking technique Also known as sirloin and porterhouse steak. Heat a browning dish on FULL for 5 mins. Add 10ml (2 tsp) oil, then the steaks, and press down well. Turn over after a third of cooking time. Cover and stand for 4 mins.

TOPSIDE

Fresh and defrosted

Quantity	Cooking time on FULL and MEDIUM in minutes		
	500W	**600W**	700W
1.4kg (3lb)	55-60	**50-55**	45-50

Cooking technique Place meat in a large bowl. Add 125ml (4 fl oz) water, 45ml (3 tbsp) tomato purée, a bouquet garni and 15ml (1 tbsp) gravy granules. Cover and cook on FULL for first 6-8 mins. then MEDIUM. Stir sauce during cooking. Stand for 20 mins.

Fillet steak

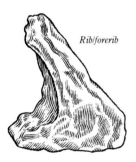

FILLET STEAK
Fresh and defrosted

Quantity	Cooking time on FULL in minutes		
	500W	600W	700W
4 × 175g (6oz)			
rare	3½-4	2½-3	2-2½
med-rare	5-5½	3½-4	2½-3
medium	6-6½	4-5	3½
well done	8-9	6½-7	4½-5

Cooking technique Place on a greased dish, sprinkle with some browning powder and cook on FULL. Turn over and pour off any juices halfway through cooking time. Cover and stand for 3 mins.

Top rib

TOP RIB
Fresh and defrosted

Quantity	Cooking time on FULL and MEDIUM in minutes		
	500W	600W	700W
per 450g (1lb), boned and rolled			
rare	13-16	10-13	7-10
medium	16-18	12-14	9-11
well done	19-22	15-18	10-12

Cooking technique Place fat side down on a roasting rack and dish and cook on FULL for first 6-8 mins. then MEDIUM. Turn over, drain off cooking juices halfway through cooking time. Cover and stand for 15 mins.

BEEFBURGERS
Fresh and defrosted

Quantity	Cooking time on FULL in minutes		
	500W	600W	700W
100g (4oz)	5½-6	4	3
225g (8oz)	9	6	5
450g (1lb)	15	10	8

Cooking technique Times refer to 50g (2 oz) or 100g (4 oz) beefburgers. Arrange on a greased dish and cook on FULL. Halfway through the cooking time, turn over, rearrange and drain off accumulated cooking juices.

MINCED BEEF
Fresh and defrosted

Quantity	Cooking time on FULL in minutes		
	500W	600W	700W
225g (8oz)	9-10	6	3
450g (1lb)	12-13	9	7

Cooking technique Put in a bowl and cook on FULL. Stir two or three times during cooking time. Add any sauce ingredients, vegetables and herbs after half the cooking time. Cook for an extra 5 mins. or until the vegetables are tender.

Rib/forerib

RIB/FORERIB
Fresh and defrosted

Quantity	Cooking time on FULL and MEDIUM in minutes		
	500W	600W	700W
per 450g (1lb)			
rare	10	7	4-5
medium	11	8	5-5½
well done	12	9	6

Cooking technique Shield the bone ends with foil. Place fat side down on a roasting rack and dish and cook on FULL for first 6-8 mins. then MEDIUM. Remove foil, turn over and drain off any liquid halfway through the cooking time. Cover and stand for 15 mins.

Brisket

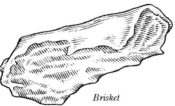

BRISKET
Fresh and defrosted

Quantity	Cooking time on MEDIUM in minutes		
	500W	600W	700W
1.4kg (3lb)	55-60	50-55	45-50

Cooking technique Plain brisket is cooked in the same way as silverside. If salted, soak overnight in cold water, then drain and cook covered with 600ml (1 pint) boiling water on MEDIUM for 25-35 mins. Drain, add 600ml (1 pint) boiling water, cover and cook for the remaining time. Stand for 15 mins.

Blade bone and chuck

BLADE BONE AND CHUCK
Fresh and defrosted

Quantity	Cooking time on FULL in minutes		
	500W	600W	700W
450g (1lb)	60-65	55-60	50-55

Cooking technique Buy as braising or stewing steak. To make a stew, cube and place in a bowl with sliced onions. Cover and cook on FULL for 5 mins. Stir in 25g (1 oz) plain flour, 300ml (½ pt) boiling stock and herbs. Cover, cook on FULL for 5 mins. then MEDIUM. Stir during cooking. Stand for 10 mins.

Pork

Pork is a meat that must be well cooked and not be pink in the centre. Check it is cooked with a meat thermometer before leaving to stand – it should read 74°C (165°F) rising to 80°C (170°F) on standing.

Spare ribs

Loin

Loin chops

LOIN

Fresh and defrosted

Quantity	Cooking time on FULL in minutes		
	500W	**600W**	700W
per 450g (1lb)			
bone-in	12-14	**10-12**	8-9
boned and rolled			
	14-15	**11-13**	9-10

Cooking technique Score the crackling and rub in some salt to improve the flavour. Place on a roasting rack and dish, fat side down. Turn over halfway through cooking time. Cover and stand for 15-20 mins.

Spare rib

SPARE RIB

Fresh and defrosted

Quantity	Cooking time on FULL and MEDIUM in minutes		
	500W	**600W**	700W
per 450g (1lb)			
	18-22	**15-17**	12-14

Cooking technique To braise, place in a dish with 120ml (8 tbsp) dry cider and herbs. Cover and cook on FULL for first 6-8 mins. then MEDIUM. Halfway through cooking turn joint over and add 2 sliced cooking apples for flavour. Stand for 20 mins.

LOIN CHOPS

Fresh and defrosted

Quantity	Cooking time on FULL in minutes		
	500W	**600W**	700W
2 × 175g (6oz)			
	5-6	**4-5**	3-4

Cooking technique Usually cut about 1.5cm (½ in) thick. Arrange on a dish with narrow ends towards the centre. Turn over after half the cooking time. To add extra flavour, split the meaty part to make a pocket and fill with a moist mixture of chopped mushrooms and herbs; cook for 1-2 mins. longer. Cover and stand for 5 mins.

Spare rib chops

SPARE RIB CHOPS

Fresh and defrosted

Quantity	Cooking time on FULL in minutes		
	500W	**600W**	700W
2 × 225g (8oz)			
	13-15	**9-11**	6-8

Cooking technique Usually about 2cm (¾ in) thick, these chops are less meaty than loin chops, but have a sweeter taste. Arrange in a dish with the thin parts towards the centre. Turn after half the cooking time. Cover and stand for 5 mins.

SPARE RIBS

Fresh and defrosted

Quantity	Cooking time on FULL and MEDIUM in minutes		
	500W	**600W**	700W
per 450g (1lb)			
	11-13	**10-11**	8-10

Cooking technique Cut into single rib pieces and place in a dish, add 90ml (6 tbsp) water. Cover and cook on FULL for first 5 mins. then MEDIUM. Halfway through, drain the ribs of fat, turn them over and brush with barbecue or sweet and sour sauce. Stand for 5 mins.

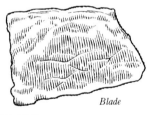

Blade

BLADE

Fresh and defrosted

Quantity	Cooking time on FULL in minutes		
	500W	**600W**	700W
900g (2lb)			
bone-in	24-30	**20-24**	16-17
boned and stuffed			
	33-35	**26-28**	19-21

Cooking technique This small joint may be cooked on the bone or boned, stuffed and rolled. Score the rind and rub in some salt and crushed garlic for flavour. Place fat side down on a roasting rack and dish. Turn after half the cooking time. Cover and stand for 15 mins.

Tenderloin or fillet

TENDERLOIN OR FILLET

Fresh and defrosted

Quantity	Cooking time on FULL and MEDIUM in minutes		
	500W	**600W**	700W
per 450g (1lb)			
	20-25	**17-21**	14-18

Cooking technique Cut a pocket the length of the fillet and add herbs or a more substantial filling. Tie with string and shield thin ends with foil. Place on a roasting rack and dish, cook on FULL for first 3-5 mins. then MEDIUM. Remove foil and turn over after half the cooking time. Cover and stand for 10 mins.

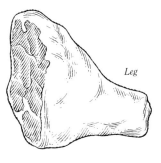

Leg

LEG

Fresh and defrosted

Quantity	Cooking time on FULL in minutes		
	500W	**600W**	700W
per 450g (1lb)			
bone-in	12-14	**10-12**	8-9
boned	14-15	**11-13**	9-10

Cooking technique Rub some salt into the crackling to improve flavour. Place on a roasting rack and dish, fat side down, and shield bone ends with foil. Turn over halfway through cooking time. Cover and stand for 15-20 mins.

Bacon steaks

BACON STEAKS

Fresh and defrosted

Quantity	Cooking time on FULL in minutes		
	500W	**600W**	700W
2 × 75g (3oz)			
	6-8	**4-5**	3-4
4 rashers	3	**3**	2

Cooking technique Snip fat at 2cm (¾ in) intervals. Place on a roasting rack and dish with narrow ends towards the centre and cover with absorbent kitchen paper. Turn over after half the cooking time. Remove paper to stop it sticking. Cover and stand for 2-3 mins. Cook rashers in the same way but do not stand.

SAUSAGES

Fresh and defrosted

Quantity	Cooking time on FULL in minutes		
	500W	**600W**	700W
225g (8oz)	8	**6**	4
450g (1lb)	12	**8**	6

Cooking technique Arrange in a dish. Brush with a browning agent, if preferred. Cover and turn and rearrange two or three times during cooking time. Allow to stand for 3 mins.

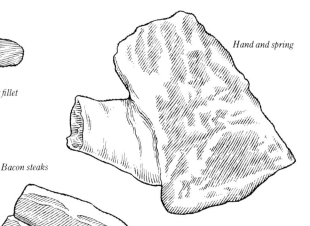

Hand and spring

HAND AND SPRING

Fresh and defrosted

Quantity	Cooking time on FULL in minutes		
	500W	**600W**	700W
per 450g (1lb)			
boned and stuffed	14-15	**11-13**	9-10

Cooking technique A large economical joint if bought whole. Cut off the knuckle end to make soup or stock. The lower part of the shoulder is ideal boned, stuffed and rolled. Cut off two or three steaks from the thin end and cook as for chump chops. To roast the rest of the joint follow the cooking technique for loin. Cover and stand for 15 mins.

GAMMON

Fresh and defrosted

Quantity	Cooking time on FULL in minutes		
	500W	**600W**	700W
per 450g (1lb)			
	15-20	**11-13**	9-10

Cooking technique Unsmoked joints microwave best as smoked gammon tends to shrink and dry up. Soak overnight in cold water to remove excess salt. Drain, dry and place fat side down on a roasting rack and dish. Turn over after half the cooking time. To glaze fat, score then brush with honey and brown under a hot grill. Cover and stand for 15 mins.

Lamb

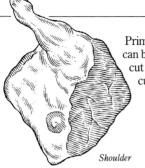

Prime joints from the loin, legs and shoulder can be microwave roasted or the meat can be cut up for kebabs and casseroles. Cheaper cuts like scrag end of neck need longer cooking, but are just as tasty.

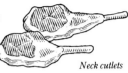

Neck cutlets

Shoulder

Middle neck

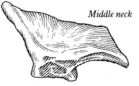

SHOULDER

Fresh and defrosted

Quantity	Cooking time on FULL in minutes		
	500W	**600W**	700W
per 450g (1lb), boned and rolled			
med-rare	14	**10**	8
well done	16-17	**12**	9
450g (1lb)			
cubed	55-60	**35-40**	30-35

Cooking technique Place on a roasting rack and dish, stick slivers of garlic and fresh rosemary leaves into the fat for flavour. Turn after half the cooking time. Cover and stand for 15 mins. Cook a whole shoulder as for leg of lamb. This meat can also be cubed and used in a casserole dish.

Riblets

RIBLETS

Fresh and defrosted

Quantity	Cooking time on FULL and MEDIUM in minutes		
	500W	**600W**	700W
900g (2lb)	35-40	**30-35**	25-30

Cooking technique Braise these strips of breast meat on the bone to make them tender. Place in a dish, add 1 sliced onion, 275ml (9 fl oz) stock and 15ml (1 tbsp) Worcestershire sauce. Cover and cook on FULL for first 5-7 mins. then MEDIUM. Stand for 10 mins.

MIDDLE NECK

Fresh and defrosted

Quantity	Cooking time on FULL and LOW in minutes		
	500W	**600W**	700W
675g (1½lb)	78-82	**70**	55-60

Cooking technique A bony, fatty cut, which is best cut up and stewed. Layer in a greased casserole with 450g (1 lb) thickly sliced potatoes, a sliced onion, 100g (4 oz) mushrooms and herbs. Add a 425g (15 oz) can chopped tomatoes and cover. Cook on FULL for first 5-7 mins. then LOW until tender. Stand for 10 mins.

Loin chops

LOIN CHOPS

Fresh and defrosted

Quantity	Cooking time on FULL in minutes		
	500W	**600W**	700W
per 450g (1lb)			
med-rare	10	**7**	5
well done	13	**10**	7

Cooking technique Place the chops in a single layer in a shallow dish with the narrow ends towards the centre. Turn over and rearrange after half the cooking time. To cook in a preheated browning dish (see chump chops), reduce cooking time by about 1 min. Cover and stand for 5 mins.

NECK CUTLETS

Fresh and defrosted

Quantity	Cooking time on FULL in minutes		
	500W	**600W**	700W
4 × 50-75g (2-3oz)			
med-rare	7	**5**	4
well done	8	**6**	5

Cooking technique These small cutlets are cut from the best end of neck. To cook, heat a browning dish for 5 mins. Add 10ml (2 tsp) oil and place the cutlets in the dish with the bony ends towards the centre; press down to seal. Turn over after a third of the cooking time. Cover and stand for 3 mins.

Best end of neck

BEST END OF NECK

Fresh and defrosted

Quantity	Cooking time on FULL in minutes		
	500W	**600W**	700W
per 450g (1lb)			
med-rare	12	**7½**	6-6½
well done	14-15	**9-10**	7½

Cooking technique This joint has 6 or 7 cutlets, cook two together to form a rack of lamb to serve 6 people. Cut away top 4cm (1½ in) of fat and meat from the rib bones. Interlock the rib bones of the two joints and tie with string. Rub the fat with garlic and herbs to flavour. Cook on a roasting rack and dish. Cover and stand for 10-15 mins.

Noisettes

Leg

Breast

NOISETTES

Fresh and defrosted

Quantity	Cooking time on FULL in minutes		
	500W	**600W**	700W
8 × 50-75g (2-3oz)			
med-rare	7	**6**	5
well done	9-9½	**8**	6½-7

Cooking technique Small, round, thick slices cut from the loin or best end cook quickly and evenly by microwave. Heat a browning dish for 5 mins. Add 10ml (2 tsp) oil. Arrange in a circle in the dish and press down. Turn and rearrange after a third of the cooking time. Cover and stand for 3 mins.

LEG

Fresh and defrosted

Quantity	Cooking time on FULL in minutes		
	500W	**600W**	700W
per 450g (1lb), bone-in			
med-rare	12-13	**9**	8
well done	15	**10**	7
450g (1lb)			
Kebabs	10-13	**7-10**	5-7

Cooking technique Wrap the joint's narrow end with smooth foil and place on a roasting rack and dish. Remove foil and turn over after half the cooking time. Cover and stand for 15 mins. For boned and rolled leg, follow shoulder of lamb timings. This lean cut can also be cubed and used for kebabs.

BREAST

Fresh and defrosted

Quantity	Cooking time on MEDIUM in minutes		
	500W	**600W**	700W
800g (1¾lb), boned and stuffed			
	45-50	**40**	30-35

Cooking technique Breast is a fatty cut, best boned, stuffed and slow roasted. An 800g (1¾ lb) breast needs about 350g (12 oz) of savoury stuffing. Spread over the lamb, fold in half crossways and tie securely with string. Place in a dish with 120ml (8 tbsp) meat stock. Turn over after half the cooking time. Cover and stand for 15 mins.

Loin

Chump chops

Scrag end of neck

LOIN

Fresh and defrosted

Quantity	Cooking time on FULL in minutes		
	500W	**600W**	700W
per 450g (1lb), bone-in			
med-rare	12-13	**9**	8
well done	15	**10**	7
per 450g (1lb), boned and rolled			
med-rare	14	**10**	8
well done	16-17	**12**	9

Cooking technique Loin is sold as a prime joint, but can also be rolled round a homemade stuffing such as minced kidney and herbs. Place on a roasting rack and dish, fat side down. Turn after half the cooking time. Cover and stand for 15 mins.

CHUMP CHOPS

Fresh and defrosted

Quantity	Cooking time on FULL in minutes		
	500W	**600W**	700W
per 450g (1lb)			
med-rare	9-10	**6-7**	4-5
well done	12-13	**9-10**	6-7

Cooking technique These meaty chops are cut from between the leg and loin. Heat a browning dish for 5 mins., add 10ml (2 tsp) oil, and press the chops down into the oil. Turn over and rearrange after half the cooking time. Cover and stand for 5 mins.

SCRAG END OF NECK

Fresh and defrosted

Quantity	Cooking time on FULL and LOW in minutes		
	500W	**600W**	700W
675g (1½lb)	80-85	**70-75**	60-65

Cooking technique This bony cut is ideal for Irish stew. Layer chunks of the meat in a dish with 675g (1½ lb) sliced potatoes and 2 large, sliced onions, topping with a potato layer. Add 250ml (8 fl oz) water and cover. Cook on FULL for first 5 mins. then LOW. Stand for 10 mins. Brown topping conventionally under a hot grill.

Poultry and game

Poultry and game cook quickly and keep moist in the microwave. Cook whole birds on a roasting rack and small ones in a roasting bag to promote browning. Cover wing tips and breast bones with foil.

CHICKEN

Fresh and defrosted

Quantity	Cooking time on FULL in minutes		
	500W	600W	700W
poussin			
450g (1lb)	10-12	8-10	6-7
spring chicken 1.25kg			
(2½lb)	24	16-18	12-13
chicken			
1.4kg (3lb)	26-28	18-20	14-16
capon			
2.75-3.5kg (6-8lb)			
	60-75	40-55	30-40

Cooking technique Different sizes of chickens are available, but they are all cooked in the same way. Place breast side down on a roasting rack inside a pierced roasting bag. Turn over after half the cooking time. Cook a capon as the instructions for turkey. Cover and stand for 10-15 mins.

Poussin

1lb

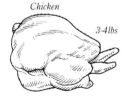

Chicken

3-4lbs

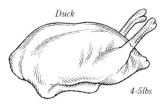

Duck

4-5lbs

CHICKEN PORTIONS

Fresh and defrosted

Quantity	Cooking time on FULL in minutes		
	500W	600W	700W
2 × 50-75g (2-3oz)			
	5	4	3
2 × 225g (8oz)			
	12	8	6

Cooking technique Arrange portions on a dish in a single layer with thinner ends towards the centre. Brush with soy or barbecue sauce for flavour. Rearrange and turn over after half the cooking time. Cover and stand for 5 mins.

BONELESS CHICKEN PORTIONS

Fresh and defrosted

Quantity	Cooking time on FULL in minutes		
	500W	600W	700W
2 × 75-100g (3-4oz)			
	8	5	4

Cooking technique Skin breasts and thighs, if necessary, and brush with herb and garlic butter, if wished. Place in a dish and cover. Turn over and rearrange halfway through cooking time. Stand for 5 mins.

DUCK

Fresh and defrosted

Quantity	Cooking time on FULL in minutes		
	500W	600W	700W
1.75kg (4lb)	38-40	26-30	20-24

Cooking technique Prick duck all over and rub skin with some salt to improve the flavour. Place breast side down on a roasting rack over a deep dish. Drain off juices and turn duck over after half the cooking time. Cover and stand for 15 mins.

HARE JOINTS

Fresh and defrosted

Quantity	Cooking time on MEDIUM in minutes		
	500W	600W	700W
per 450g (1lb)			
	20-24	14-18	11-14

Cooking technique Trim off fat and place in a dish with 225g (8 oz) sliced vegetables, chopped herbs, 425g (15 oz) can chopped tomatoes and 150ml (¼ pint) stock and cover. Turn over, rearrange the portions and stir after half the cooking time. Stand for 5 mins.

RABBIT JOINTS

Fresh and defrosted

Quantity	Cooking time on FULL and MEDIUM in minutes		
	500W	600W	700W
575g (1¼lb)	25-29	19-23	16-19

Cooking technique Trim joints and place in dish. In another dish, cook 225g (8 oz) sliced carrots, 1 chopped onion in some oil on FULL for 5 mins. Stir in 10ml (2 tsp) grated orange rind, 30ml (2 tbsp) flour and 300ml (½ pint) hot stock. Add to rabbit joints, cover and cook on MEDIUM for remaining time. Stir once and stand for 5 mins.

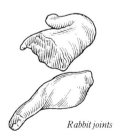

Rabbit joints

TURKEY

Fresh and defrosted

Quantity	Cooking time on FULL in minutes		
	500W	**600W**	700W
2.75-3.5kg (6-8lb)	60-75	**40-55**	30-40

Cooking technique Place on one side of the breast on a roasting rack and dish. Turn onto the other breast after a third of the cooking time and right over for final third. Shield any parts that are over-cooking with pieces of foil. Cover and stand for 20 mins.

TURKEY PORTIONS

Fresh and defrosted

Quantity	Cooking time on FULL in minutes		
	500W	**600W**	700W
450g (1lb)	10-12	**8-10**	6-7
900g (2lb)	16-20	**13-15**	9-12

Cooking technique Place turkey portions such as whole breast or a boneless roll on a roasting rack and dish, meaty side down. Wrap bony parts with foil. Remove the foil and turn after half the cooking time. Cover and stand for 10 mins. Cook 4 duck quarters in the same way as 900g (2 lb) of turkey portions.

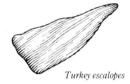

Turkey escalopes

TURKEY ESCALOPES

Fresh and defrosted

Quantity	Cooking time on FULL in minutes		
	500W	**600W**	700W
4×75g (3oz)	12	**9**	7

Cooking technique Cook these thin breast slices in a browning dish, preheated for 5 mins. Coat in egg and breadcrumbs if you like. Add 15ml (1 tbsp) oil to the hot dish, then the escalopes and press down. Turn after a third of cooking time. Cover and stand for 3 mins.

Saddle of venison

Goose

GOOSE

Fresh and defrosted

Quantity	Cooking time on FULL in minutes		
	500W	**600W**	700W
2.75-3.5kg (6-8lb)	60-75	**40-55**	30-40

Cooking technique Goose has a slightly gamey flavour. It is very fatty so prick the skin before cooking. Place breast down on a roasting rack over a deep dish. Drain off juices and turn over after half the cooking time. Cover and stand for 20 mins.

GUINEA FOWL

Fresh and defrosted

Quantity	Cooking time on FULL in minutes		
	500W	**600W**	700W
per 450g (1lb)	12-15	**8-10**	6-8

Cooking technique These small birds, now bred for cooking, range in size from 575g (1¼ lb) birds known as squabs and larger chicks up to fowls weighing up to 1.75kg (4 lb). Place breast down on a roasting rack and dish inside a pierced roasting bag. Turn over after half the cooking time. Cover and stand for 10 mins.

VENISON

Fresh and defrosted

Quantity	Cooking time on FULL in minutes		
	500W	**600W**	700W
per 450g (1lb)	9-11	**14-16**	11-14

Cooking technique Marinate joints overnight in a bowl with 150ml (¼ pint) red wine, 1 sliced onion, 1 sliced carrot and herbs. Drain before cooking and place on a roasting rack and dish in a pierced roasting bag. Turn over after half the cooking time. Stand for 15 mins.

6-8lbs

PHEASANT

Fresh and defrosted

Quantity	Cooking time on FULL in minutes		
	500W	**600W**	700W
1 × 900g (2lb)	30	**20**	15

Cooking technique Pheasants dry out easily so cover the breast with streaky bacon. Place breast down on a roasting rack and dish in a pierced roasting bag. Turn over halfway through cooking time. Protect any parts that overcook with small pieces of foil. Cover and stand for 5 mins.

Pheasant

2½-3lbs

Guinea fowl

2-2¼lbs

Offal

Offal has always been much maligned but with careful cooking it is tender and tasty as well as nutritious. The finer types of liver and kidney especially will toughen and harden if they are overcooked at all.

LIVER

Fresh and defrosted

Quantity	Cooking time on FULL in minutes		
	500W	**600W**	700W
225g (8oz)	6-7	**4-5**	3-4
450g (1lb)	10-11	**7-8**	5-6

Cooking technique Peel skin and cut out any tough membranes. Soak pig's and ox's liver in milk for some hours to mellow. Cook pig's and ox's liver whole but slice calf's and lamb's liver. Cook in a browning dish preheated for 5 mins., add a little oil and press liver down. Turn after a third of the cooking time. Do not overcook, the liver should be slightly pink inside. Cover and stand for 3 mins. Cook pig's and ox's liver further in a savoury stock for 25-30 mins. or until tender. Stand for 5 mins.

Calf kidney

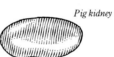

Ox kidney

Lamb kidney

Pig kidney

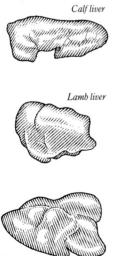

Calf liver

Lamb liver

Pig liver

HEARTS

Fresh and defrosted

Quantity	Cooking time on MEDIUM in minutes		
	500W	**600W**	700W
450g (1lb)	55-60	**45-50**	40-45

Cooking technique Ox's and pig's hearts are very tough and are best chopped and used in stews. Lamb's and calf's can be stuffed with an onion and sage mixture and braised. Allow 1 heart per person, snip out arteries and tendons before stuffing, and fasten with a wooden cocktail stick. Place in a dish, add stock, chopped vegetables and cover. Turn and stir halfway through cooking time. Stand for 10 mins.

KIDNEY

Fresh and defrosted

Quantity	Cooking time on FULL in minutes		
	500W	**600W**	700W
225g (8oz)	9-10	**7-8**	5-6
450g (1lb)	13-14	**11-12**	8-9

Cooking technique Calf's and ox's kidneys are only used in slow cooked pies and stews. For lamb's and pig's kidneys, remove outer membrane, halve lamb's kidneys and chop pig's kidneys and snip out the white core. Cook in a browning dish preheated for 5 mins., add 15ml (1 tbsp) oil and press down. Stir once. To "devil" them, add some mustard, Worcestershire sauce and dry sherry after half the cooking time. Cover and stand for 3 mins.

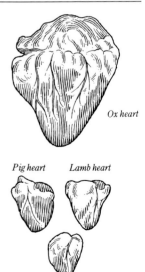

Ox heart

Pig heart   *Lamb heart*

Calf heart

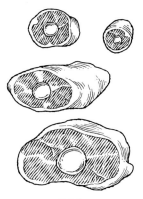

Oxtail

BRAINS

Fresh and defrosted

Quantity	Cooking time on FULL and MEDIUM in minutes		
	500W	600W	700W
450g (1lb)	25	22	19

Cooking technique Brains are always sold in sets. Calf's have a more delicate flavour than lamb's. Place in a bowl and cover with stock. Cook on FULL for 6-8 mins. then MEDIUM for 10-12 mins. Drain and slice, coat with egg and breadcrumbs and cook on FULL in a browning dish preheated for 5 mins., add 25g (1oz) butter, press down and cook for 3-5 mins. stirring once. Serve at once.

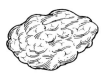

Calf brain

Lamb brain

OXTAIL

Fresh and defrosted

Quantity	Cooking time on FULL and MEDIUM in minutes		
	500W	600W	700W
900g (2lb)	80-85	70-75	60-65

Cooking technique Oxtail is sold skinned and jointed into 5cm (2 in) pieces for stewing. Cook in browning dish preheated for 5 mins., add some oil, press down and cook for 6-8 mins. turning once. Add 2 sliced onions, 225g (8 oz) sliced carrots, 2 sliced celery stalks, 30ml (2 tbsp) flour and 300ml (½ pint) hot stock. Cover and cook on FULL for first 6-8 mins. then MEDIUM. Stir during cooking. Stand for 10 mins.

Calf sweetbreads

Lamb sweetbreads

SWEETBREADS

Fresh and defrosted

Quantity	Cooking time on FULL and MEDIUM in minutes		
	500W	600W	700W
450g (1lb)	17-20	14-17	11-14

Cooking technique Calf's and lamb's sweetbreads have a subtle flavour. Soak in a dish of cold water for a few hours to remove blood. Drain, cover with cold water and cook on FULL until boiling. Drain, remove black veins and membrane. Add 150ml (¼ pint) stock and some butter. Cover and cook on FULL for first 3-5 mins. then MEDIUM. Serve with a creamy sauce. Stand for 3 mins.

TONGUE

Fresh and defrosted

Quantity	Cooking time on FULL and MEDIUM in minutes		
	500W	600W	700W
1kg (2¼lb)	80-85	70-75	60-65

Cooking technique Fresh (not salted) ox's and lamb's tongues need slow cooking. Trim bones and gristle then place in a large dish with 300ml (½ pint) boiling water, 2.5ml (½ tsp) salt, some peppercorns and an onion. Cover and cook on FULL until boiling then MEDIUM. Remove skin when cool, slice and serve with parsley sauce.

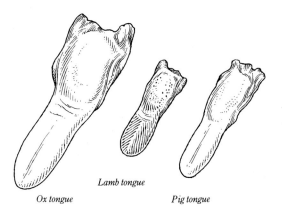

Ox tongue *Lamb tongue* *Pig tongue*

Veal

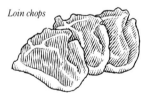

Loin

Veal has a delicate flavour, but can dry out. Marinating joints, then cooking them in a roasting bag, helps to keep the meat moist. Don't overcook chops and cutlets, let them finish cooking in the standing time.

Knuckle or shin

Best end neck cutlets

LOIN

Fresh and defrosted

Quantity	Cooking time on FULL in minutes		
	500W	**600W**	700W
per 450g (1lb), bone-in	12-14	**10-12**	8-9
per 450g (1lb), boned and rolled	12-15	**10-13**	8-10

Cooking technique Marinate overnight in oil, wine, lemon rind and tarragon to flavour and tenderize. Drain and place on a roasting rack and dish, fat side down, inside a pierced roasting bag. Turn over after half the cooking time. Stand for 5 mins. Shoulder of veal can be cooked in the same way as rolled loin.

BEST END NECK CUTLETS

Fresh and defrosted

Quantity	Cooking time on FULL in minutes		
	500W	**600W**	700W
4 × 175g (6oz)	13-15	**12-13**	9-11

Cooking technique The whole best end of neck is normally cut into cutlets. Place with 10ml (2 tsp) oil, narrow ends towards the centre, in a browning dish preheated for 5 mins. Turn over after a third of the cooking time. Cover and stand for 5 mins.

KNUCKLE OR SHIN

Fresh and defrosted

Quantity	Cooking time on FULL and MEDIUM in minutes		
	500W	**600W**	700W
1.25kg (2½lb)	38-40	**33-36**	28-30

Cooking technique This cut is ideal for Osso Bucco stew. Place 15ml (1 tbsp) oil in a large dish with 1 sliced onion, 1 chopped carrot and some sliced celery stalks. Cover and cook for 3-5 mins. then stir in 30ml (2 tbsp) flour, add the veal and cover. Cook on FULL for first 10 mins. then MEDIUM. Stand for 10 mins.

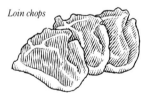

Loin chops

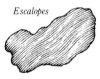

Escalopes

Pie veal

LOIN CHOPS

Fresh and defrosted

Quantity	Cooking time on FULL in minutes		
	500W	**600W**	700W
2 × 225kg (8oz)	10-13	**7-10**	5-7

Cooking technique Heat a browning dish for 5 mins. and add 10ml (2 tsp) oil. Put in the chops with the narrow ends towards the centre and press down. Turn over after a third of the cooking time. Cover and stand for 5 mins.

ESCALOPES

Fresh and defrosted

Quantity	Cooking time on FULL and MEDIUM in minutes		
	500W	**600W**	700W
2 × 100g (4oz)	7	**6**	5

Cooking technique Beat out these veal slices thinly and coat with flour. Heat a browning dish for 5 mins., add 10ml (2 tsp) oil and 15g (½ oz) butter. Add the escalopes, press down and cook on FULL for 1 minute both sides then MEDIUM. Cover and stand for 2 mins.

PIE VEAL

Fresh and defrosted

Quantity	Cooking time on FULL and MEDIUM in minutes		
	500W	**600W**	700W
450g (1lb)	50-55	**45-50**	40-45

Cooking technique Use for slow cooked stews. For a blanquette of veal, cook 1 sliced onion and garlic clove in some oil for 3-5 mins. in a dish. Add the veal, 600ml (1 pint) white sauce and 100g (4 oz) chopped mushrooms. Cover, cook on FULL for first 8-10 mins. then on MEDIUM. Stir during cooking. Stand for 5 mins.

RECIPES

The delight of using a microwave is that it will cook more quickly and efficiently many of the foods that you cook conventionally. Where foods do not brown very well, as with joints of meat or poultry, a microwave browning dish can be used which will finish the dish off perfectly giving the desired golden-brown effect.

A wide variety of recipes has been included in this section so that you have a good selection to choose from when cooking for friends and family. If you are having a dinner party you can plan your menu from the range of soups and starters, main courses, vegetable accompaniments and desserts. If a vegetarian friend is coming to dinner, don't worry, as there are several vegetarian main courses to choose from. Appetizing sauce and preserve recipes are included to add that extra spice and flavour to the main dishes. Teatime is also featured, with several delicious cake and biscuit recipes, plus some tasty and easy to make bread recipes.

All the recipes have been tested in 500W, 600W and 700W ovens so that you can see at a glance the correct cooking times for your own microwave. Adapt a recipe, where necessary, by increasing or decreasing the cooking time if you find that the food is not finished to your liking.

Recipe guidelines

E ach recipe is supplied with a range of symbols so that you can see how much time you should allow for preparation and cooking, how many servings it will make, whether you can reheat it or freeze it, and whether you should make it in advance.

KEY TO THE SYMBOLS

The time allowed for preparing the ingredients: measuring, scrubbing, chopping, mixing, blending.

The total cooking time required in a 600-650W microwave oven.

The power settings used.

This dish reheats well.

This dish freezes well.

This dish should be made in advance to allow for chilling times or for the various flavours to blend.

The approximate number of servings. These will depend upon size of appetite and whether the dish is being served as a starter, a side dish or a main course.

POINTS TO REMEMBER

● The timings in the recipes are for the quantities of food stated. If you alter the amounts, you'll need to adjust the timings accordingly. As a rule, extend the cooking time by a third to a half again when doubling the amount and reduce by the same amount when cooking less.

● Notice that ingredients are given in both metric and imperial measures. Use one system or the other, but don't mix the two.

● Follow the recipe instructions for covering, piercing, stirring and rearranging. Never cover dishes so they are airtight.

● Follow any recipe instructions on the size and type of container. Use smaller ones when reducing amounts.

● Always leave the food to stand for the time specified as this is an essential part of the cooking process.

● Use oven gloves when removing containers from the microwave.

COMPARISON OF POWER OUTPUTS USED IN RECIPES

The wattage of your microwave oven determines how long different foods take to cook. All the recipes in this book give timings for 600W (700W and 500W) ovens respectively. Occasionally you'll see that timings are the same for all powers either because they are so short or because of the food type. However, as microwave ovens vary appreciably from one manufacturer to another and even from one model to another, you may need to adapt some of the timings slightly to suit your own oven.

The chart below shows the power settings employed to test the following recipes as well as some of the descriptions used by different manufacturers.

Description on 700W and 600-650W oven	Keep warm	Low	Stew	Medium	Bake	Medium-High	Full
500W oven	Warm	Defrost		Simmer	Roast	Reheat	Full
% power output	20%	25-30%	40%	50%	60-70%	75-80%	100%
Approximate power output							
700W oven	140W	170-210W	280W	350W	420-450W	525-550W	700W
600-650W oven	100-150W	150-200W	250W	300W	370-400W	435-470W	600-650W
500W oven	100W	125-175W	200W	255W	300-350W	375-400W	500W

Figures in bold = *settings used in* R E C I P E S

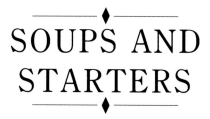

SOUPS AND STARTERS

Chestnut and tomato soup

INGREDIENTS

50g (2 oz) dried chestnuts
600ml (1 pint) boiling water
10ml (2 tsp) sunflower oil
1 medium onion, finely chopped
225g (8 oz) carrots, diced
2 bay leaves
400g (14 oz) can tomatoes
15-30ml (1-2 tbsp) tomato purée
5-10ml (1-2 tsp) shoyu
salt and black pepper
Garnish
fresh parsley

The sweet flavour of the chestnuts blends well with the carrots, and together they balance any acidity in the tomatoes.

1 Put the chestnuts in a medium bowl and pour over the boiling water. Leave to soak for 1 hour, then cover and ▨ FULL for 5 mins. 600W *(4 mins. 700W; 6 mins. 500W)* until boiling, then ▨ MEDIUM for 15 mins. 600W *(12-13 mins. 700W; ▨ DEFROST for 22 mins. 500W)* or until tender, stirring several times. Leave to stand for 5 mins., then drain, reserving the stock.

2 Put the oil in a medium dish and ▨ FULL for 1 min. 600W *(30 secs. 700W; 1 min. 500W)*. Add onion, then ▨ FULL for 2 mins. 600W *(1½ mins. 700W; 2½ mins. 500W)*.

3 Add the carrots, chestnuts and bay leaves. Cover and ▨ FULL for 3 mins. 600W *(2½ mins. 700W; 3½ mins. 500W)*.

4 Add the tomatoes, tomato purée and 300ml (½ pint) of the chestnut stock. Re-cover and ▨ FULL for 10 mins. 600W *(8½ mins. 700W; 12½ mins. 500W)*, stirring several times.

5 Cool slightly, remove the bay leaves, then liquidize, adding a little more chestnut stock if necessary. Season well with shoyu, salt and pepper. To reheat, cover and ▨ FULL for 1-2 mins., then garnish with parsley before serving it.

⭐ **Preparation:**
15 minutes, plus 1 hour soaking

▧ **Cooking time:**
37 minutes

⊘ **Power settings:**
FULL and MEDIUM

▧ **Good reheated**

◎ **Serves 4-6**

⭐ If you don't have time to soak the chestnuts, you can cook them from dried. Cover with plenty of boiling water and ▨ FULL for 10 mins. *(all powers)*. Continue ▨ MEDIUM for 20-25 mins. 600W *(and 700W; ▨ FULL for 20-25 mins. 500W)*.

Illustrated on p. 53

Onion and cider soup

INGREDIENTS

15ml (1 tbsp) sunflower oil
350g (12 oz) onions, thinly sliced
2 cloves garlic, crushed
300ml (½ pint) boiling vegetable stock
300ml (½ pint) medium dry cider
5ml (1 tsp) chopped fresh sage
5ml (1 tsp) mustard powder
15-30ml (1-2 tbsp) shoyu
15ml (1 tbsp) miso, dissolved in a little water

For the topping

15ml (1 tbsp) olive oil
40g (1½ oz) wholemeal breadcrumbs
25g (1 oz) chopped nuts
2.5ml (½ tsp) mustard powder

This tasty version of French onion soup has a delicious crunchy topping in place of the traditional toasted slice of French bread with Gruyère cheese. Alternatively, serve with some croûtons.

1 Put the oil in a medium dish and ⊗ FULL for 1 min. 600W *(30 secs. 700W; 1 min. 500W)*. Stir in the onions and ⊗ FULL for 2 mins. 600W *(1½ mins. 700W; 2½ mins. 500W)*.

2 Add the garlic, cover and ⊗ FULL for 2 mins. 600W *(1½ mins. 700W; 2½ mins. 500W)*.

3 Add the stock, cider, seasonings and shoyu and ⊗ FULL for 5 mins. 600W *(4 mins. 700W; 6 mins. 500W)*, then ⊗ MEDIUM for 10 mins. 600W *(8 mins. 700W; ⊗ DEFROST for 15 mins. 500W)*, stirring once or twice.

4 Add the miso to the soup and ⊗ MEDIUM for 1 min. 600W *(30 secs. 700W; ⊗ DEFROST for 1½ mins. 500W)*.

5 For the topping, put the oil in a medium dish and ⊗ FULL for 1 min. 600W *(30 secs. 700W; 1 min. 500W)*. Stir in the breadcrumbs, nuts and mustard powder until well coated with hot oil. ⊗ FULL for 2 mins. 600W *(1½ mins. 700W; 2½ mins. 500W)*. Sprinkle over the soup, either in the serving dish or in individual bowls. Reheat for 1-2 mins. before serving, if necessary.

★ **Preparation:**
20 minutes

⊗ **Cooking time:**
24 minutes

∅ **Power settings:**
FULL and MEDIUM

◎ **Serves 4**

★ To make croûtons, heat 15ml (1 tbsp) oil for 1 min. Add 50g (2 oz) small bread cubes and stir. ⊗ FULL for 2 mins. 600W *(1½ mins. 700W; 2½ mins. 500W)*, stirring halfway through. Cover and allow to stand for 2 mins. before using.

Illustrated opposite

Top: **Onion and cider soup** (*see opposite*); Bottom: **Chestnut and tomato soup** (*see p. 51*)

Cream of lettuce soup

INGREDIENTS

600ml (1 pint) skimmed milk
½ medium onion
1 bay leaf
6 peppercorns
15ml (1 tbsp) sunflower oil
3 spring onions, trimmed and chopped
1 clove garlic, crushed
2.5ml (½ tsp) celery seeds
2.5ml (½ tsp) grated nutmeg
1 large crisp or flat lettuce, shredded
Garnish
chopped spring onion tops or chives

To make a good lettuce soup, you need a well-flavoured milk base or stock. It's quick and easy to infuse milk in the microwave using a measuring jug, but make sure that it is large enough to allow for any liquid expansion.

1 Put the milk, onion, bay leaf and peppercorns in a large jug or bowl and ☒ FULL for 4 mins. 600W (*3 mins. 700W; 5 mins. 500W*). Leave to stand for 3 mins., then strain.

2 Put the oil in a medium dish and ☒ FULL for 1 min. 600W (*30 secs. 700W; 1 min. 500W*). Stir in the onions, garlic, celery seeds and nutmeg. Cover and ☒ FULL for 1½ mins. 600W (*1 min. 700W; 1½ mins. 500W*).

3 Stir in the shredded lettuce, re-cover and ☒ FULL for 3 mins. 600W (*2½ mins. 700W; 3½ mins. 500W*).

4 Pour in the infused milk, then liquidize.

5 Return the soup to the dish, cover and ☒ FULL for 1-2 mins. to reheat.

6 Garnish with the chopped spring onion tops or chives.

★ **Preparation:** 15 minutes

☒ **Cooking time:** 10½ minutes

⊘ **Power setting:** FULL

≈ **Good reheated**

◎ **Serves 4**

★ Warmed bread rolls are always delicious with soup. To heat them through, place in the oven and ☒ FULL for about 30 secs.

Illustrated on p. 57

Cream of garlic soup

INGREDIENTS

15ml (1 tbsp) olive oil
1 head garlic (10-12 cloves), crushed
225g (8 oz) parsnips, diced
600ml (1 pint) boiling stock
4 eggs
10-15ml (2-3 tsp) vinegar
salt and black pepper

Despite the large amount of garlic, this creamy soup has a delicious, subtle flavour.

1 Put the oil in a medium dish and ☒ FULL for 1 min. 600W (*30 secs. 700W; 1 min. 500W*). Add the garlic and ☒ MEDIUM for 2 mins. 600W (*1½ mins. 700W; ☒ DEFROST for 3 mins. 500W*).

2 Add parsnips and stock, cover and ☒ MEDIUM for 6 mins. 600W (*5 mins. 700W; ☒ DEFROST for 9 mins. 500W*), stir once.

3 In a separate bowl, beat the eggs with the vinegar, then add to the soup. Re-cover and ☒ MEDIUM for a further 2 mins. 600W (*1½ mins. 700W; ☒ DEFROST for 3 mins. 500W*), whisking once. Season and serve hot.

★ **Preparation:** 10 minutes

☒ **Cooking time:** 11 minutes

⊘ **Power settings:** FULL and MEDIUM

≈ **Good reheated**

◎ **Serves 4**

≈ Reheat on LOW or DEFROST to prevent the mixture from curdling.

Oriental mushroom soup

INGREDIENTS

8 dried shitake mushrooms
300ml (½ pint) boiling water
15ml (1 tbsp) groundnut oil
50g (2 oz) shallots, chopped
2.5ml (½ tsp) grated fresh root ginger
175g (6 oz) button mushrooms, wiped and thinly sliced
100g (4 oz) carrots, sliced into thin rings
7.5g (¼ oz) arame seaweed
450ml (¾ pint) boiling vegetable stock
15-30ml (1-2 tbsp) shoyu
15ml (1 tbsp) sherry

Dried mushrooms are an invaluable ingredient for adding extra flavour and texture to soups. The microwave speeds up the process of reconstituting them, making this recipe extremely quick to prepare.

1 Put the mushrooms in a medium dish and pour over the boiling water. Cover and ❈ FULL for about 2 mins. *(all powers)*. Leave to soak for 10-15 mins., then slice the mushrooms and reserve the water.

2 Put the oil in a medium dish and ❈ FULL for 1 min. 600W *(30 secs. 700W; 1 min. 500W)*. Add the shallots and grated root ginger, stir well, then ❈ FULL for 2 mins. 600W *(1½ mins. 700W; 2½ mins. 500W)*.

3 Add the dried and button mushrooms and the carrots. Cover and ❈ FULL for 2 mins. 600W *(1½ mins. 700W; 2½ mins. 500W)*, stirring once or twice.

4 Add the seaweed, stock, mushroom water, shoyu and sherry. Re-cover and ❈ FULL for 3-4 mins. 600W *(2-3 mins. 700W; 4-5 mins. 500W)*.

5 Leave to stand for 5 mins., then season to taste and serve.

Preparation: 20 minutes

Cooking time: 10 minutes

Power setting: FULL

Good reheated

Serves 4

Illustrated on p. 57

Borsch

INGREDIENTS

15ml (1 tbsp) sunflower oil
1 small onion, finely chopped
2 sticks celery, diced
1 medium carrot, diced
1 medium parsnip, diced
225g (8 oz) uncooked beetroot, diced
200g (7 oz) can tomatoes, puréed
10ml (2 tsp) caraway seeds
15ml (1 tbsp) dill weed
45ml (3 tbsp) fresh parsley
300ml (½ pint) boiling meat stock
juice of ½ lemon
salt and black pepper
2.5ml (½ tsp) caster sugar
For serving
soured cream
chopped chives (optional)

This microwave version of borsch is quick to make, and the flavour retains all the freshness of raw vegetables.

1 Put the oil in a large bowl and 🕸 FULL for 1 min. 600W (*30 secs. 700W; 1 min. 500W*).

2 Stir in the chopped onion and celery, then 🕸 FULL for 2 mins. 600W (*1½ mins. 700W; 2½ mins. 500W*), stirring once during cooking.

3 Add the carrot, parsnip, beetroot, puréed tomatoes, caraway seeds, chopped herbs and boiling stock. Cover and 🕸 FULL for 7 mins. 600W (*6 mins. 700W; 8½ mins. 500W*).

4 Cool slightly, then liquidize to make either a textured or smooth consistency.

5 Add lemon juice and sugar to taste, then season well with salt and pepper. Chill thoroughly.

6 Add a swirl of soured cream and chopped chives, if using, to the soup just before serving it.

★ Preparation: 20 minutes, plus chilling

🕸 Cooking time: 10 minutes

⊘ Power setting: FULL

▤ Make in advance

◎ Serves 4

Illustrated opposite

Yellow split pea and parsnip soup

INGREDIENTS

15ml (1 tbsp) sunflower oil
1 onion, finely chopped
1 clove garlic, crushed
225g (8 oz) parsnips, diced
2 sticks celery, diced
30ml (2 tbsp) chopped fresh parsley
5ml (1 tsp) fresh thyme
100g (4 oz) yellow split peas
450ml (¾ pint) boiling vegetable stock
5ml (1 tsp) miso
salt and black pepper

A warming soup for cold winter evenings.

1 Put the oil in a medium dish and 🕸 FULL for 1 min. 600W (*30 secs. 700W; 1 min. 500W*). Stir in the onion and garlic and 🕸 FULL for 1 min. 600W (*30 secs. 700W; 1 min. 500W*).

2 Add the parsnips, celery and herbs, cover and 🕸 FULL for 3 mins. 600W (*2½ mins. 700W; 3½ mins. 500W*).

3 Add the split peas and stock, re-cover and 🕸 FULL for 30 mins. 600W (*25 mins. 700W; 37 mins. 500W*), stirring several times.

4 Cool slightly, then liquidize. Stir in the miso, dissolved in a little water, and season.

5 Return the soup to the dish, cover and 🕸 FULL for 1-2 mins. to reheat.

★ Preparation: 25 minutes

🕸 Cooking time: 36 minutes

⊘ Power setting: FULL

🕸 Good reheated

❄ Freezes well

◎ Serves 4

Top: **Borsch** (*see opposite*); Centre: **Oriental mushroom soup** (*see p. 55*); Bottom: **Cream of lettuce soup** (*see p. 54*)

Chunky chowder

INGREDIENTS

15ml (1 tbsp) sunflower oil
1 onion, finely sliced
100g (4 oz) baby mushrooms, quartered
1 red pepper, quartered and finely sliced
30ml (2 tbsp) plain flour
600ml (1 pint) milk
pinch of saffron threads
350g (12 oz) smoked haddock, cubed
300g (11 oz) can sweetcorn, drained
salt and black pepper

Saffron threads are expensive, but give the soup a lovely delicate flavour. You can substitute saffron powder, but don't be tempted to use ground turmeric – the flavour is too strong and quite different.

1 Put the oil and onion in a large bowl and cover. ≋ FULL for 5 mins. 600W (*4 mins. 700W; 6 mins. 500W*), stirring once.

2 Add the mushrooms and pepper and re-cover. ≋ FULL for 2 mins. 600W (*1½ mins. 700W; 2½ mins. 500W*), stirring once.

3 Stir in the flour, then gradually add the milk. Cover and ≋ FULL for 5 mins. 600W (*4 mins. 700W; 6 mins. 500W*), or until thickened, stirring two or three times.

4 Stir in the saffron, haddock and sweetcorn, cover and ≋ FULL for 12 mins. 600W (*10 mins. 700W; 15 mins. 500W*) until the fish is cooked, stirring once. Season to taste with salt and pepper (if the fish is salty, you may only need to add pepper).

5 Leave to stand for 5 mins., then serve while still hot.

★	**Preparation:** 5 minutes
≋	**Cooking time:** 24 minutes
⊘	**Power setting:** FULL
≋	**Good reheated**
◎	**Serves 4**
★	You can substitute other firm white or smoked fish like whiting or cod in the chowder.

Illustrated on p. 60

Beef and bean soup

INGREDIENTS

225g (8 oz) lean minced beef
1 stick celery, sliced
1 small onion, sliced
1 clove garlic, crushed
75g (3 oz) mushrooms, sliced
225g (8 oz) green beans, cut into 2.5cm (1 in) lengths
425g (15 oz) can black-eye beans, drained
225g (8 oz) can chopped tomatoes
900ml (1½ pint) boiling beef stock
15ml (1 tbsp) soy sauce
salt and black pepper
15ml (1 tbsp) cornflour

A colourful, hearty soup with a dash of soy sauce added for extra flavour. Serve with some crusty, wholemeal rolls for a filling winter lunch.

1   Put the mince in a large bowl and ⊠ FULL for 1 min. 600W *(30 secs. 700W; 1 min. 500W)*. Stir well, breaking up the mince thoroughly, then ⊠ FULL for 2½-3 mins. 600W *(2-2½ mins. 700W; 3-3½ mins. 500W)*, stirring two or three times, until the mince has lost its pink colour. Drain off the excess fat.

2   Stir in the celery, onion, garlic and mushrooms. Cover and ⊠ FULL for 4 mins. 600W *(3 mins. 700W; 5 mins. 500W)*, stirring once.

3   Stir in the green and black-eye beans, tomatoes, stock and soy sauce. Re-cover and ⊠ FULL for 15 mins. 600W *(12½ mins. 700W; 18 mins. 500W)*, until the green beans are tender, stirring two or three times. Season to taste.

4   Blend the cornflour with a little water and stir into the soup, ⊠ FULL for 2 mins. 600W *(1½ mins. 700W; 2½ mins. 500W)*, stirring two or three times until thickened slightly. Serve hot.

★ **Preparation:** 10 minutes

⊠ **Cooking time:** 24½ minutes

⊘ **Power setting:** FULL

⊠ **Good reheated**

◎ **Serves 6**

★ You can substitute frozen cut green beans for the fresh ones. ⊠ FULL for 2-3 mins. *(all powers)* extra, or until tender.

Illustrated on p. 60

Top: **Beef and bean soup** (*see p. 59*); Bottom: **Chunky chowder** (*see p. 58*)

Mushrooms
stuffed with garlic vegetables

INGREDIENTS

4 large field mushrooms	
For the filling	
15ml (1 tbsp) olive oil	
3 spring onions, trimmed and diced	
2 cloves garlic, crushed	
1 courgette, diced	
5ml (1 tsp) dried oregano	
30ml (2 tbsp) tomato purée	
5ml (1 tsp) shoyu	
salt and black pepper	

Choose large field mushrooms as their broad caps make shallow shells and are easy to stuff. Chop the filling ingredients finely, so that they bind together with the tomato purée.

1 Wipe the mushrooms carefully. Remove the stalks and some of the centre to form a shell. Chop the stalks finely.

2 Put the oil in a medium dish and ▩ FULL for 1 min. 600W *(30 secs. 700W; 1 min. 500W)*. Stir in the onions and garlic and ▩ FULL for 2 mins. 600W *(1½ mins. 700W; 2½ mins. 500W)*, stirring halfway through.

3 Add the chopped mushroom stalks and all the remaining ingredients, except the whole mushrooms and seasoning. Cover and ▩ FULL for 4 mins. 600W *(3 mins. 700W; 5 mins. 500W)*, stirring once.

4 Season the filling to taste with salt and pepper, then pile it into the mushroom caps. Place in a shallow dish, cover and ▩ FULL for 4 mins. 600W *(3 mins. 700W; 5 mins. 500W)*, rearranging halfway through.

5 Leave to stand for 2-3 mins. before serving.

Preparation:
15 minutes

Cooking time:
11 minutes

Power setting:
FULL

Serves 4

Illustrated on p. 65

Lentil and coconut pâté

INGREDIENTS

100g (4 oz) split red lentils
400ml (14 fl oz) boiling water
50g (2 oz) creamed coconut, grated
juice of ½ lemon
4-5 drops Tabasco sauce
1.25ml (¼ tsp) grated nutmeg
salt and black pepper

This makes a delicious creamy pâté with a subtle flavour. Red lentils are particularly quick to cook in the microwave, but be sure to put them in a large bowl or the cooking liquid will froth over the top. Serve the pâté with crudités or Melba toast.

1 Place the red lentils in a deep bowl and pour over the boiling water. Cover and ≋ FULL for 10 mins. (*all powers*), stirring several times. Drain well, if necessary, reserving any liquid.

2 Stir in the creamed coconut, lemon juice, Tabasco sauce and nutmeg. Liquidize until smooth, adding a little of the reserved lentil stock, or water, if necessary.

3 Season to taste with salt and pepper, then chill thoroughly before serving.

★ **Preparation:** 10 minutes, plus chilling

≋ **Cooking time:** 10 minutes

⊘ **Power setting:** FULL

▤ **Make in advance**

◎ **Serves 4**

Illustrated on p. 65

Coriander ramekins

INGREDIENTS

3 eggs
150ml (¼ pint) yogurt
45ml (3 tbsp) chopped fresh coriander
salt and black pepper

If fresh coriander is unavailable, try using mixtures of other fresh herbs, such as chives, parsley or tarragon, or chopped spinach, sorrel or cooked leeks.

1 Beat the eggs thoroughly, then add in the yogurt. Fold in the coriander, and season to taste with salt and pepper.

2 Spoon the mixture into four ramekin dishes. Cover, then arrange the dishes in a circle in the microwave and ≋ FULL for 3 mins. 600W (2½ mins. 700W; 3 mins. 500W), rearranging halfway through.

3 Leave to stand for 3 mins. before serving.

★ **Preparation:** 5 minutes

≋ **Cooking time:** 3 minutes

⊘ **Power setting:** FULL

◎ **Serves 4**

≋ These should be quite soft when served; if overcooked they can become rubbery in texture.

Illustrated on p. 65

Stuffed avocados

INGREDIENTS

25g (1 oz) raisins
juice of 1 orange
50g (2 oz) short-grain brown rice
300ml (½ pint) boiling water
25g (1 oz) sunflower seeds
3 spring onions, finely chopped
5ml (1 tsp) shoyu
5ml (1 tsp) grated fresh root ginger
2 avocados

Hot stuffed avocados make an unusual alternative to the more usual avocado vinaigrette. The microwave heats up the avocado halves without drying them out or making them bitter.

1 Put the raisins in a small bowl, pour over the orange juice and ▨ FULL for 1 min. 600W (*30 secs. 700W; 1 min. 500W*) to plump them up.

2 Put the rice in a medium dish with the boiling water. Cover and ▨ FULL for 18 mins. (*all powers*), stirring 2-3 times. Leave to stand for 5 mins.

3 Spread out the sunflower seeds on a small plate and ▨ FULL for 2 mins. 600W (*1½ mins. 700W; 2½ mins. 500W*), shaking halfway through.

4 Mix the raisins, cooked rice, toasted seeds, onions, shoyu and root ginger together.

5 Halve the avocados, scoop out the flesh and dice. Mix the flesh with the other ingredients, then spoon back into each of the avocado halves.

6 Arrange the halves in a large round dish with the thicker ends outwards. Cover and ▨ FULL for 2 mins. 600W (*1½ mins. 700W; 2½ mins. 500W*). Serve at once.

★ **Preparation:** 20 minutes

▨ **Cooking time:** 23 minutes

⊘ **Power setting:** FULL

◎ **Serves 4**

★ To get more juice from oranges and lemons, microwave individually for 30 secs. before squeezing.

Aubergine dip

INGREDIENTS

1 large aubergine
10ml (2 tsp) sesame seeds
10ml (2 tsp) sunflower seeds
30ml (2 tbsp) olive oil
2 cloves garlic, crushed
juice of ½ lemon
2.5ml (½ tsp) ground coriander
salt and black pepper

Aubergines cook very quickly in the microwave, saving time and the need to heat an entire oven simply to make this tasty dip. Choose aubergines that feel heavy for their size and have smooth, glossy skins.

1 Trim the aubergine, then pierce the skin. Wrap in absorbent paper and ☷ FULL for 5 mins. 600W *(4 mins. 700W; 6 mins. 500W)*, turning once. Leave to stand for 4 mins.

2 Spread out the seeds on a small plate and ☷ FULL for 3 mins. 600W *(2½ mins. 700W; 3½ mins. 500W)*, shaking halfway through. Crush lightly.

3 Scoop out the aubergine flesh, mash well and mix with the oil, garlic, lemon juice and coriander. Season well with salt and pepper, then stir in the crushed, toasted seeds. Serve warm as a dip with crudités or strips of toast, or serve as a spread.

★ **Preparation:** 10 minutes

☷ **Cooking time:** 8 minutes

⊘ **Power setting:** FULL

▤ **Make in advance**

◎ **Serves 4**

☷ Wrapping aubergines in absorbent paper prevents them collapsing during cooking.

Illustrated opposite

Leek vinaigrette

INGREDIENTS

450g (1 lb) young leeks, trimmed weight
90ml (6 tbsp) olive oil
30ml (2 tbsp) lemon juice
15ml (1 tbsp) cider vinegar
10ml (2 tsp) capers
5ml (1 tsp) coarse-grained mustard
1 clove garlic, crushed
salt and black pepper

Vegetables cooked in the microwave retain a crisp, fresh flavour and are excellent served chilled in a vinaigrette dressing. The same recipe can be used for artichoke hearts, mushrooms or French beans.

1 Chop the leeks into 2.5cm (1 in) pieces and wash thoroughly.

2 Arrange in a dish with 30ml (2 tbsp) water. Cover and ☷ FULL for 4 mins. 600W *(3 mins. 700W; 5 mins. 500W)*, shaking the dish once or twice during cooking. Drain well.

3 Combine all the remaining ingredients, except the seasoning, and add to the cooked leeks. Cover and ☷ FULL for 1 min. 600W *(30 secs. 700W; 1 min. 500W)*.

4 Leave to cool completely. Season well with salt and pepper, then chill thoroughly. Serve with brown bread or with a crisp green salad.

★ **Preparation:** 15 minutes, plus chilling

☷ **Cooking time:** 5 minutes

⊘ **Power setting:** FULL

▤ **Make in advance**

◎ **Serves 4**

Clockwise from top left: **Lentil and coconut pâté** (*see p. 62*); **Aubergine dip** (*see opposite*); **Mushrooms stuffed with garlic vegetables** (*see p. 61*); **Coriander ramekins** (*see p. 62*)

Seafood shells

INGREDIENTS

4 fresh scallops (shells reserved)
225g (8 oz) cod steaks
75g (3 oz) mushrooms, sliced
25g (1 oz) butter
25g (1 oz) plain flour
about 150ml (¼ pint) milk
15ml (1 tbsp) dry sherry
30ml (2 tbsp) double cream
salt and black pepper
45ml (3 tbsp) Parmesan cheese
45ml (3 tbsp) wholewheat breadcrumbs

For the potato border

450g (1 lb) potatoes, cut into chunks
15g (½ oz) butter
30ml (2 tbsp) double cream
30ml (2 tbsp) chopped fresh parsley

Make a few scallops go further when serving four people, by combining with cod in a creamy sauce, topped with cheesy breadcrumbs. The potato border won't brown in the microwave, but looks and tastes good, speckled with chopped fresh parsley instead.

1 To make the potato border: put the potatoes in a large bowl with 60ml (4 tbsp) water. Cover and ☷ FULL for 12 mins. 600W (*10 mins. 700W; 15 mins. 500W*), stirring once.

2 Leave to stand for 5 mins., then drain and mash with the butter and cream. Stir in the parsley and spoon into a large piping bag fitted with a star nozzle. Pipe a border round the edge of four scallop shells.

3 Put the scallops on a plate and cover. ☷ MEDIUM for 2½-3 mins. 600W (*2-2½ mins. 700W; 3-3½ mins. 500W*) or until just cooked, stirring once. Leave to stand for 5 mins., then drain and reserve the liquid. Cut off the orange coral and slice the white muscle thickly.

4 Put the cod steaks on a plate, scatter with the mushrooms and ☷ FULL for 3 mins. 600W (*2½ mins. 700W; 3½ mins. 500W*) until just cooked, turning over once. Leave to stand for 5 mins., drain and reserve liquid.

5 Put the butter in a medium bowl and ☷ FULL for 1 min. 600W (*30 secs. 700W; 1 min. 500W*). Stir in the flour. Combine the fish cooking liquids and make up to 300ml (½ pint) with the milk and stir into the flour mixture. ☷ FULL for 3-4 mins. (*all powers*), until thickened, stirring twice.

6 Add the sherry and cream and season to taste. Flake the cod, removing any skin and bones, and add to the sauce with the mushrooms and scallops. Spoon into the prepared scallop shells.

7 Combine the cheese and crumbs and sprinkle over the sauce. ☷ FULL for 5 mins. 600W (*4 mins. 700W; 6 mins. 500W*). Leave to stand for 3 mins., then serve at once.

★ **Preparation:** 10 minutes

☷ **Cooking time:** 26½ minutes

⊘ **Power settings:** FULL and MEDIUM

◎ **Serves 4**

★ The deep shells from scallops make good individual dishes. Scrub them thoroughly before use.

Crab and prawn cocktail

INGREDIENTS

15ml (1 tbsp) sunflower oil
½ small onion, finely chopped
1 small garlic clove, crushed
175g (6 oz) cooked, peeled prawns
200g (7 oz) can white crab meat, drained
grated rind and juice of ½ orange
1 mango, peeled, stoned and thinly sliced
1 orange, peeled and cut into segments
12 small lettuce leaves
For the dressing
90ml (6 tbsp) mayonnaise
grated rind and juice of ½ orange
salt and black pepper
Garnish
4 whole prawns .

This cocktail has a lovely tropical taste. You can make it up to 24 hours in advance, but don't add the sliced mango until the last minute or its strong taste will overpower all the other flavours.

1 Put the oil, onion and garlic in a medium bowl, cover and ☒ FULL for 3 mins. 600W (*2½ mins. 700W; 3½ mins. 500W*), stirring once. Leave to cool, then add the prawns, crab, orange rind and juice and stir well.

2 To make the dressing: mix the mayonnaise with the orange rind and juice and season to taste. Stir into the prawn and crab mixture and chill until ready to serve.

3 Reserve four pieces of mango and orange for the garnish and mix the remainder into the prawn mixture until well coated in the dressing.

4 Arrange the lettuce leaves on four individual plates and spoon the prawn mixture on top, dividing it into equal portions.

5 Garnish each cocktail with a whole prawn, a slice of mango and a segment of orange. Serve at once, with granary bread.

★ Preparation: 10 minutes, plus chilling

Cooking time: 3 minutes

Power setting: FULL

Make in advance

◎ Serves 4

★ To thaw frozen prawns, spread in a shallow dish and ☒ LOW for 4 mins. 600W (*3 mins. 700W; 5 mins. 500W*), stirring once. Leave to stand for 5 minutes before using.

Illustrated on p. 69

Chicken liver pâté

INGREDIENTS

100g (4 oz) butter

1 small onion, finely chopped

225g (8 oz) chicken livers, chopped

50g (2 oz) mushrooms, chopped

1 clove garlic, crushed

15ml (1 tbsp) dry sherry

15ml (1 tbsp) chopped fresh parsley

salt and black pepper

Garnish

a few lettuce leaves, and tomato wedges (optional)

A rich butter-topped pâté that is very quick and easy to make in the microwave. For a dinner party, garnish with a few pink-tinged, curly lettuce leaves.

1 Put 50g (2 oz) of the butter and onion in a medium bowl and cover. ᠍ FULL for 4 mins. 600W (*3 mins. 700W; 5 mins. 500W*) until softened, stirring once.

2 Stir in the livers, mushrooms and garlic, re-cover and ᠍ MEDIUM-HIGH for 4 mins. 600W (*3 mins. 700W; 5 mins. 500W*), or until the livers are no longer pink, stirring twice.

3 Pour the liver mixture into a blender and liquidize until smooth. Add the sherry, parsley and seasoning to taste and mix together until well blended.

4 Spoon either into four individual dishes or one large dish and smooth the surface. Put the remaining butter in a small bowl and ᠍ FULL for 1½ mins. 600W (*1 min. 700W; 1½-2 mins. 500W*) to melt.

5 Spoon the melted butter over the pâté and leave to set, then chill for 6-8 hours or overnight. Serve with toast and garnish with lettuce leaves, if liked.

★ **Preparation:** 20 minutes, plus chilling

᠍ **Cooking time:** 9½ minutes

▨ **Power settings:** FULL and MEDIUM-HIGH

▤ **Make in advance**

◎ **Serves 4**

★ Check over the livers carefully and cut away any green-tinged parts, which would give the pâté a bitter taste.

Illustrated opposite

Top: **Chicken liver pâté** (*see opposite*); **Crab and prawn cocktail** (*see p. 67*).

Fruity spare ribs

INGREDIENTS

675g (1½ lb) pork spare ribs
45ml (3 tbsp) undiluted blackcurrant drink
5ml (1 tsp) lemon juice
15ml (1 tbsp) honey
45ml (3 tbsp) tomato ketchup
15ml (1 tbsp) soy sauce
Garnish
lemon slices

These ribs have a delicious sweet and sour taste. The only way to eat them is with your fingers, so provide thick napkins and finger bowls so that your guests can easily clean up afterwards.

1 Cut the spare ribs into single rib pieces and place in a large shallow dish in a single layer. Add 90ml (6 tbsp) water and cover. ≋ FULL for 3½ mins. 600W (*3 mins. 700W; 4 mins. 500W*). Rearrange and turn over the ribs and drain off the cooking liquid.

2 Re-cover and ≋ FULL for 3½ mins. 600W (*3 mins. 700W; 4 mins. 500W*). Leave to stand for 4 mins., then drain off the cooking juices.

3 Mix together the blackcurrant drink, lemon juice, honey, tomato ketchup, soy sauce and 25ml (1 tbsp) water. Brush the sauce over the ribs to coat completely.

4 Arrange the ribs on a microwave roasting rack over a shallow dish and cover with greaseproof paper. ≋ MEDIUM for 8-10 mins. 600W (*6½-8½ mins. 700W; 10-12½ mins. 500W*), rearranging ribs and basting with the sauce two or three times.

5 Cover and leave to stand for 5 mins. Garnish with lemon slices and serve at once with any remaining sauce poured over.

Preparation: 5 minutes

Cooking time: 15 minutes

Power settings: FULL and MEDIUM

Serves 4

Cover the ribs with a firm lid for the first part of cooking, then loosely with greaseproof paper (which lets the steam escape, but prevents splashing) for the second part.

MAIN COURSES
FISH AND SHELLFISH

Sole Véronique

INGREDIENTS

15g (½ oz) butter
450g (1 lb) lemon sole fillets, skinned
salt and black pepper
60ml (4 tbsp) dry white wine
60ml (4 tbsp) fish stock
few sprigs of parsley
bay leaf
60ml (4 tbsp) double cream
7.5ml (1½ tsp) cornflour
100g (4 oz) seedless green grapes

Rolled fillets of sole can be coated with a variety of sauces. Cooked in the microwave, they keep moist and tender. This light wine and cream sauce includes tiny seedless grapes which add a delicious sweetness to the dish.

1 Put a knob of butter on the skinned side of the fillets, season with salt and pepper and roll up from the tail end. Arrange the rolls in a greased dish.

2 Pour in the wine and stock, and add the parsley and bay leaf. Cover and ❋ FULL for 4 mins. 600W (*3 mins. 700W; 5 mins. 500W*) until the fish is opaque and flaky, rearranging once.

3 Drain off the cooking liquid from the fish and discard the herbs. Cover the fish and keep warm while you make the sauce. Pour the liquid into a jug and ❋ FULL for 2 mins. 600W (*1½ mins. 700W; 2½ mins. 500W*) until reduced by about half.

4 Blend the cream with the cornflour, stir into the reduced stock and mix until smooth. ❋ FULL for 1-1½ mins. 600W (*1 min. 700W; 1½-2 mins. 500W*), stirring twice until hot.

5 Season to taste, add the grapes and ❋ FULL for 1 min. 600W (*30 secs. 700W; 1 min. 500W*) to heat through. Pour over the fish and serve at once.

Preparation:
5 minutes

Cooking time:
8 minutes

Power setting:
FULL

Serves 4

Moules marinière

INGREDIENTS

1.4kg (3 lb) fresh mussels
1 small onion, finely chopped
90ml (6 tbsp) dry white wine
25g (1 oz) butter
5ml (1 tsp) plain flour
10ml (2 tsp) tomato purée

Garnish

15ml (1 tbsp) chopped fresh parsley

Preparation:
15 minutes

Cooking time:
10 minutes

Power setting:
FULL

Serves 2-3

There is always a chance that some grit will escape the washing process, so it is a good idea to strain the sauce into the serving dish.

Illustrated opposite

This classic dish cooks very well in the microwave. However, mussels are very bulky so if you increase the quantities, cook the extra mussels in another batch so that they have a chance to cook evenly. This quantity will also serve up to four as a starter.

1 Discard any mussels with broken shells, tap open ones sharply and discard any that do not close. Scrub the rest under cold running water, scraping off any barnacles. Use a sharp knife to pull away the beards. Shake the mussels in several changes of water to remove any traces of grit.

2 Put the onion and wine in a large bowl. Cover and ⌇ FULL for 3 mins. 600W (2½ mins. 700W; 3½ mins. 500W), to soften.

3 Add the mussels, re-cover and ⌇ FULL for 4-5 mins. 600W (3-4 mins. 700W; 5-6 mins. 500W), or until they are almost all open, stirring two or three times.

4 Spoon the mussels into a warm serving dish, cover and leave to stand for 3 mins., then discard any that remain tightly closed.

5 Mix the butter and flour together and whisk a little at a time into the cooking liquid. Add the tomato purée and ⌇ FULL for 3 mins. 600W (2½ mins. 700W; 3½ mins. 500W) until boiling and thickened, stirring two or three times.

6 Pour all of the sauce over the mussels and garnish with the chopped parsley. Serve immediately.

Top: **Salmon with tarragon sauce** (*see p. 74*); Bottom: **Moules marinière** (*see opposite*).

Salmon with tarragon sauce

INGREDIENTS

4 × 100-175g (4-6 oz) salmon steaks

juice of 1 lemon

For the sauce

25g (1 oz) butter

grated rind of 1 lemon

30ml (2 tbsp) plain flour

150ml (¼ pint) milk

150ml (¼ pint) fish stock

1 egg yolk

30ml (2 tbsp) double cream

30ml (2 tbsp) chopped fresh tarragon

salt and black pepper

Garnish

four sprigs of tarragon and ¼ slices of lemon

Salmon steaks cook so amazingly quickly by microwave that you need to make the sauce first. Reheat it while the fish is standing for a short time.

1 To make the sauce: put the butter and lemon rind in a small bowl and 🌊 FULL for 1 min. 600W (*30 secs. 700W; 1 min. 500W*) to melt.

2 Stir in the flour, then the milk and fish stock. 🌊 FULL for 4 mins. 600W (*3 mins. 700W; 5 mins. 500W*) until boiling and thickened, stirring every minute.

3 Beat the yolk and cream together, then blend in a little of the hot sauce. Whisk back into the rest of the sauce and 🌊 FULL for 30 secs. (*all powers*).

4 Stir in the tarragon and leave to stand while you cook the steaks. Place the steaks in a dish with the narrow ends towards the centre. Sprinkle with the lemon juice and cover. 🌊 FULL for 6-8 mins. 600W (*5-6½ mins. 700W; 7-10 mins. 500W*), turning over halfway through cooking.

5 Leave to stand for 3 mins. and reheat the sauce, 🌊 FULL for 2 mins. 600W (*1½ mins. 700W; 2½ mins. 500W*). Season to taste, pour over the steaks and garnish with the tarragon sprigs and the lemon slices.

⭐ **Preparation:** 10 minutes

🌊 **Cooking time:** 13½ minutes

▨ **Power setting:** FULL

◎ **Serves 4**

⭐ It's not worth using dried tarragon for this delicately flavoured sauce – if you can't get fresh tarragon, use a mixture of fresh parsley and chives instead.

Illustrated on p. 73

Fish lasagne

INGREDIENTS

6 sheets spinach lasagne
1.15 litres (2 pints) boiling water
15ml (1 tbsp) sunflower oil
350g (12 oz) whiting fillets
350g (12 oz) trout fillets
100g (4 oz) mozzarella cheese, grated
100g (4 oz) Cheddar cheese, grated
salt and black pepper
For the tomato sauce
400g (14 oz) can chopped tomatoes
30ml (2 tbsp) tomato purée
5ml (1 tsp) chopped fresh oregano
5ml (1 tsp) dried thyme
1 bay leaf
pinch of garlic salt
black pepper
For the white sauce
25g (1 oz) butter
25g (1 oz) plain flour
about 250ml (8 fl oz) milk

This filling main course is full of rich flavours – it is easy to make, but time consuming because there are four different parts to microwave. To save time, you can cook the lasagne conventionally while the fish and sauces are microwaving.

1 Put the lasagne, water and oil into a large dish and ⊠ FULL for 6-8 mins. *(all powers)* until just tender, stirring two or three times. Leave to stand for 5 mins.

2 Arrange the fish fillets in a dish and cover. ⊠ FULL for 4-6 mins. 600W *(3-5 mins. 700W; 5-7 mins. 500W)*, until flaking easily. Leave to stand for 3 mins. Drain off the juices and make up to 300ml (½ pint) with the milk for the white sauce. Flake the fish, removing any skin and bones.

3 To make the tomato sauce: put the tomatoes, tomato purée, oregano, thyme, bay leaf, garlic salt and pepper in a bowl and cover. ⊠ FULL for 10 mins. 600W *(8½ mins. 700W; 12½ mins. 500W)*, stirring once. Set aside and remove bay leaf.

4 To make the white sauce: put the butter in a large bowl and ⊠ FULL for 1 min. 600W *(30 secs. 700W; 1 min. 500W)* to melt. Stir in the flour and flavoured milk and ⊠ FULL for 3-4 mins. 600W *(2½-3 mins. 700W; 3½-5 mins. 500W)*, until boiling and thickened, stirring twice.

5 Mix together the cheeses and stir half into the white sauce with the fish. Season to taste. Grease a large roasting dish and spread one third of the tomato sauce in the base, add two sheets of lasagne in a single layer and cover with one-third of the white sauce. Repeat these layers twice more, then sprinkle with the rest of the cheese.

6 ⊠ MEDIUM for 15-20 mins. 600W *(12-17 mins. 700W; 18-25 mins. 500W)* until hot, rotating the dish twice. Leave to stand for 5 mins., then serve hot with a crisp salad and wholewheat bread.

Preparation: 10 minutes

Cooking time: 39 minutes

Power settings: FULL and MEDIUM

Good reheated

Freezes well

Serves 4

Illustrated on p. 76

Top right: **Prawn and coconut curry** (*see opposite*); Middle: **Fish lasagne** (*see p. 75*). Bottom: **Seafood paella** (*see p. 78*).

Prawn and coconut curry

INGREDIENTS

100g (4 oz) creamed coconut
450ml (¾ pint) boiling water
30ml (2 tbsp) sunflower oil
1 onion, finely sliced
1 clove garlic, crushed
2 courgettes, diced
1 red pepper, diced
45ml (3 tbsp) wholewheat flour
5ml (1 tsp) curry paste
350g (12 oz) cooked shelled prawns
salt and black pepper

This mild curry sauce makes a delicious base for prawns. The flavour of the sauce is improved if made in advance, so if you have time, make it without the prawns and add them just for the final reheating.

1 Put the creamed coconut and water in a bowl and leave to stand for 5 mins., stirring occasionally until the coconut dissolves.

2 Put the oil, onion and garlic in a large bowl and cover. 🍲 FULL for 4 mins. 600W (*3 mins. 700W; 5 mins. 500W*) until softened, stirring once. Stir in the courgettes and pepper and 🍲 FULL for 3 mins. 600W (*2½ mins. 700W; 3½ mins. 500W*) to soften.

3 Stir in the flour and curry paste and 🍲 FULL for 1 min. 600W (*30 secs. 700W; 1 min. 500W*). Pour in the coconut mixture, stir well and 🍲 FULL for 5 mins. 600W (*4 mins. 700W; 6 mins. 500W*) until boiling and thickened, stirring two or three times.

4 Season to taste, and stir in the prawns and cover. 🍲 FULL for 4 mins. 600W (*3 mins. 700W; 5 mins. 500W*) until heated through. Leave to stand for 3 mins., then serve hot with rice.

⭐ **Preparation:** 10 minutes

🍲 **Cooking time:** 17 minutes

⊘ **Power setting:** FULL

〰 **Good reheated**

◎ **Serves 4**

⭐ Cooked prawns just need heating through and if microwaved for too long will become tough and chewy, so watch them carefully.

Illustrated opposite

Seafood paella

INGREDIENTS

225g (8 oz) fresh mussels, cleaned (see page 37)
30ml (2 tbsp) sunflower oil
1 onion, sliced
1 clove garlic, crushed
225g (8 oz) long grain rice
1.2ml (¼ tsp) saffron threads
700ml (1¼ pint) boiling fish stock
225g (8 oz) white fish, cut into large chunks
1 red pepper, sliced
1 yellow pepper, sliced
75g (3 oz) frozen peas
100g (4 oz) cooked shelled prawns
10ml (2 tsp) chopped fresh basil
salt and black pepper

Garnish
sprigs of basil

Paella is a colourful dish that combines many different flavours and textures. It takes almost as long to make in a microwave as it does the conventional way, but in the microwave the dish needs much less attention and cooks to perfection without any sticking problems.

1 Put the mussels in a bowl and cover. ☷ FULL for about 1½ mins. 600W (*1 min. 700W; 2 mins. 500W*), until the shells open. Leave to stand for 5 mins., then remove the mussels from their shells and set aside.

2 Put the oil, onion and garlic in a large bowl and cover. ☷ FULL for 4 mins. 600W (*3 mins. 700W; 5 mins. 500W*) to soften.

3 Stir in the rice, saffron and stock and cover. ☷ FULL for 5 mins. 600W (*4 mins. 700W; 6 mins. 500W*), or until boiling, stirring once.

4 Add the fish and peppers, stir gently and re-cover. ☷ FULL for 4 mins. 600W (*3 mins. 700W; 5 mins. 500W*), stir in the peas, prawns, mussels, basil and seasoning and ☷ FULL for 3-5 mins. 600W (*2½-4 mins. 700W; 3½-6 mins. 500W*), until cooked, and almost all the liquid has been absorbed, stirring two or three times.

5 Leave to stand for 5 mins., then serve at once, garnished with the basil.

★ **Preparation:** 15 minutes

☷ **Cooking time:** 17½ minutes

⊘ **Power setting:** FULL

◎ **Serves 4**

★ Paella should be moist but not wet, so if there is any stock left in the base of the dish after standing, uncover and ☷ FULL for a further 2-3 mins. (*all powers*), stirring once.

Illustrated on p. 76

Stuffed trout with fennel sauce

INGREDIENTS

4 × 225g (8 oz) trout, scored both sides

For the stuffing

50g (2 oz) butter
1 small onion, finely chopped
50g (2 oz) button mushrooms, chopped
grated rind and juice of 1 lemon
15ml (1 tbsp) chopped fresh fennel
50g (2 oz) fresh breadcrumbs
1 egg yolk
salt and black pepper

For the sauce

75g (3 oz) butter
3 egg yolks
15ml (1 tbsp) lemon juice
15ml (1 tbsp) chopped fresh fennel

Garnish

fresh fennel leaves

The mild aniseed flavour of fennel goes very well with trout and the feathery leaves also make a very pretty garnish.

1 To make the stuffing: put the butter in a bowl and ❈ FULL for 1½ mins. 600W (*1 min. 700W; 1½-2 mins. 500W*) to melt. Stir in the onion, mushrooms, lemon rind and juice and fennel. Cover and ❈ FULL for 6 mins. 600W (*5 mins. 700W; 7 mins. 500W*), stirring the mixture once.

2 Leave to cool slightly, then stir in the breadcrumbs and egg yolk and mix well. Season to taste. Divide the stuffing between the trout. Arrange the fish in a shallow dish and cover.

3 ❈ FULL for 7-9 mins. 600W (*6-7 mins. 700W; 11-13 mins. 500W*), turning over halfway through cooking. Leave to stand for 5 mins.

4 Meanwhile, make the sauce: put the butter in a medium bowl and ❈ FULL for 2 mins. 600W (*1½ mins. 700W; 2½ mins. 500W*) to melt. Whisk the egg yolks and lemon juice until frothy, then gradually whisk into the butter. ❈ FULL for 45 secs. 600W (*30 secs. 700W; 1 min. 500W*), whisking every 15 seconds, until thickened slightly.

5 Whisk the fennel into the sauce and season to taste. Serve the trout at once with a little of the sauce poured over each of them. Garnish with the fennel leaves.

Preparation: 10 minutes

Cooking time: 17¼ minutes

Power setting: FULL

Serves 4

Arrange the trout head to tail in the dish, turning once for even cooking.

Illustrated on p. 81

Lemony sea bass

INGREDIENTS

800g (1¾ lb) sea bass
1 lemon
1 bay leaf
For the stuffing
25g (1 oz) wholewheat breadcrumbs
30ml (2 tbsp) chopped fresh parsley
grated rind of 1 lemon
salt and black pepper
a little beaten egg

Sea bass is considered to be as fine a fish as salmon – cook it simply with herbs and seasonings "en papillote". Keep the accompanying sauce very light; just stir a little single cream and chopped herbs into the cooking juices.

1 To make the stuffing: mix together the breadcrumbs, parsley, lemon rind and salt and pepper with enough beaten egg to bind.

2 Cut four very thin slices from the lemon and squeeze the juice from the rest. Sprinkle the juice into the cavity of the fish and season to taste. Spoon the stuffing into the cavity, then score each side of the fish carefully with a sharp knife.

3 Place the fish on a large sheet of buttered greaseproof paper and tuck the lemon slices and bay leaf underneath. Fold the edges of the paper together to make a parcel, completely enclosing the fish. Place on a large shallow dish.

4 ▨ FULL for 7-10½ mins. 600W (*6-8½ mins. 700W; 8½-12½ mins. 500W*) until the fish flakes easily, turning over once during cooking. Leave to stand for 5 mins. Serve hot.

⬛ **Preparation:**
8 minutes

▨ **Cooking time:**
7 minutes

▨ **Power setting:**
FULL

◎ **Serves 4**

▨ Scoring both sides of the fish two or three times with a sharp knife helps the thickest parts cook more quickly.

Top left: **Cod steaks Niçoise** (*see p. 83*); Middle: **Orange and parsley monkfish kebabs** (*see p. 82*); Bottom: **Stuffed trout with fennel sauce** (*see p. 79*).

Orange and parsley monkfish kebabs ◆

INGREDIENTS

450g (1 lb) monkfish tail fillet
grated rind and juice of ½ orange
15g (½ oz) butter
1 spring onion, finely chopped
15ml (1 tbsp) plain flour
120ml (8 tbsp) milk
10ml (2 tsp) chopped fresh parsley
30ml (2 tbsp) double cream
salt and black pepper
Garnish
orange slices and parsley sprigs

The firm white flesh of monkfish becomes tender and moist during microwaving, but doesn't fall apart once it's cooked so is very suitable for kebabs. Marinate the fish in orange juice for extra flavour.

1 Cut the fish into twelve 1 × 10cm (½ × 4 in) strips and thread onto 12 small wooden skewers. Place in a single layer in a shallow dish and sprinkle with the orange juice. Cover and leave to marinate for up to 2 hours.

2 Put the butter and spring onion in a small bowl and 🌊 FULL for 2 mins. 600W (*1½ mins. 700W; 2½ mins. 500W*). Stir in the flour, milk, orange rind and parsley and 🌊 FULL for 2 mins. 600W (*1½ mins. 700W; 2½ mins. 500W*), until boiling and thickened, stirring twice. Cover and set aside.

3 Baste the kebabs with the orange juice, re-cover and 🌊 FULL for 2½-3 mins. 600W (*2-2½ mins. 700W; 3-3½ mins. 500W*), until the fish goes white, rearranging once. Drain the cooking juices into the sauce, then leave the kebabs to stand for 2-3 mins.

4 Stir the cream and seasoning into the sauce and 🌊 FULL for 1 min. 600W (*30 secs. 700W; 1 min. 500W*). Pour the sauce over the kebabs, garnish with the orange slices and parsley sprigs and serve at once.

Preparation: 15 minutes

Cooking time: 7½ minutes

Power setting: FULL

Make in advance

Serves 4

Always use wooden or bamboo skewers for microwaving – they can be bought in Oriental supermarkets.

Illustrated on p. 81

Cod steaks Niçoise

INGREDIENTS

4 × 225g (8 oz) cod steaks
juice of ½ lemon
For the sauce
15ml (1 tbsp) sunflower oil
1 medium onion, sliced
1 clove garlic, crushed
10ml (2 tsp) chopped fresh basil
1 green pepper, sliced
1 red pepper, sliced
400g (14 oz) can chopped tomatoes
30ml (2 tbsp) tomato purée
25g (1 oz) pitted black olives, sliced
salt and black pepper

In this dish the colourful blend of vegetables complements the cod perfectly. But the versatile sauce is also good with hamburgers, chops and chicken.

1 To make the sauce: put the oil and onion in a medium bowl and cover. ☒ FULL for 5 mins. 600W (*4 mins. 700W; 6 mins. 500W*). Add the garlic, basil and peppers and ☒ FULL for 2 mins. 600W (*1½ mins. 700W; 2½ mins. 500W*).

2 Stir in the tomatoes, tomato purée, olives and seasoning to taste. ☒ FULL for 4 mins. 600W (*3 mins. 700W; 5 mins. 500W*), stirring twice. Cover and leave to stand for 5 mins.

3 Arrange the steaks in a large shallow dish with the narrow ends towards the centre. Sprinkle with the lemon juice and cover. ☒ FULL for 8 mins. 600W (*6½ mins. 700W; 10 mins. 500W*).

4 Drain off the cooking juices and spoon the tomato sauce over the steaks. Re-cover and ☒ FULL for 3-4 mins. 600W (*2½-3 mins. 700W; 3½-5 mins. 500W*) until the fish flakes easily. Leave to stand for 3 mins., then serve hot.

★ **Preparation:** 10 minutes

☒ **Cooking time:** 22 minutes

⊘ **Power setting:** FULL

◎ **Serves 4**

★ The bones in cod steaks sometimes "pop" during microwaving; this is just the sound of little bursts of steam escaping.

Illustrated on p. 81

Chilli con carne

INGREDIENTS

30ml (2 tbsp) plain flour
5-10ml (1-2 tsp) chilli powder
10ml (2 tsp) ground cumin
10ml (2 tsp) dried oregano
450g (1 lb) chuck steak, cubed
400g (14 oz) can chopped tomatoes
30ml (2 tbsp) tomato purée
150ml (¼ pint) boiling beef stock
425g (15 oz) can kidney beans, drained
2 cloves garlic, crushed
salt and black pepper

You can make this dish as mild or hot as you like, depending on whether you like really spicy food. The rich tomato-flavoured sauce is enhanced with cumin and oregano, which give it a good rounded taste. Serve with brown rice and a green salad tossed in a sharp vinaigrette dressing.

1 Mix together the flour, chilli powder to taste, ground cumin and oregano. Add the cubed beef and toss well to coat with all the spices.

2 Place in a large bowl, add the tomatoes, tomato purée, stock, kidney beans and garlic. Stir the mixture thoroughly.

3 Cover and ⊠ FULL for 10 mins. 600W *(8½ mins. 700W; 12½ mins. 500W)* or until boiling, stirring twice. ⊠ MEDIUM for 30-35 mins. 600W *(25-30 mins. 700W; 35-40 mins. 500W)* or until tender, stirring once.

4 Leave to stand for 5 mins. Serve with the rice and the salad.

Preparation: 15 minutes

Cooking time: 40 minutes

Power settings: FULL and MEDIUM

Good reheated

Serves 4

Cut the beef into small, neat cubes to ensure that it cooks evenly.

Illustrated opposite

Top: **Chilli con carne** (*see opposite*); Bottom: **Kidneys in cream sauce** (*see p. 87*).

Steak and kidney pudding

INGREDIENTS

30ml (2 tbsp) sunflower oil	
2 onions, sliced	
450g (1 lb) chuck steak, cubed	
250g (8 oz) ox kidney, chopped	
45ml (3 tbsp) seasoned flour	
150ml (¼ pint) brown ale	

For the pastry

225g (8 oz) wholewheat self-raising flour	
100g (4 oz) shredded vegetable suet	
about 150ml (¼ pint) cold water	

The flavour of this rich meat filling benefits from the double cooking – once on its own and once inside the pastry shell. Eat the pudding as soon as it is cooked because the pastry will start to harden as it cools.

1 Put the oil and the onions in a large bowl and cover. ▨ FULL for 5 mins. 600W *(4 mins. 700W; 6 mins. 500W)* to soften. Toss the steak and kidney in the seasoned flour, then stir into the onions. Re-cover and ▨ FULL for 10 mins. 600W *(8½ mins. 700W; 12½ mins. 500W)*, stirring two or three times.

2 Stir in the ale, re-cover and ▨ MEDIUM for 40 mins. 600W *(34 mins. 700W; 50 mins. 500W)*, or until tender, stirring two or three times. Leave to cool.

3 To make the pastry: sift the flour into a mixing bowl, tipping in the bran from the sieve. Add the suet and enough of the water to mix to a soft dough, but make sure it is not sticky. Knead lightly and roll out on a floured board to a 25cm (10 in) circle. Cut out a quarter and set aside for the lid.

4 Line a 900ml (1½ pint) pudding basin with the pastry, brush the seam with water and press to seal. Roll out the reserved pastry to a circle to fit the top of the basin.

5 Spoon the steak and kidney mixture into the basin. Brush the edge with water and press on the lid, pinching the edges together to seal firmly. Cover loosely with cling film.

6 ▨ FULL for 8-10 mins. 600W *(6½-8½ mins. 700W; 10-12½ mins. 500W)*. Leave to stand for 5 mins., then invert onto a serving dish and serve at once.

Preparation:
10 minutes, plus cooling

Cooking time:
63 minutes

Power setting:
FULL

Make in advance

Serves 4

Leave the meaty filling to cool completely before assembling the pudding, otherwise the pastry will become soggy.

Kidneys in cream sauce

INGREDIENTS

25g (1 oz) butter
1 small onion, chopped
1 clove garlic, chopped
8 lamb's kidneys, skinned, cored and quartered
30ml (2 tbsp) plain flour
150ml (¼ pint) boiling beef stock
150ml (¼ pint) single cream
salt and black pepper
Garnish
fresh chopped parsley

This tasty dish makes a lovely light main course, served with rice or pasta, but it is also delicious as a filling starter or supper dish, served on top of buttered wholewheat toast.

1 Put the butter in a medium bowl and ⧆ FULL for 1 min. 600W (*30 secs. 700W; 1 min. 500W*) to melt. Add the onion and garlic and cover. ⧆ FULL for 4 mins. 600W (*3 mins. 700W; 5 mins. 500W*) to soften.

2 Stir in the kidneys, re-cover and ⧆ FULL for 11-12 mins. 600W (*9-10 mins. 700W; 13½-15½ mins. 500W*), until the kidneys are no longer pink in the centre, stirring two or three times.

3 Stir in the flour, mixing well, then stir in the stock and cream and ⧆ FULL for 3-4 mins. 600W (*2½-3 mins. 700W; 3-5 mins. 500W*), until just boiling and thickened, stirring two or three times.

4 Season to taste, cover and leave to stand for 5 mins. Garnish with parsley and serve hot with boiled rice or pasta shells.

Preparation:
20 minutes

Cooking time:
15 minutes

Power setting:
FULL

Serves 4

Illustrated on p. 85

Top: **Sweet and sour pork** (*see p. 91*); Middle: **Lemony lamb kebabs** (*see p. 90*); Bottom: **Bacon steaks with orange and raisin sauce** (*see opposite*).

Bacon steaks with orange and raisin sauce

INGREDIENTS

4 × 75g (3 oz) bacon steaks	
15ml (1 tbsp) sunflower oil	

For the sauce

100g (4 oz) soft light brown sugar	
15ml (1 tbsp) cornflour	
1.5ml (¼ tsp) ground cinnamon	
1.5ml (¼ tsp) mustard powder	
300ml (½ pint) orange juice	
75g (3 oz) raisins	
15g (½ oz) butter	

Preparation: 10 minutes

Cooking time: 11 minutes

Power setting: FULL

Serves 4

Illustrated opposite

Bacon steaks can be cooked either on a microwave roasting rack or on a browning dish. With the latter, the steaks brown a little more and keep very moist. Serve with a sweet tangy sauce to complement the savoury taste of the bacon steaks.

1 Preheat a browning dish, ⊠ FULL for 5 mins. 600W (*4 mins. 700W; 6 mins. 500W*), or according to the manufacturer's instructions. Snip the fat off the steaks at 1cm (½ in) intervals to prevent it curling.

2 Pour the oil into the hot dish and swirl to coat the base. Add the steaks and press them down well. Cover and ⊠ FULL for 8-9 mins. 600W (*6½-7½ mins. 700W; 10-11½ mins. 500W*), turning over and rearranging once. Leave to stand for 3 mins.

3 Meanwhile, to make the sauce: put the sugar, cornflour, cinnamon and mustard into a medium bowl and mix well. Stir in the orange juice, raisins and butter and ⊠ FULL for 3 mins. 600W (*2½ mins. 700W; 3½ mins. 500W*), or until boiling, stirring twice. Serve hot, poured over the steaks.

Lemony lamb kebabs

INGREDIENTS

450g (1 lb) boned leg of lamb
2 small onions, quartered
2 courgettes, each cut into 8 chunks
30ml (2 tbsp) olive oil
5ml (1 tsp) chopped fresh thyme
grated rind and juice of 1 lemon
2.5ml (½ tsp) cornflour

Lamb cubes threaded onto skewers cook quickly and stay tender when cooked in the microwave. To keep them really moist, stop cooking when the cubes are still slightly pink and leave to stand in a warm place while microwaving the sauce.

1 Cut the lamb into 24 even-sized chunks. Thread the lamb onto eight short wooden skewers, alternately with the onion and courgette chunks. Lay them in a shallow dish.

2 Mix together the olive oil, thyme, lemon rind and juice and spoon over the kebabs. Leave them in a cool place to marinate for about 30 mins., basting with the marinade occasionally.

3 Drain the kebabs and reserve the marinade. Place on a microwave roasting rack over a shallow dish and ▨ FULL for 12-14 mins. 600W (*10-11 mins. 700W; 15-17 mins. 500W*) until just cooked, basting with the marinade and turning and rearranging two or three times. Drain the cooking juices into a bowl, then cover the kebabs and leave to stand for 3 mins.

4 Mix the cornflour to a paste with a little water and stir into the juices, then add any remaining marinade and mix well. ▨ FULL for 1-1½ mins. 600W (*½-1 min. 700W; 1-2 mins. 500W*), until boiling and thickened, stirring every 30 secs. Pour over the kebabs and serve at once with a mixed salad.

Preparation:
15 minutes, plus marinating

Cooking time:
13 minutes

Power setting:
FULL

Make in advance

Serves 4

Thread the smaller-sized chunks of lamb onto the centre of the skewers, keeping any slightly larger chunks at the ends, where they will cook more quickly.

Illustrated on p. 88

Sweet and sour pork

INGREDIENTS

15ml (1 tbsp) sunflower oil

450g (1 lb) pork fillet, cut into thin strips

2 carrots, thinly sliced

4 spring onions, cut into 2.5cm (1 in) pieces

1 green pepper, quartered and sliced

30ml (2 tbsp) soft light brown sugar

15ml (1 tbsp) cornflour

pinch of garlic salt

15ml (1 tbsp) white wine vinegar

30ml (2 tbsp) soy sauce

15ml (1 tbsp) tomato ketchup

225g (8 oz) can pineapple chunks

Garnish

50g (2 oz) roasted cashew nuts

By first cooking the pork and vegetables separately, then quickly heating them through in the sweet and sour sauce, everything keeps its individual flavour. The pork remains very tender and the vegetables stay pleasantly crisp.

1 Preheat a browning dish, ⊠ FULL for 5 mins. 600W *(4 mins. 700W; 6 mins. 500W)*, or according to the manufacturer's instructions. Add the oil and swirl to coat the base. Spread the pork in an even layer in the hot dish and press down well for a few seconds, then stir and press down again until the sizzling stops.

2 Cover and ⊠ FULL for 4 mins. 600W *(3 mins. 700W; 5 mins. 500W)*, stirring once, until the pork is no longer pink. Remove the pork from the dish with a slotted spoon and set aside.

3 Add the carrots, onions and green pepper to the juices in the dish and cover. ⊠ FULL for 4-5 mins. 600W *(3-4 mins. 700W; 5-6 mins. 500W)*, until just tender, stirring once.

4 Mix the sugar, cornflour and garlic salt with the vinegar, soy sauce and tomato ketchup. Pour onto the vegetables, add the pineapple and its juice and stir well.

5 Stir in the pork and ⊠ FULL for 4-6 mins. 600W *(3-5 mins. 700W; 5-7 mins. 500W)*, until the sauce is boiling and thickened. Stir twice during cooking. Serve hot garnished with the cashew nuts, accompanied by rice.

Preparation:
15 minutes

Cooking time:
12 minutes

Power setting:
FULL

Serves 4

Illustrated on p. 88

Duck with cherry sauce

INGREDIENTS

4 duck quarters
For the sauce
425g (15 oz) can pitted black cherries
grated rind and juice of 1 orange
5ml (1 tsp) chopped fresh mint
45ml (3 tbsp) port
30ml (2 tbsp) black cherry jam
10ml (2 tsp) arrowroot
Garnish
sprigs of mint

Balance the rich flavour of duck with a sharp sauce. This quick, colourful cherry sauce can be made while the duck is standing and still cooking through.

1 Put the duck portions (with the thinner parts to the centre) in a shallow dish and 🌊 FULL for 13-15 mins. 600W (*10-12½ mins. 700W; 16-18 mins. 500W*), rearranging and turning over after halfway through cooking. Cover and leave to stand for 5 mins.

2 To make the cherry sauce: drain the cherries and reserve the juice. Put the cherries, orange rind and juice, mint, port and cherry jam in a small bowl. Mix the arrowroot with 60ml (4 tbsp) of the cherry juice and stir into the cherry mixture.

3 🌊 FULL for 2-3 mins. 600W (*1½-2½ mins. 700W; 2½-3½ mins. 500W*) until boiling and thickened, stirring twice. Serve hot, poured over the duck and garnish with the mint sprigs.

⭐ **Preparation:** 10 minutes

🌊 **Cooking time:** 15 minutes

▢ **Power setting:** FULL

◎ **Serves 4**

⭐ Skim the fat from the cooking juices and add to the sauce for extra flavour.

Illustrated opposite

Top: **Duck with cherry sauce** (*see opposite*); Bottom: **Roast chicken with redcurrants** (*see p. 94*).

Roast chicken with redcurrants

INGREDIENTS

1 × 1.4kg (3 lb) chicken
chicken browning spice
For the stuffing
150g (5 oz) redcurrant jelly
grated rind and juice of 1 lemon
40g (1½ oz) butter
50g (2 oz) wholewheat breadcrumbs
50g (2 oz) chopped toasted hazelnuts
salt and black pepper

Stuffing the chicken under the skin rather than in the cavity ensures that it cooks thoroughly and has the added advantage of making the breast meat moist and full of flavour.

1 To make the stuffing: put the redcurrant jelly and lemon rind and juice in a jug and ⧖ FULL for 2 mins. 600W (*1½ mins. 700W; 2½ mins. 500W*), then stir to melt. Put the butter in a separate bowl and ⧖ FULL for 1 min. 600W (*30 secs. 700W; 1 min. 500W*) to melt.

2 Reserve one-third of the butter for basting the chicken and pour the rest into a mixing bowl. Stir in the breadcrumbs, hazelnuts, seasoning to taste and three-quarters of the redcurrant jelly mixture and mix well.

3 Loosen the skin over the breast of the chicken, then stuff the neck end, pushing the stuffing in an even layer, over the breast, under the skin. Secure the neck flap with a wooden skewer.

4 Brush the chicken with the reserved butter and sprinkle with the browning spice. Place the prepared chicken on a microwave roasting rack and dish, breast-side down and ⧖ FULL for 9 mins. 600W (*7 mins. 700W; 13 mins. 500W*).

5 Turn the chicken over and drain off the cooking juices. Sprinkle with a little more browning spice and ⧖ FULL for 9-11 mins. 600W (*7½-9 mins. 700W; 11½-13½ mins. 500W*) until the juices run clear. Cover and leave to stand for 10 minutes.

6 Just before serving, pour the remaining redcurrant jelly mixture into a small bowl and ⧖ FULL for 1 min. 600W (*30 secs. 700W; 1 min. 500W*). Serve hot with the sliced chicken and stuffing.

Preparation:
25 minutes

Cooking time:
22 minutes

Power setting:
FULL

Serves 4

Illustrated on p. 93

Chicken korma

INGREDIENTS

1 medium onion, chopped
30ml (2 tbsp) sunflower oil
120ml (8 tbsp) natural yogurt
8 chicken drumsticks
15ml (1 tbsp) chopped fresh coriander
15ml (1 tbsp) lemon juice
For the curry sauce
50g (2 oz) unsalted cashew nuts
2.5cm (1 in) piece fresh root ginger, finely grated
5ml (1 tsp) chilli powder
5ml (1 tsp) ground cinnamon
1.5ml (¼ tsp) cardamon seeds
1.5ml (¼ tsp) ground cloves
15ml (1 tbsp) poppy seeds
15ml (1 tbsp) ground coriander
10ml (2 tsp) ground cumin
2.5ml (½ tsp) saffron threads
30ml (2 tbsp) boiling water
Garnish
slices of lemon
sprigs of fresh coriander

This mild curry with its wonderful blend of spices cooks quickly, but it really needs to be left for a few hours after cooking to allow the flavours to develop properly. It's ideal for a dinner party as it can be made the day before.

1 To make the sauce: put the cashew nuts, ginger and all the spices except the saffron in a blender with 150ml (¼ pint) water and liquidize until smooth. Add the saffron to the boiling water and leave to soak.

2 Put the onion and oil in a large bowl and cover. 🦐 FULL for 4 mins. 600W (*3 mins. 700W; 5 mins. 500W*) to soften. Stir in the sauce and yogurt and 🦐 FULL for 3 mins. 600W (*2½ mins. 700W; 3½ mins. 500W*).

3 Add the chicken drumsticks, placing the narrow parts towards the centre, and spoon over the sauce to cover. Add the soaked saffron and the fresh coriander.

4 Cover and 🦐 FULL for 5 mins. 600W (*4 mins. 700W; 6 mins. 500W*). Stir, re-cover and 🦐 MEDIUM for 20-25 mins. 600W (*17-21 mins. 700W; 25-30 mins. 500W*), until the chicken is tender, stirring once.

5 Uncover and leave to cool, then cover and keep in a cool place for at least 2 hours (overnight if possible). To serve, 🦐 FULL for 10-12 mins. 600W (*8½-10 mins. 700W; 12½-15 mins. 500W*), stirring once until heated through. Leave to stand for 5 mins., then serve at once, garnished with the coriander sprigs and lemon slices.

Preparation: 10 minutes

Cooking time: 28 minutes

Power settings: FULL and MEDIUM

Make in advance

Good reheated

Serves 4

Top: **Turkey tetrazzini** (*see opposite*); Bottom: **Roast pheasant with port and lemon sauce** (*see p. 98*).

Turkey tetrazzini

INGREDIENTS

100g (4 oz) macaroni
1.2 litres (2 pints) boiling salted water
450g (1 lb) turkey breast
25g (1 oz) butter
225g (8 oz) button mushrooms, quartered
50g (2 oz) grated Cheddar cheese
30ml (2 tbsp) wholewheat breadcrumbs
For the sauce
40g (1½ oz) butter
40g (1½ oz) plain flour
150ml (½ pint) turkey or chicken stock
30ml (2 tbsp) dry vermouth (optional)
75ml (5 tbsp) double cream
salt and black pepper

This dish is based on an American recipe. It was originally made with turkey leftovers and tastes equally good made with chicken.

1 Put the macaroni and water in a deep bowl. Cover and ❄ FULL for 8 mins. (*all powers*), stirring two or three times. Leave to stand for 5 mins., then drain.

2 Put the turkey, butter and mushrooms in a shallow dish and ❄ FULL for 8-10 mins. 600W (*6-8½ mins. 700W; 10-12½ mins. 500W*), turning the turkey over halfway through cooking. Leave to stand for 5 mins., then slice the turkey thickly.

3 To make the sauce: put the butter in a medium bowl and ❄ FULL for 1 min. 600W (*30 secs. 700W; 1 min. 500W*) to melt. Stir in the flour, then the stock and ❄ FULL for 3-4 mins. 600W (*2½-3 mins. 700W; 3½-5 mins. 500W*) until boiling, stirring twice.

4 Stir in vermouth, if liked, and the cream and seasoning to taste, then mix in the turkey, mushrooms and macaroni. Spoon into individual ramekin dishes and spread evenly.

5 Mix the cheese and crumbs together and sprinkle over the tops. ❄ FULL for 4-6 mins. 600W (*3-5 mins. 700W; 5-7 mins. 500W*) until bubbling and hot, giving the dishes a half turn once. Leave to stand for 3 mins., then serve hot.

★ **Preparation:** 10 minutes

❄ **Cooking time:** 24 minutes

⊘ **Power setting:** FULL

❄ **Good reheated**

◎ **Serves 4**

Illustrated opposite

Roast pheasant with port and lemon sauce

INGREDIENTS

2 × 900g (2 lb) oven-ready hen pheasants
1 lemon
6 sprigs of fresh thyme
salt and black pepper
25g (1 oz) butter
5ml (1 tsp) soy sauce
4 rashers streaky bacon
For the sauce
5ml (1 tsp) cornflour
120ml (8 tbsp) port
10ml (2 tsp) chopped fresh thyme
5ml (1 tsp) soft brown sugar
5-10ml (1-2 tsp) lemon juice

Pheasant has quite a strong flavour so it needs a rich sauce to accompany it. It is traditionally served with game chips, which are difficult to make – ready salted crisps, heated under a grill, make a perfectly acceptable substitute.

1 Wipe the pheasant with a clean cloth, then dry the skin. Cut the lemon into six wedges and reserve four for the garnish. Place one of the remaining lemon wedges and a sprig of thyme inside each pheasant. Season with salt and pepper.

2 Put the butter in a small bowl and ⊠ FULL for 1 min. 600W (*30 secs. 700W; 1 min. 500W*) to melt. Stir in the soy sauce and brush over the birds. Cover the breast of the birds with the bacon and truss neatly. Place them breast-side down on a roasting rack in a large roasting bag.

3 ⊠ FULL for 32 mins. 600W (*25 mins. 700W; 48 mins. 500W*), until the juices run clear, turning the birds over halfway through cooking. Drain the juices into a small bowl and leave the birds to stand for 5 mins.

4 To make the sauce: blend the cornflour with 30ml (2 tbsp) water, then add the cooking juices, port, chopped thyme and sugar. ⊠ FULL for 2-2½ mins. 600W (*1½-2 mins. 700W; 2½-3 mins. 500W*) until boiling and thickened, stirring two or three times. Add the lemon juice and season to taste.

5 Cut the pheasants in half, and pour over the port and lemon sauce. Garnish with the remaining lemon wedges and sprigs of thyme and serve at once.

★ **Preparation:**
15 minutes

⧀ **Cooking time:**
32 minutes

⊘ **Power setting:**
FULL

◎ **Serves 4**

★ Tie the end of the roasting bag loosely with either string or an elastic band, so that steam can escape during cooking.

Illustrated on p. 96

Crunchy Chinese vegetables

INGREDIENTS

225g (8 oz) carrots, cut into julienne strips
225g (8 oz) turnips, diced
225g (8 oz) mangetout, sliced
100g (4 oz) mooli (white radish), cut into julienne strips
salt and black pepper
For the sauce
15ml (1 tbsp) sunflower oil
1 clove garlic, crushed
2 spring onions, chopped
150ml (¼ pint) boiling vegetable stock
15ml (1 tbsp) wine vinegar
30ml (2 tbsp) honey
15ml (1 tbsp) shoyu
15ml (1 tbsp) sherry
100g (4 oz) fresh pineapple, grated
5ml (1 tsp) aniseed
10ml (2 tsp) arrowroot

This is a microwave version of a stir-fry where the vegetables are cooked very quickly. The difference is that here the sauce is made before they are cooked and is used as a marinade.

1 Prepare all the vegetables and arrange in a large dish.

2 For the sauce, put the oil in a medium dish and ⊠ FULL for 1 min. 600W (*30 secs. 700W; 1 min. 500W*). Stir in the garlic and spring onions and ⊠ FULL for 30 secs.

3 Add the remaining ingredients, except the arrowroot, and ⊠ FULL for 3 mins. 600W (*2½ mins. 700W; 3½ mins. 500W*), stirring once or twice.

4 Dissolve the arrowroot in a little water, then stir into the sauce. ⊠ FULL for 2 mins. 600W (*1½ mins. 700W; 2½ mins. 500W*), stirring once.

5 Pour the sauce over the vegetables, stir well, then cover and ⊠ FULL for 5 mins. (*4 mins. 700W; 6 mins. 500W*), stirring once or twice.

6 Leave to stand for 2 mins., then season to taste. Serve with noodles or rice.

★ **Preparation:** 25 minutes

≋ **Cooking time:** 11½ minutes

⊘ **Power setting:** FULL

≋ **Good reheated**

❉ **Freezes well**

◎ **Serves 4**

★ Vary the ingredients according to the seasons. Mooli is a spicy-flavoured white radish which is available in specialist shops and large supermarkets.

Stuffed cabbage leaves

INGREDIENTS

100g (4 oz) pot barley
600ml (1 pint) boiling water
75g (3 oz) sunflower seeds
15ml (1 tbsp) sunflower oil
1 medium onion, finely chopped
175g (6 oz) button mushrooms, diced
100g (4 oz) cabbage, shredded
1 apple, grated
5ml (1 tsp) caraway seeds
100g (4 oz) carrots, grated
15ml (1 tbsp) shoyu
salt and black pepper
8-12 cabbage leaves

For the sauce

225g (8 oz) cooked carrots
30ml (2 tbsp) orange juice
60ml (4 tbsp) yogurt
2.5ml (½ tsp) grated nutmeg
salt and black pepper

Garnish

some cumin seeds

Barley is an underrated grain all too often confined to soups. It has a delicate flavour and is ideal as a vegetable filling.

1 Put the barley in a deep dish and pour over the boiling water. Leave to soak for 1 hour. Cover and ⌇ FULL for 20 mins. (*all powers*), stirring 2-3 times. Stand for 5 mins., then drain.

2 Spread out the sunflower seeds on a small plate and ⌇ FULL for 2 mins. 600W (*1½ mins. 700W; 2½ mins. 500W*).

3 Put the oil in a medium dish and ⌇ FULL for 1 min. 600W (*30 sec. 700W; 1 min. 500W*). Add the onion and ⌇ FULL for 2 mins. 600W (*1½ mins. 700W; 2½ mins. 500W*). Stir in the mushrooms, shredded cabbage, apple and caraway seeds. Cover and ⌇ FULL for 4 mins. 600W (*3 mins. 700W; 5 mins. 500W*).

4 Mix the cooked vegetables and barley with the raw carrot, sunflower seeds and shoyu. Season well with salt and pepper.

5 To soften the cabbage leaves, place in a large dish with 30ml (2 tbsp) water. Cover and ⌇ FULL for 2 mins. 600W (*1½ mins. 700W; 2½ mins. 500W*). Spoon 15-30ml (1-2 tbsp) filling on to each cabbage leaf, then roll up to make parcels. Arrange these in a shallow dish, cover and ⌇ FULL for 3 mins. 600W (*2½ mins. 700W; 3½ mins. 500W*) or until warmed.

6 To make the sauce, purée the cooked carrots with the orange juice and yogurt, and season well. ⌇ FULL for 1½ mins. 600W (*1 min. 700W; 2 mins. 500W*), then serve garnished with cumin seeds.

★ **Preparation:**
25 minutes

⌇ **Cooking time:**
44 minutes

⊘ **Power setting:**
FULL

◎ **Serves 4**

★ Choose dark cabbage leaves such as the outer leaves of a January King or Savoy for this recipe or the end result will look pale.

Illustrated opposite

Stuffed tomatoes

INGREDIENTS

4 large beef tomatoes
50g (2 oz) peanuts
15ml (1 tbsp) sesame seeds
5ml (1 tsp) cumin seeds
5ml (1 tsp) coriander seeds
50-75g (2-3 oz) wholewheat breadcrumbs
50g (2 oz) black olives, stoned and chopped
2 sticks celery, diced
4 spring onions, diced
15ml (1 tbsp) tomato purée
10ml (2 tsp) miso, dissolved in a little stock
salt and black pepper

The spicy flavour of the roasted nut and seed filling complements the sweet, moist beef tomatoes perfectly.

1 Slice a lid from the base of each tomato, then scoop out the flesh and chop well.

2 Mix the peanuts, sesame seeds and spices together, spread out on a small plate and 🍲 FULL for 3 mins. 600W *(2½ mins. 700W; 3½ mins. 500W)*, shaking the plate once or twice. Grind quite finely.

3 Mix the ground nuts and seeds with about half of the tomato flesh and the remaining ingredients, seasoning well with salt and pepper. Fill the tomatoes with the mixture and cover each one with its lid.

4 Arrange the tomatoes in a large dish, cover and 🍲 FULL for 7 mins. 600W *(6 mins. 700W; 8½ mins. 500W)*, rearranging once or twice during cooking.

5 Serve hot with a spicy tomato sauce (*see page 147*) or sharp yogurt dressing.

Preparation: 25 minutes

Cooking time: 10 minutes

Power setting: FULL

Serves 4

Be careful not to overcook the tomato shells or they will collapse. Miso is a soya bean paste which is available in health stores and Japanese and Chinese shops.

Illustrated below

Left: **Stuffed tomatoes** (*see above*); Right: **Stuffed cabbage leaves** (*see opposite*)

Hazelnut roast

INGREDIENTS

100g (4 oz) short-grain brown rice
450ml (¾ pint) boiling water
100g (4 oz) hazelnuts
15ml (1 tbsp) sunflower oil
1 medium onion, finely chopped
2 cloves garlic, crushed
5ml (1 tsp) celery seeds
100g (4 oz) carrots, diced
15ml (1 tbsp) wholewheat flour
150ml (¼ pint) red wine
30ml (2 tbsp) tomato purée
salt and black pepper

Using grains instead of breadcrumbs in a nut roast makes the mixture chewy in texture, but lighter and more moist.

1 Put the rice in a deep dish and pour over the boiling water. Cover and 🌊 FULL for 18 mins. (*all powers*), stirring 2-3 times. Leave to stand for 5 mins.

2 Spread out the hazelnuts on a small plate and 🌊 FULL for 4 mins. 600W (*3 mins. 700W; 5 mins. 500W*), shaking the plate once or twice. Cool and grind.

3 Put the oil in a medium dish and 🌊 FULL for 1 min. 600W (*30 secs. 700W; 1 min. 500W*). Stir in the onion, then 🌊 FULL for 1 min. 600W (*30 secs. 700W; 1 min. 500W*).

4 Add the garlic, celery seeds and carrots and 🌊 FULL for 4 mins. 600W (*3 mins. 700W; 5 mins. 500W*).

5 Sprinkle over the flour and 🌊 FULL for 30 secs.

6 Stir in the wine and tomato purée, cover and 🌊 FULL for 2 mins. 600W (*1½ mins. 700W; 2½ mins. 500W*).

7 Mix the ground nuts and the rice into the sauce and season well with salt and pepper.

8 Line a 450g (1 lb) loaf dish with greaseproof paper and spoon in the mixture. Cover with more paper and stand the dish on an upturned plate or saucer in the microwave. 🌊 FULL for 10-12 mins. 600W (*8½-10 mins. 700W; 12½-15 mins. 500W*), giving the dish a quarter turn every 3 mins. Leave to stand for 4 mins. before turning out and serving while still hot.

⭐ **Preparation:** 20 minutes

🌊 **Cooking time:** 40½ minutes

▨ **Power setting:** FULL

◎ **Serves 4**

🌊 Nut roasts are best when slightly undercooked and then left to stand. If overcooked, the outsides become dry and hard.

Spicy layered mango pilaff

INGREDIENTS

15ml (1 tbsp) sunflower oil
3 spring onions, finely chopped
1-2 cloves garlic, crushed
5ml (1 tsp) garam masala
5ml (1 tsp) cumin seeds
2.5ml (½ tsp) turmeric
50g (2 oz) pine kernels
175g (6 oz) long-grain brown rice
750ml (1¼ pints) boiling water
1 mango, peeled and diced
juice of ½ lemon
salt and black pepper
For the filling
15ml (1 tbsp) sunflower oil
225g (8 oz) mushrooms, diced
1 clove garlic, chopped
100g (4 oz) French beans, diced
15ml (1 tbsp) shoyu

The filling for this pilaff consists of a simple mixture of fresh vegetables which can be varied according to availability.

1 Put the oil in a medium dish and ⊠ FULL for 1 min. 600W *(30 secs. 700W; 1 min. 500W)*. Stir in the onion and garlic and ⊠ FULL for 30 secs.

2 Mix the spices with a little water. Add to the onions with the pine kernels and ⊠ FULL for 30 secs.

3 Add the rice and boiling water. Cover and ⊠ FULL for about 18 mins. *(all powers)*, stirring 2-3 times. Leave to stand for 5 mins. Then add the mango and the lemon juice. Season well.

4 For the filling, put the oil in a medium dish and ⊠ FULL for 1 min. 600W *(30 secs. 700W; 1 min. 500W)*. Stir in the diced mushrooms and garlic, cover and ⊠ FULL for 3 mins. 600W *(2½ mins. 700W; 3½ mins. 500W)*.

5 Add the beans, shoyu and 15ml (1 tbsp) water. Re-cover and ⊠ FULL for 4 mins. 600W *(3 mins. 700W; 5 mins. 500W)*. Season well.

6 Put half the rice into a large dish and cover with the mushroom and bean mixture. Spoon over the remaining rice, cover and ⊠ FULL for 3 mins. 600W *(2½ mins. 700W; 3½ mins. 500W)*.

⬛ **Preparation:** 25 minutes

⊠ **Cooking time:** 31 minutes

⊘ **Power setting:** FULL

❄ **Freezes well**

◎ **Serves 4**

⊠ The cooking time for rice will vary according to the age and variety of the grain. If it's not quite tender at the end of the time recommended here, cook for a little longer, adding more boiling water, if necessary.

Illustrated on p. 105

Leek and cauliflower cobbler

INGREDIENTS

10ml (2 tsp) sunflower oil
1 medium leek, diced
450g (1 lb) cauliflower, divided into florets
For the sauce
15g (½ oz) margarine
15ml (1 tbsp) wholewheat flour
300ml (½ pint) skimmed milk
1 bay leaf
2.5ml (½ tsp) grated nutmeg
5ml (1 tsp) mustard powder
For the topping
75g (3 oz) wholewheat flour
75g (3 oz) cornmeal
7.5ml (1½ tsp) baking powder
2.5ml (½ tsp) salt
5ml (1 tsp) caraway seeds
2.5ml (½ tsp) mustard powder
1 egg
150ml (¼ pint) milk
15ml (1 tbsp) olive oil
50g (2 oz) Cheddar cheese, grated

In this dish the lightly cooked vegetables retain a good crisp texture, the sauce is easy to prepare, and the scone topping provides a tasty and wholesome finish.

1 Put the oil in a medium dish and ≋ FULL for 1 min. 600W (*30 secs. 700W; 1 min. 500W*). Add the leek and cauliflower, cover and ≋ FULL for 4 mins. 600W (*3 mins. 700W; 5 mins. 500W*). Leave to stand.

2 For the sauce, put the margarine in a 600ml (1 pint) jug and ≋ FULL for 1 min. 600W (*30 secs. 700W; 1 min. 500W*). Add the flour and ≋ FULL for 30 secs. Pour in the milk, stirring well. Add the bay leaf and spices, then ≋ FULL for 2 mins. 600W (*1½ mins. 700W; 2½ mins. 500W*), stirring every 30 secs. Season well, then mix into the vegetables.

3 For the topping, mix the wholewheat flour, cornmeal, baking powder, salt and spices together.

4 In a separate jug, beat the egg thoroughly, then add the milk and olive oil. Pour the mixture over the dry ingredients and mix to a stiff dough. Add the cheese. Roll out the dough and cut into 2.5cm (1 in) rounds about 1cm (½ in) deep.

5 Put the vegetables and sauce in a medium dish and cover with the scone rounds. ≋ FULL for 5 mins. 600W (*4 mins. 700W; 6 mins. 500W*), then brown under a preheated conventional grill.

★ **Preparation:** 30 minutes `

≋ **Cooking time:** 13½ minutes

⦸ **Power setting:** FULL

◎ **Serves** 4

≋ If wished, top with a little more grated cheese before browning under a conventional grill.

Illustrated opposite

Top: **Spicy layered mango pilaff** (*see p. 103*); Bottom: **Leek and cauliflower cobbler** (*see opposite*)

Saffron rice with mangetout

INGREDIENTS

15ml (1 tbsp) sesame oil
1 medium onion, chopped
1 clove garlic, crushed
1cm (½ in) piece fresh root ginger, grated
5ml (1 tsp) ground coriander
200g (7 oz) can tomatoes, drained and sieved
5ml (1 tsp) ground saffron
175g (6 oz) brown rice
750ml (1¼ pints) boiling water
225g (8 oz) mangetout
1 medium green pepper, deseeded and diced
75g (3 oz) mung bean sprouts
½ cucumber, diced
For the sauce
juice of 1 orange
juice of ½ lemon
15ml (1 tbsp) shoyu
15ml (1 tbsp) sherry
5ml (1 tsp) arrowroot

Grain dishes topped with mixtures of lightly cooked vegetables are really easy to cook in the microwave. Here, saffron, ginger and coriander add an exotic flavour to the rice while the vegetables give a fresh, crisp texture.

1 Put the oil in a medium dish and ▨ FULL for 1 min. 600W (*30 secs. 700W; 1 min. 500W*). Stir in the onion and garlic and ▨ FULL for 30 secs. Stir well.

2 Add the ginger, coriander, tomatoes, saffron and rice. Pour over the boiling water, cover and ▨ FULL for 18 mins. (*all powers*), stirring 2-3 times.

3 Add the vegetables, re-cover and ▨ FULL for 4 mins. 600W (*3 mins. 700W; 5 mins. 500W*). Leave to stand for 4 mins.

4 For the sauce, mix the fruit juices, shoyu and sherry together in a small jug, then ▨ FULL for 2 mins. 600W (*1½ mins. 700W; 2½ mins. 500W*).

5 Dissolve the arrowroot in a little water, then stir into the sauce. ▨ FULL for 2 mins. 600W (*1½ mins. 700W; 2½ mins. 500W*), stirring twice.

6 Pour the sauce over the rice and vegetables and serve immediately.

Preparation: 20 minutes

Cooking time: 27½ minutes

Power setting: FULL

Serves 4

Borlotti bean casserole

INGREDIENTS

225g (8 oz) borlotti or pinto beans, soaked overnight

1.2 litres (2 pints) boiling water

15ml (1 tbsp) olive oil

1 onion, finely chopped

1 clove garlic, crushed

225g (8 oz) courgettes, diced

1 medium green pepper, deseeded and diced

400g (14 oz) can tomatoes, sieved

1 bay leaf

15ml (1 tbsp) tomato purée

salt and black pepper

For the pesto

25g (1 oz) pine kernels

15g (½ oz) Parmesan cheese, grated

60ml (4 tbsp) chopped fresh basil

15ml (1 tbsp) olive oil

1-2 cloves garlic

salt and black pepper

Pesto sauce adds a wonderful flavour to any savoury dish. It is particularly good in microwaved stews where the quick cooking means the flavours of the ingredients don't have much time to blend.

1 To make the pesto, grind the pine kernels using a pestle and mortar, then work in the other ingredients to form a smooth paste. Set aside.

2 Drain the beans, put in a deep dish and pour over the boiling water. Cover and 🌊 FULL for 22 mins. (*all powers*), stirring 2-3 times and adding more boiling water if necessary. Leave to stand for 10 mins., then drain.

3 Put the oil in a medium dish and 🌊 FULL for 1 min. (*30 secs. 700W; 1 min. 500W*). Stir in the onion and garlic and 🌊 FULL for 2 mins. 600W (*1½ mins. 700W; 2½ mins. 500W*).

4 Add the courgettes, pepper and cooked beans, stir well and 🌊 FULL for 5 mins. 600W (*4 mins. 700W; 6 mins. 500W*), stirring once or twice.

5 Add the tomatoes, bay leaf and purée. Cover and 🌊 FULL for 5 mins. 600W (*4 mins. 700W; 6 mins. 500W*).

6 Add the pesto sauce and 🌊 FULL for 5 mins. 600W (*4 mins. 700W; 6 mins. 500W*). Leave to stand for 5 mins., then season to taste. Serve hot, accompanied by rice, noodles, pasta or jacket potatoes.

Preparation:
20 minutes, plus overnight soaking

Cooking time:
40 minutes

Power setting:
FULL

Good reheated

Serves 4

Illustrated on p. 108

Top: **Borlotti bean casserole** (*see p. 107*); Bottom right: **Lentil and vegetable loaf** (*see opposite*); Bottom left: **Aubergine layer** (*see p. 110*)

Lentil and vegetable loaf

INGREDIENTS

50g (2 oz) continental or brown lentils
600ml (1 pint) boiling water
1 potato, weighing about 175g (6 oz)
15ml (1 tbsp) sunflower oil
100g (4 oz) leeks, trimmed and diced
1 medium carrot, diced
100g (4 oz) mushrooms, chopped
10ml (2 tsp) chopped fresh sage
10ml (2 tsp) miso (see p. 101)
50ml (2 fl oz) bean stock or dark vegetable stock
15ml (1 tbsp) tomato purée
50g (2 oz) porridge oats
25g (1 oz) breadcrumbs
15g (½ oz) sunflower margarine
15g (½ oz) wholewheat flour
15ml (1 tbsp) shoyu
5ml (1 tsp) yeast extract
black pepper

This hearty savoury loaf is full of rich flavours and moist vegetables. It is a good dish to serve for family supper with baked potatoes and green vegetables.

1 Put the lentils in a deep dish and pour over the boiling water. Cover and ☒ FULL for 12 mins. (*all powers*), stirring 2-3 times. Leave to stand for 5 mins., then drain.

2 Pierce the potato and wrap in absorbent paper. ☒ FULL for 6 mins. 600W (*5 mins. 700W; 7½ mins. 500W*), turning over halfway through. Leave to cool slightly, then dice.

3 Put the oil in a medium dish and ☒ FULL for 1 min. 600W (*30 secs. 700W; 1 min. 500W*). Stir in the leeks and ☒ FULL for 3 mins. 600W (*2½ mins. 700W; 3½ mins. 500W*).

4 Add the carrot, mushrooms, potato, sage and the miso dissolved in a little of the stock. Cover and ☒ FULL for 5 mins. (*4 mins. 700W; 6 mins. 500W*), stirring once or twice. Stir in the tomato purée, oats, breadcrumbs and lentils.

5 Put the margarine in a separate dish and ☒ FULL for 30 secs. Stir in the flour and ☒ FULL for 30 secs. Add the remaining bean stock, shoyu and yeast extract. ☒ FULL for 1-1½ mins., stirring once.

6 Stir the sauce into the lentil and vegetable mixture. Season to taste. Spoon into 450g (1 lb) loaf dish and ☒ FULL for 10 mins. 600W (*8½ mins. 700W; 12½ mins. 500W*). Leave to stand for 5 mins. before turning out and serving.

★ **Preparation:** 20 minutes

☒ **Cooking time:** 39 minutes

▨ **Power setting:** FULL

☒ **Good reheated**

❅ **Freezes well**

◎ **Serves 4**

☒ Savoury loaves also cook well in savarin moulds as the microwaves can easily penetrate the food from all sides.

Illustrated opposite

Aubergine layer

INGREDIENTS

1 large aubergine, weighing about 350g (12 oz)
1 large potato, weighing about 225g (8 oz)
15ml (1 tbsp) olive oil
1 medium onion, finely chopped
1-2 cloves garlic, crushed
3 sticks celery, diced
1 medium green pepper, deseeded and diced
1 medium red pepper, deseeded and diced
400g (14 oz) can tomatoes
30ml (2 tbsp) chopped fresh basil
salt and black pepper
100g (4 oz) hard Greek cheese (Haloumi), cubed

This deliciously rich dish is much easier to prepare in the microwave. Whole aubergines and potatoes take only a few minutes to bake and the dish is completed with a quick sauce.

1 Trim the aubergine and pierce the skin. Wrap in absorbent paper and ⊠ FULL for 3 mins. 600W *(2½ mins. 700W; 3½ mins. 500W)* until tender but still firm, turning over halfway through. Leave to stand for 4 mins., then slice thinly.

2 Pierce the potato and wrap in absorbent paper. ⊠ FULL for 4 mins. 600W *(3 mins. 700W; 5 mins. 500W)*, turning over halfway through. Leave to stand for 5 mins., then slice thinly.

3 Put the oil in a medium dish and ⊠ FULL for 1 min. 600W *(30 secs. 700W; 1 min. 500W)*. Stir in the onion and ⊠ FULL for 2 mins. 600W *(1½ mins. 700W; 2½ mins. 500W)*.

4 Add the garlic, celery and peppers. Stir well, cover and ⊠ FULL for 4 mins. 600W *(3 mins. 700W; 5 mins. 500W)*.

5 Add the tomatoes and basil. Cover and ⊠ FULL for 5 mins. 600W *(4 mins. 700W; 6 mins. 500W)*, stirring once. Season well with salt and pepper.

6 Put a layer of sauce in the base of a deep, medium-sized dish and cover with layers of sliced potato, aubergine and cubes of cheese. Continue layering, finishing with sauce then cheese.

7 ⊠ MEDIUM-HIGH for 8 mins. *(6 mins. 700W; ⊠ FULL for 6-7 mins. 500W)* until the cheese has just melted, giving the dish a quarter turn every 2 mins. Leave to stand for 4 mins. before serving.

★ **Preparation:** 25 minutes

≋ **Cooking time:** 27 minutes

⊘ **Power settings:** FULL and MEDIUM-HIGH

≋ **Good reheated**

❈ **Freezes well**

◎ **Serves 4**

Illustrated on p. 108

Marinated tofu with vegetables

INGREDIENTS

225g (8 oz) firm tofu, cut into 2.5cm (1 in) squares

For the marinade

75ml (3 fl oz) red wine

30ml (2 tbsp) shoyu

15ml (1 tbsp) concentrated apple juice (CAJ)

15ml (1 tbsp) mild mustard powder

2.5ml (½ tsp) chopped fresh rosemary

2.5ml (½ tsp) chopped fresh sage

1 clove garlic, crushed

For the vegetable accompaniment

15ml (1 tbsp) sunflower oil

350g (12 oz) leeks, cut into chunks

225g (8 oz) broccoli, divided into florets

100g (4 oz) turnips, cut into julienne strips

100g (4 oz) carrots, cut into julienne strips

salt and black pepper

The microwave is ideal for making quick marinades. Tofu benefits greatly from being marinated as it acts like blotting paper, soaking up all the flavours of the marinade ingredients. Use firm tofu which slices easily and does not fall apart during cooking.

1 Mix the marinade ingredients together in a shallow dish. Add the tofu, baste well, cover and ☒ FULL for 3 mins. 600W (*2½ mins. 700W; 3½ mins. 500W*), stirring once. Leave to stand for 10-15 mins.

2 For the vegetables, put the oil in a medium dish and ☒ FULL for 1 min. 600W (*30 secs. 700W; 1 min. 500W*). Stir in the chopped leeks and ☒ FULL for 2 mins. 600W (*1½ mins. 700W; 2½ mins. 500W*).

3 Add the broccoli, turnips and carrots. Cover and ☒ FULL for 2 mins. 600W (*1½ mins. 700W; 2½ mins. 500W*).

4 Add 30ml (2 tbsp) of the marinade, re-cover and ☒ FULL for 4-5 mins. 600W (*3-4 mins. 700W; 5-6 mins. 600W*), stirring once. Leave to stand for 2 mins., then season to taste with salt and pepper.

5 Meanwhile reheat the tofu mixture, cover and ☒ FULL for 2 mins. 600W (*1½ mins. 700W; 2½ mins. 500W*).

6 Serve with the vegetables and some brown rice, either mixing the tofu with the vegetables or keeping them separate.

★ **Preparation:**
25 minutes

☒ **Cooking time:**
14 minutes

∅ **Power setting:**
FULL

☒ **Good reheated**

◎ **Serves 4**

☒ The cooking time given in this recipe produces crisp vegetables; cook for longer if a softer texture is preferred.

Illustrated on p. 113

Vegetable gado gado

INGREDIENTS

100g (4 oz) peanuts
30ml (2 tbsp) groundnut oil
1 onion, finely chopped
1 clove garlic, crushed
1 bay leaf
5ml (1 tsp) grated fresh root ginger
1 green chilli, diced
juice of 1 lemon
15ml (1 tbsp) honey
300ml (½ pint) boiling light stock
15ml (1 tbsp) shoyu
salt and black pepper
For the vegetables
4 spring onions, diced
225g (8 oz) mangetout, sliced
100g (4 oz) mooli, diced (see p. 99)
2 red peppers, diced
350g (12 oz) green beans
Garnish
Chopped spring onion

The rich peanut sauce is quick and easy to make in the microwave. The vegetables should be crunchy but hot, so serve them as soon as they are cooked.

1 Spread out the peanuts in a shallow dish and ⊠ FULL for 3 mins. 600W (*2½ mins. 700W; 3½ mins. 500W*), shaking the dish halfway through. Grind to a fine powder.

2 Put the oil in a medium dish and ⊠ FULL for 1½ mins. 600W (*1 min. 700W; 1½ mins. 500W*). Stir in the onion and garlic and ⊠ FULL for 1 min. 600W (*30 secs. 700W; 1 min. 500W*).

3 Add the remaining ingredients, including the peanuts. Season to taste with salt and pepper, and ⊠ FULL for 8 mins. 600W (*6½ mins. 700W; 10 mins. 500W*), stirring 3-4 times.

4 Prepare all the vegetables and slice them finely. Mix together in a large dish and add 30ml (2 tbsp) water. Cover and ⊠ FULL for 4 mins. 600W (*3 mins. 700W; 5 mins. 500W*), stirring once or twice.

5 Pour the sauce over the vegetables and garnish with the spring onion. Serve with brown rice, pot barley or wholemeal noodles.

★ **Preparation:**
25 minutes

⌇ **Cooking time:**
17½ minutes

⊘ **Power setting:**
FULL

⌇ **Good reheated**

◎ **Serves 4**

Illustrated opposite

Top: **Vegetable gado gado** (*see opposite*); Bottom: **Marinated tofu with vegetables** (*see p. 111*)

Creamy onion flan

INGREDIENTS

100g (4 oz) wholewheat flour
pinch of salt
50g (2 oz) sunflower margarine or white vegetable fat and butter mixed
1 egg, beaten, plus a little milk or 30-45ml (2-3 tbsp) milk or soya milk

For the filling

15ml (1 tbsp) sunflower oil
225g (8 oz) onions, finely chopped
1 egg
30ml (2 tbsp) soured cream, cream cheese or thick yogurt
30ml (2 tbsp) chopped fresh parsley
pinch of grated nutmeg
salt and black pepper

Pastry made with egg or milk as the binding agent gives the best result in the microwave. Covering the pastry with absorbent paper and a plate ensures that all the moisture is absorbed and the pastry stays crisp.

1 Mix the flour and salt together in a bowl, then rub in the margarine or fat and butter until the mixture resembles fine breadcrumbs. Mix in the egg to form a smooth dough, adding a little milk if necessary. Alternatively use all milk or soya milk. Cover and leave to rest in a cool place for 15 mins.

2 Roll out the pastry and line a 20cm (8 in) flan dish. Prick the sides and base with a fork. Cover with absorbent paper and a plate and ⊗ FULL for 5 mins. 600W (*4 mins. 700W; 6 mins. 500W*), giving the dish a quarter turn every 1½ mins. Uncover and leave to cool.

3 For the filling, put the oil in a medium dish and ⊗ FULL for 1 min. 600W (*30 secs. 700W; 1 min. 500W*). Stir in the onions and ⊗ FULL for 3 mins. 600W (*2½ mins. 700W; 3½ mins. 500W*), stirring once or twice.

4 Cool slightly, then beat in the egg, soured cream, parsley and nutmeg. Season to taste with salt and pepper.

5 Pour the filling into the pastry case and ⊗ FULL for 2½ mins. 600W (*2 mins. 700W; 3 mins. 500W*) until just set.

Preparation:
30 minutes

Cooking time:
11½ minutes

Power setting:
FULL

Good reheated

Serves 4

Choose fillings that do not need much cooking once they are in the pastry case. Purées of lentils, split peas or vegetables such as parsnips are ideal.

VEGETABLE ACCOMPANIMENTS

Hungarian marrow

INGREDIENTS

450-700g (1-1½ lb) marrow
15ml (1 tbsp) sunflower oil
1 clove garlic, crushed
5ml (1 tsp) paprika
30ml (2 tbsp) white wine
5ml (1 tsp) dill weed
pinch of cayenne
salt and black pepper
Garnish
sprigs of dill

There is no need to add any extra water when cooking this marrow recipe as its texture will remain firm and crisp, and it will easily absorb the full flavours of the ingredients.

1 Peel the marrow if the skin is tough or the marrow a little old, otherwise leave it on. Slice the marrow in half, discard the seeds and chop the flesh into 1cm (½ in) cubes. The flesh should weigh about 450-700g (1-1½ lb).

2 Put the oil and garlic in a medium dish and ≋ FULL for 2 mins. 600W *(1½ mins. 700W; 2½ mins. 500W)*. Add the marrow and paprika and ≋ FULL for 2 mins. 600W *(1½ mins. 700W; 2½ mins. 500W)*.

3 Add the wine, dill weed and cayenne. Stir well, cover and ≋ FULL for 3 mins. 600W *(2½ mins. 700W; 3½ mins. 500W)*, stirring halfway through.

4 Season to taste with salt and pepper. Serve hot or cold, garnished with dill.

★ **Preparation:**
15 minutes

≋ **Cooking time:**
7 minutes

⊘ **Power setting:**
FULL

◎ **Serves 4**

★ Substitute courgettes when marrows are out of season.

Illustrated on p. 117

Green bean, mushroom and artichoke medley

INGREDIENTS

350g (12 oz) green beans, trimmed and sliced in half
100g (4 oz) button mushrooms, quartered
100g (4 oz) artichoke hearts, halved
1 medium tomato, skinned
15ml (1 tbsp) tomato purée
1 small onion, finely chopped
1 clove garlic, crushed
15ml (1 tbsp) shoyu
25ml (1 fl oz) stock
salt and black pepper

Liven up different assortments of cooked vegetables with tasty sauces like this tomato-based one, which can be heated up in seconds. The speed of the cooking means that the sauce is not absorbed by the vegetables, it simply highlights their individual flavours.

1 Put the beans in a large bowl with 30ml (2 tbsp) water, cover and ⧈ FULL for 5 mins. 600W *(4 mins. 700W; 6 mins. 500W)*, stirring once.

2 Add the mushrooms and artichoke hearts. Re-cover and ⧈ FULL for 3 mins. 600W *(2½ mins. 700W; 3½ mins. 500W)*. Drain, reserving all the liquid to be used as stock.

3 Liquidize the tomato, tomato purée, onion, garlic, shoyu and stock until smooth.

4 Stir the sauce into the vegetables. Cover and ⧈ FULL for 1 min., then season well with salt and pepper. Serve hot or cold.

Preparation: 15 minutes

Cooking time: 9 minutes

Power setting: FULL

Serves 4

Illustrated opposite

Top: **Hungarian marrow** (*see p. 115*); Centre: **Green bean, mushroom and artichoke medley** (*see opposite*);
Bottom: **Spiced cauliflower** (*see p. 118*)

Spiced cauliflower

INGREDIENTS

7.5ml (1½ tsp) sesame seeds
7.5ml (1½ tsp) cumin seeds
7.5ml (1½ tsp) mustard seeds
15ml (1 tbsp) sesame oil
1 onion, finely chopped
1 clove garlic, crushed
1 small cauliflower, divided into small, even-sized florets
150ml (¼ pint) yogurt
salt and black pepper

Garnish

sprigs of coriander

Cauliflower cooked by this method in the microwave retains the crisp texture and nutty flavour of the raw vegetable. The mixture of aromatic spices gives extra flavour and transforms it into an unusual and tasty dish.

1 Put all the seeds on a small plate and 🔆 FULL for 1 min. 600W *(30 secs. 700W; 1 min. 500W)* to develop their flavour. Grind to a powder.

2 Put the oil in a medium dish and 🔆 FULL for 1 min. 600W *(30 secs. 700W; 1 min. 500W)*. Stir in the chopped onion and the garlic and 🔆 FULL for 2 mins. 600W *(1½ mins. 700W; 2½ mins. 500W)*.

3 Add the cauliflower florets, seeds and 15ml (1 tbsp) water, stir well, then cover and 🔆 FULL for 2 mins. 600W *(1½ mins. 700W; 2½ mins. 500W)*.

4 Stir in the yogurt, then re-cover and 🔆 LOW for 2 mins. 600W *(1½ mins. 700W; 🔆 DEFROST for 2 mins. 500W)*. It is important that the yogurt doesn't boil or it will curdle.

5 Season well with salt and pepper and serve hot or cold, garnished with coriander.

Preparation: 15 minutes

Cooking time: 7½ minutes

Power settings: FULL and LOW

Serves 4

Chop the cauliflower stalk into small pieces and use to make up a vegetable stock or soup.

Illustrated on p. 117

Runner beans with walnut sauce

INGREDIENTS

450g (1 lb) runner beans,
trimmed and cut into
2.5cm (1 in) lengths.

For the sauce

15g (½ oz) sunflower
margarine

15g (½ oz) wholewheat flour

150ml (¼ pint) skimmed milk

50g (2 oz) chopped walnuts

salt and black pepper

Garnish

whole walnut

Fresh runner beans are a true sign of summer. Their strong flavour goes particularly well with this creamy sauce enriched with crunchy walnut pieces.

1   Put the beans in a large bowl with 45ml (3 tbsp) water. Cover and 🟰 FULL for 5 mins. 600W *(4 mins. 700W; 6 mins. 500W)*. Strain, reserving the liquid. Make up the liquid to 150ml (¼ pint) with water.

2   Put the margarine in a medium dish and 🟰 FULL for 30 secs. Stir in the flour and 🟰 FULL for 30 secs.

3   Stir in the milk and the bean cooking water. Cover and 🟰 FULL for 4 mins. 600W *(3 mins. 700W; 5 mins. 500W)*, stirring several times.

4   Stir in the chopped walnuts and season well. Pour the sauce over the beans and 🟰 FULL for 30 secs. to reheat. Serve hot, garnished with the walnut.

★ **Preparation:**
15 minutes

🟰 **Cooking time:**
10½ minutes

⊘ **Power setting:**
FULL

◎ **Serves 4**

★ Any variety of green bean can be used instead of runner beans, if preferred.

Illustrated on p. 120

Spinach cream

INGREDIENTS

450g (1 lb) spinach

100g (4 oz) cottage cheese

50g (2 oz) cream cheese

1 egg

2.5ml (½ tsp) grated nutmeg

salt and black pepper

Garnish

slices of lemon

sprigs of dill

This dish can also make a delicious starter, or a light meal when served with a tomato salad and wholemeal rolls. Use 175g (6 oz) ricotta in place of the cottage cheese and cream cheese mixture if you prefer.

1   Wash the spinach and shred finely. Place in a medium dish, cover and 🟰 FULL for 2 mins. 600W *(1½ mins. 700W; 2½ mins. 500W)*.

2   Drain the spinach, then liquidize until smooth. Add the cheeses and blend until smooth. Beat in the egg and the nutmeg. Season well with salt and pepper.

3   Divide the mixture between four ramekin dishes, then 🟰 FULL for 3 mins. 600W *(2½ mins. 700W; 3½ mins. 500W)*. The cream should still be soft at this stage – do not let it become rubbery. Serve hot, garnished with lemon and dill.

★ **Preparation:**
15 minutes

🟰 **Cooking time:**
5 minutes

⊘ **Power setting:**
FULL

◎ **Serves 4**

★ Plain spinach cooks beautifully in the microwave, especially if you buy young tender leaves which can be cooked in seconds. The water that clings to the leaves after washing is sufficient to cook all the spinach.

Illustrated on p. 120

Clockwise from the top: **Runner beans with walnut sauce** (*see p. 119*); **Baby beetroots with orange sauce**
(*see opposite*); **Spinach cream** (*see p. 119*); **Ratatouille** (*see opposite*)

Baby beetroots with orange sauce

INGREDIENTS

350g (12 oz) uncooked baby beetroots, scrubbed

For the sauce

150ml (¼ pint) orange juice

juice of ½ lemon

15ml (1 tbsp) concentrated apple juice (CAJ)

1cm (½ in) fresh root ginger, grated

1.25ml (¼ tsp) celery seeds

7.5ml (1½ tsp) arrowroot

parsley sprigs, to garnish

Hot beetroot is just as delicious as cold, but it needs a sauce to balance its slightly dry texture, and the sweetness of orange juice is ideal.

1 Pierce each beetroot once or twice, then arrange around the edge of a medium dish, evenly spacing each one. Cover and ⊠ FULL for 8 mins. 600W *(6½ mins. 700W; 10 mins. 500W)*, rearranging twice during the cooking time. Leave to stand for 3 mins., then peel, if wished.

2 Meanwhile, mix all the sauce ingredients together, except the arrowroot, in a medium dish. ⊠ FULL for 2 mins. 600W *(1½ mins. 700W; 2½ mins. 500W)*, stirring several times.

3 Dissolve the arrowroot in a little water, then stir into the sauce. ⊠ FULL for 2 mins. 600W *(1½ mins. 700W; 2½ mins. 500W)* until the liquid boils and clears.

4 Pour the sauce over the beetroot and serve hot. Garnish with parsley for colour.

★ **Preparation:**
15 minutes

≋ **Cooking time:**
12 minutes

⊘ **Power setting:**
FULL

≋ **Good reheated**

◎ **Serves 4**

Illustrated opposite

Ratatouille

INGREDIENTS

15ml (1 tbsp) olive oil

1 medium onion, finely chopped

1 clove garlic, crushed

1 aubergine, weighing about 225g (8 oz), diced

225g (8 oz) courgettes, diced

1 medium green or red pepper, deseeded and diced

400g (14 oz) can tomatoes

15ml (1 tbsp) tomato purée

10ml (2 tsp) chopped fresh thyme

5ml (1 tsp) chopped fresh marjoram

1 bay leaf

salt and pepper

Vegetable stews such as ratatouille work very well in the microwave. They are simple to prepare, the texture remains good and the flavours infuse well into the sauce.

1 Put the oil in a medium dish and ⊠ FULL for 1 min. 600W *(30 secs. 700W; 1 min. 500W)*.

2 Stir in the chopped onion and the garlic and ⊠ FULL for 2 mins. 600W *(1½ mins. 700W; 2½ mins. 500W)*.

3 Add the diced aubergine, courgettes, and pepper. ⊠ FULL for 3 mins. 600W *(2½ mins. 700W; 3½ mins. 500W)*.

4 Add the remaining ingredients, except the seasoning, stir well, then cover and ⊠ FULL for 8 mins. 600W *(6½ mins. 700W; 10 mins. 500W)*, stirring once or twice.

5 Season to taste with salt and pepper and serve hot.

★ **Preparation:**
20 minutes

≋ **Cooking time:**
14 minutes

⊘ **Power setting:**
FULL

≋ **Good reheated**

◎ **Serves 4**

★ Different combinations of vegetables can be used in this recipe – try fresh broad beans, green beans and mushrooms.

Illustrated opposite

Marinated beef tomatoes

INGREDIENTS

15ml (1 tbsp) olive oil
3 spring onions, finely chopped
1 clove garlic, crushed
50g (2 oz) fennel, chopped, or 5ml (1 tsp) fennel seeds
45ml (3 tbsp) red wine
30ml (2 tbsp) tomato purée
5ml (1 tsp) shoyu
5ml (1 tsp) chopped fresh tarragon
450g (1 lb) beef tomatoes
30ml (2 tbsp) chopped fresh parsley
salt and black pepper

The large Italian beef tomatoes make a delicious side vegetable. Their flavour is enhanced with this simple marinade, which is easy and quick to make using the microwave.

1 Put the oil in a medium dish and ▨ FULL for 1 min. 600W *(30 secs. 700W; 1 min. 500W)*.

2 Stir in the onions, garlic and fennel or fennel seeds and ▨ FULL for 30 secs.

3 Mix in the wine, tomato purée, shoyu and tarragon. Add a little more olive oil if the dressing is too sharp.

4 Slice the tomatoes and lay them in the dressing, basting well. Sprinkle with parsley, cover and ▨ FULL for 5 mins. 600W *(4 mins. 700W; 6 mins. 500W)*.

5 Season with salt and pepper and serve hot or chilled.

★ **Preparation:** 10 minutes

▨ **Cooking time:** 6½ minutes

⊘ **Power setting:** FULL

◎ **Serves 4**

Cheese and potato layer

INGREDIENTS

175g (6 oz) Cheddar cheese, grated
550g (1¼ lb) potatoes, scrubbed and thinly sliced
225g (8 oz) onions, cut into thin rings
5ml (1 tsp) chopped fresh sage
5ml (1 tsp) chopped fresh thyme
150ml (¼ pint) skimmed milk
1.25ml (¼ tsp) grated nutmeg
salt and black pepper

This dish could be served as a side vegetable with a rich stew or on its own as an easy, light supper snack. It is best finished off under a conventional grill so that the cheese is golden and bubbling.

1 Set aside 25g (1 oz) of the cheese for the topping. Layer the potatoes, onions and cheese in a medium dish, sprinkling the herbs over each of the layers. Finish with a layer of cheese.

2 Mix the milk and nutmeg together and season well with salt and pepper.

3 Pour the milk over the vegetables and cheese, cover and ▨ FULL for 15 mins. 600W *(12½ mins. 700W; 17-18 mins. 500W)*, giving the dish a quarter turn every 5 mins.

4 Leave to stand for 4 mins. Sprinkle with the reserved cheese and melt under a preheated conventional grill. Serve hot.

★ **Preparation:** 30 minutes

▨ **Cooking time:** 15 minutes

⊘ **Power setting:** FULL

≋ **Good reheated**

✳ **Freezes well**

◎ **Serves 4**

★ Add other vegetables or cooked beans to make a more substantial, filling dish.

Braised fennel
in tomato and apricot sauce

INGREDIENTS

700g (1½ lb) fennel bulbs, trimmed

For the sauce

15ml (1 tbsp) olive oil

1 medium onion, finely chopped

1 clove garlic, crushed

25g (1 oz) dried apricots, cut into slivers

400g (14 oz) can tomatoes, mashed

15ml (1 tbsp) tomato purée

15ml (1 tbsp) chopped fennel fronds or 2.5ml (½ tsp) fennel seeds

salt and black pepper

Fennel cooked in the microwave retains its delicate flavour, and the texture remains pleasantly crunchy. To make a more substantial dish, cover with grated cheese and brown under a conventional grill, or serve with pasta and Parmesan cheese or chopped nuts.

1 For the sauce, put the oil in a medium dish and ☷ FULL for 1 min. 600W *(30 secs. 700W; 1 min. 500W)*. Stir in the chopped onion and garlic and ☷ FULL for 1 min. 600W *(30 secs. 700W; 1 min. 500W)*.

2 Add the apricots, tomatoes, tomato purée and fennel fronds or seeds. Cover and ☷ FULL for 10 mins. 600W *(8½ mins. 700W; 12½ mins. 500W)*, stirring several times.

3 Slice the fennel into four chunks, or if using two bulbs, slice each one into four.

4 Arrange the fennel in a shallow dish, add 30ml (2 tbsp) water, cover and ☷ FULL for 6 mins. 600W *(5 mins. 700W; 7½ mins. 500W)*, turning once or twice. Cook for longer if a softer vegetable is preferred. Drain, reserving the liquid.

5 Add the cooking liquid to the tomato sauce, then liquidize until smooth. Season well with salt and pepper.

6 Pour the sauce over the fennel in the dish and ☷ FULL for 1 min. to reheat. Serve hot.

Preparation:
20 minutes

Cooking time:
19 minutes

Power settings:
FULL

Serves 4

Barbecue-style baked potatoes

INGREDIENTS

100g (4 oz) pinto beans, soaked overnight	
900ml (1½ pints) boiling water	
4 large potatoes	

For the sauce

225ml (8 fl oz) tomato juice

45ml (3 tbsp) red wine

60ml (4 tbsp) lemon juice

30ml (2 tbsp) wine vinegar

30ml (2 tbsp) concentrated apple juice (CAJ)

100g (4 oz) mushrooms, diced

2 sticks celery

30ml (2 tbsp) chopped fresh parsley

5ml (1 tsp) chopped fresh thyme

salt and black pepper

It's easy to make a wholesome meal out of a baked potato by mixing the flesh with a selection of ingredients. Here are four tasty fillings, all of which cook beautifully in the microwave. You can easily speed up this first recipe by using pre-cooked beans.

1 Drain the beans and place in a deep bowl. Pour over the boiling water. Ensure that it covers the beans by 3-5cm (1-2 in). Add more if necessary. Cover and ⊠ FULL for 25 mins. 600W (*21 mins. 700W; 30 mins. 500W*) until just soft. Drain.

2 Pierce each potato, wrap in absorbent paper and ⊠ FULL for 15 mins. 600W (*12½ mins. 700W; 18 mins. 500W*), turning over and rearranging halfway through. Stand for 5 mins.

3 For the sauce, mix all the ingredients together, then stir into the cooked beans.

4 Slice the potatoes in half and scoop out the flesh. Mix with the beans and sauce. Fill the potato halves with the mixture, piling it up into a mound.

5 Arrange the potato halves on a plate and ⊠ FULL for 3 mins. 600W (*2½ mins. 700W; 3½ mins. 500W*) or until heated through, rearranging once.

★ **Preparation:**
15 minutes

⊠ **Cooking time:**
43 minutes

⊘ **Power setting:**
FULL

⊠ **Good reheated**

◎ **Serves 4**

★ Use cider vinegar instead of wine vinegar if preferred. Red kidney beans can be used instead of pinto beans, but they should be boiled on the top of the stove for 10 minutes before cooking in the microwave.

Illustrated opposite

Clockwise from top right: **Barbecue-style baked potatoes** (*see opposite*); **Leek and horseradish filling** (*see p. 126*); **Peanut and yogurt filling** (*see p. 126*); **Cheese filling** (*see p. 126*)

Baked potato fillings

VARIATIONS

Leek and horseradish filling

INGREDIENTS

225g (8 oz) leeks, finely chopped

30-45ml (2-3 tbsp) water

5ml (1 tsp) horseradish sauce

30ml (2 tbsp) yogurt

salt and black pepper

2 baked potatoes

Garnish

sprigs of coriander

1 Put the leeks in a medium dish with the water. Cover and ⊠ FULL for 3 mins. 600W (*2½ mins. 700W; 3½ mins. 500W*), stirring once. Drain well.

2 Liquidize the leeks with the horseradish and yogurt. Season to taste with salt and pepper.

3 Scoop out a little of the potato flesh, add to the purée, then spoon back into the potatoes. ⊠ FULL for 2 mins. 600W (*1½ mins. 700W; 2½ mins. 500W*) or until hot. Serve, garnished with coriander.

 Fills 2 potatoes

★ To bake 2 potatoes, follow the same method as above but bake for 8 mins. 600W (*7 mins. 700W; 10 mins. 500W*), remembering to turn over and rearrange halfway through. Leave for 3-4 mins. to soften.

Illustrated on p. 125

Peanut and yogurt filling

INGREDIENTS

15ml (1 tbsp) peanut butter

15ml (1 tbsp) yogurt

5ml (1 tsp) shoyu

2 baked potatoes

Garnish

sprigs of rosemary

1 Cream the ingredients together.

2 Halve the baked potatoes and scoop out some of the flesh. Combine with the sauce and spoon back into the potato cases.

3 ⊠ FULL for 3 mins. 600W (*2½ mins. 700W; 3½ mins. 500W*). Serve, garnished with rosemary.

 Fills 2 potatoes

Illustrated on p. 125

Cheese filling

INGREDIENTS

50g (2 oz) cheese, grated

25g (1 oz) margarine

2.5ml (½ tsp) caraway seeds

2.5ml (½ tsp) mustard seeds

black pepper

2 baked potatoes

Garnish

some cumin seeds

1 Beat the cheese and margarine together in a small dish, then add the remaining ingredients.

2 Scoop out a little of the potato flesh, and add to the cheese mixture. Spoon the filling into the hot potatoes, then ⊠ FULL for 2 mins. 600W (*1½ mins. 700W; 2½ mins. 500W*). Serve, garnished with cumin.

◎ **Fills 2 potatoes**

Illustrated on p. 125

Broccoli with olives and garlic

INGREDIENTS

15ml (1 tbsp) olive oil
1 small onion, finely chopped
350g (12 oz) broccoli, divided into small, even-sized florets
8-12 large olives, stoned
1 medium tomato, skinned
15ml (1 tbsp) red wine vinegar
1 clove garlic
2.5ml (½ tsp) garam masala
salt and black pepper

The pungent olive and tomato sauce with garlic and spices gives the broccoli a rich and exotic flavour. Everything is heated so quickly that the broccoli remains crisp yet tender.

1   Put the oil in a medium dish and ⊠ FULL for 1 min. 600W *(30 secs. 700W; 1 min. 500W)*. Stir in the onion and ⊠ FULL for 2 mins. 600W *(1½ mins. 700W; 2½ mins. 500W)*.

2   Stir in the broccoli, then add 30ml (2 tbsp) water. Cover and ⊠ FULL for 5 mins. 600W *(4 mins. 700W; 6 mins. 500W)*, stirring once. Leave to stand for 2-3 mins.

3   Meanwhile, liquidize the olives, tomato, vinegar, garlic and garam masala to make a coarse-textured sauce.

4   Drain the vegetables, then toss in the sauce. Cover and ⊠ FULL for 1 min. to reheat. Season well with salt and pepper. Serve hot or cold.

★ **Preparation:** 20 minutes

⊠ **Cooking time:** 8 minutes

▨ **Power setting:** FULL

◎ **Serves 4**

Illustrated on p. 129

Creamy carrot and parsnip bake

INGREDIENTS

450g (1 lb) mixed carrots and parsnips, diced
75g (3 oz) quark
10ml (2 tsp) sesame oil
salt and black pepper
15-30ml (1-2 tbsp) sesame seeds

Mixtures of mashed root vegetables are always popular, and using quark gives this vegetable purée a lovely creamy flavour.

1   Put the carrots and parsnips in a large bowl with 30ml (2 tbsp) water. Cover and ⊠ FULL for 5 mins. 600W *(4 mins. 700W; 6 mins. 500W)*. Leave to stand for 2-3 mins. to finish cooking, then drain.

2   Liquidize the carrots and parsnips with the quark and sesame oil, then season well with salt and pepper.

3   Sprinkle the sesame seeds thickly over the base of a small dish and ⊠ FULL for 2 mins. 600W *(1½ mins. 700W; 2½ mins. 500W)*, shaking the dish halfway through.

4   Spread the purée over the top of the seeds, then ⊠ FULL for 30 secs. to reheat. Turn out and serve in wedges.

★ **Preparation:** 15 minutes

⊠ **Cooking time:** 7½ minutes

▨ **Power setting:** FULL

◎ **Serves 4**

★ Make the purée with a mixture of carrots and swede instead of parsnip, if preferred.

Illustrated on p. 129

Braised red cabbage

INGREDIENTS

15ml (1 tbsp) sunflower oil
1 onion, sliced into rings
1 clove garlic, crushed
175g (6 oz) fennel or celery, diced
5ml (1 tsp) fennel or caraway seeds
450g (1 lb) red cabbage, shredded
50g (2 oz) raisins
45ml (3 tbsp) red wine
15ml (1 tbsp) honey
salt and black pepper

Using the microwave is a marvellously quick way to make this delicious vegetable side dish. Try adding nuts like walnuts or extra fruit, such as fresh apple or dried apricots.

1 Put the oil in a medium dish and ⊠ FULL for 1 min. 600W (*30 secs. 700W; 1 min. 500W*). Stir in the sliced onion and the garlic and ⊠ FULL for 2 mins. 600W (*1½ mins. 700W; 2½ mins. 500W*).

2 Add the fennel or celery, the seeds and 15ml (1 tbsp) water. Cover and ⊠ FULL for 4 mins. 600W (*3 mins. 700W; 5 mins. 500W*), stirring once.

3 Stir in the remaining ingredients, except the seasoning, re-cover and ⊠ FULL for 10 mins. 600W (*8½ mins. 700W; 12½ mins. 500W*), stirring 3 times.

4 Leave to stand for 3 mins., then season well with salt and pepper. Serve hot or cold.

⋆ **Preparation:** 20 minutes

⊠ **Cooking time:** 17 minutes

⊘ **Power setting:** FULL

⊠ **Good reheated**

◎ **Serves 4**

⊠ To produce cabbage with a slightly softer texture, cook for a few minutes longer than the time given in this recipe.

Illustrated opposite

Marinated peppers

INGREDIENTS

4 medium peppers, preferably 2 red, 1 yellow and 1 green
salt
For the marinade
90ml (6 tbsp) olive oil
30ml (2 tbsp) red wine vinegar
5ml (1 tsp) grain mustard
10ml (2 tsp) capers, chopped
15ml (1 tbsp) finely chopped fresh parsley
5ml (1 tsp) chopped fresh thyme
1-2 cloves garlic, crushed
salt and black pepper
Garnish
15ml (1 tbsp) finely chopped fresh parsley

This is a rich, tasty idea for an interesting starter or a salad accompaniment. The salad can be made with aubergines instead of peppers.

1 Slit the skin of the peppers, then arrange on a plate and ⊠ FULL for 15 mins. 600W (*12½ mins. 700W; 19 mins. 500W*), turning over and rearranging halfway through. Drop the peppers into a bowl of cold water, leave for 5 mins., then remove the skin and deseed.

2 Cut each pepper into four or six pieces and place in a small, deep dish.

3 Mix all the marinade ingredients together, except the seasoning, and pour over the peppers. Cover and ⊠ FULL for 2 mins. 600W (*1½ mins. 700W; 2½ mins. 500W*).

4 Leave until cold, then season to taste with salt and pepper. Serve straight from the dish or drain the peppers and place on individual plates. Garnish with parsley.

⋆ **Preparation:** 20 minutes

⊠ **Cooking time:** 18 minutes

⊘ **Power setting:** FULL

◎ **Serves 4**

⋆ It doesn't matter if the peppers collapse a little during the microwaving, they need to be well cooked in order to remove the skins.

Top: **Broccoli with olives and garlic** (*see p. 127*); Centre: **Braised red cabbage** (*see opposite*); Bottom:
Creamy carrot and parsnip bake (*see p. 127*).

Hot green salad

INGREDIENTS

15ml (1 tbsp) olive oil

4 spring onions, trimmed and chopped

4 sticks celery, diced

½ avocado, peeled and diced

1 green pepper, deseeded and diced

1 Cos lettuce, chopped

½ cucumber, diced

For the dressing

5ml (1 tsp) mustard powder

15ml (1 tbsp) white wine vinegar

30ml (2 tbsp) olive oil

10ml (2 tsp) chopped fresh herbs, e.g. chives and basil

salt and black pepper

An unusual idea for a side salad that is only possible with a microwave. The salad ingredients remain crisp, but the avocado melts to give an extra buttery flavour to the dressing. This dish also makes a delicious starter.

1 Put the oil in a medium dish and ▨ FULL for 1 min. 600W (*30 secs. 700W; 1 min. 500W*).

2 Stir in the spring onions and ▨ FULL for 1 min. 600W (*30 secs. 700W; 1 min. 500W*).

3 Add all the salad ingredients.

4 Mix all the dressing ingredients together and toss into the salad. Cover and ▨ FULL for 3 mins. 600W (*2½ mins. 700W; 3½ mins. 500W*).

5 Toss the salad, then leave to stand for 2 mins. Serve hot.

Preparation:
20 minutes

Cooking time:
5 minutes

Power setting:
FULL

Serves 4

DESSERTS

Apricot petit pots

INGREDIENTS

100g (4 oz) dried apricots
600 ml (1 pint) boiling water
2 eggs
25g (1 oz) cornmeal
150ml (¼ pint) skimmed milk
2.5ml (¼ tsp) ground cardamom
15-30ml (1-2 tbsp) honey (optional)

Decoration

15g (½ oz) flaked almonds, chopped

Egg custards and cornmeal custards work extremely well in the microwave and can be flavoured with different fruit purées or a variety of spices and sweeteners.

1 Cover the apricots with boiling water. Cover and 🔆 FULL for 5 mins. 600W (*4 mins. 700W; 6 mins. 500W*). Leave until cool and plump. Drain, then purée.

2 Whisk together all the remaining ingredients, sweetening to taste with honey if wished. Mix in the apricot purée.

3 Divide the mixture between four ramekin dishes. 🔆 FULL for 5 mins. 600W (*4 mins. 700W; 6 mins. 500W*), rearranging the dishes halfway through.

4 Arrange the almonds on a small plate and toast on 🔆 FULL for about 3 mins. 600W (*2 mins. 700W; 4 mins. 500W*), stirring at least once a minute to prevent scorching.

5 Decorate with the flaked almonds.

Preparation:
15 minutes, plus cooling

Cooking time:
10 minutes

Power setting:
FULL

Serves 4

Illustrated on pp. 132-133

Plum and banana crumble

INGREDIENTS

450g (1 lb) plums, stoned and chopped
2 bananas, sliced
30ml (2 tbsp) concentrated apple juice (CAJ)
For the topping
50g (2 oz) wholewheat flour
50g (2 oz) coarse oatmeal
50g (2 oz) sunflower margarine
25g (1 oz) sunflower seeds
30ml (2 tbsp) demerara sugar

Choose mixtures of dried and fresh fruits for natural sweetness and a better flavour.

1   Mix the fruit and CAJ in a medium dish. Cover and ≋ FULL for 4 mins. 600W *(3 mins. 700W; 5 mins. 500W).*

2   Mix flour and oatmeal together. Rub in margarine and add seeds and sugar.

3   Add the crumble to the fruit, then ≋ FULL for 3 mins. 600W *(2½ mins. 700W; 3½ mins. 500W);* turn often. Serve hot.

★ **Preparation:**
15 minutes

≋ **Cooking time:**
7 minutes

⊘ **Power setting:**
FULL

◎ **Serves** 4

Illustrated below

From left to right: **Summer compote** (*see opposite*); **Apricot petit pots** (*see p. 131*); **Plum and banana crumble** (*see above*)

Summer compote

INGREDIENTS

225g (8 oz) blackcurrants
225g (8 oz) redcurrants
10ml (2 tsp) arrowroot
15ml (1 tbsp) concentrated apple juice (CAJ)
30ml (2 tbsp) honey

This refreshing fruit pudding is simple to make in the microwave.

1 String the currants, then liquidize or mash half of them. Dissolve arrowroot in the CAJ mixed with 25ml (1 fl oz) water. Add honey and stir into fruit purée.

2 Put in a medium dish, cover and ⊠ FULL for 4 mins. 600W (*3 mins. 700W; 5 mins. 500W*); stir once. Add other fruit and ⊠ FULL for 1 min. 600W (*30 secs. 700W; 1 min. 500W*). Serve chilled.

Preparation: 15 minutes, plus chilling

Cooking time: 5 minutes

Power setting: FULL

Serves 4

Top with yogurt and redcurrants.

Illustrated below

Baked pears with mango sauce

INGREDIENTS

4 large pears
300ml (½ pint) orange juice
juice of ½ lemon
2.5cm (1 in) fresh root ginger, cut into slivers
1 mango, peeled and diced
10ml (2 tsp) arrowroot

A delicious, light dessert with an interesting combination of fruits. Use ripe William or Packham pears and choose a ripe mango by its distinctive scent.

1   Peel the pears, halve and core them. Arrange around the outside of a large round dish, cut side down, with the thicker ends pointing outwards.

2   Pour over the orange and lemon juice and add the ginger. Cover and ◙ FULL for 5 mins. 600W (*4 mins. 700W; 6 mins. 500W*), giving the dish a quarter turn every 1½ mins.

3   Strain off the excess juice, then liquidize the mango in the fruit juice until smooth.

4   Dissolve the arrowroot in a little of the fruit juice, then stir into the remainder.

5   Pour into a jug and ◙ FULL for 4 mins. 600W (*3 mins. 700W; 5 mins. 500W*), stirring once every minute until the sauce has boiled and thickened.

6   Pour the sauce over the pears and ◙ FULL for 1 min. to reheat if necessary.

★ **Preparation:** 15 minutes

▧ **Cooking time:** 9 minutes

▨ **Power setting:** FULL

◎ **Serves 4**

Carob and raisin chiffon pie

INGREDIENTS

50g (2 oz) sunflower margarine
15ml (1 tbsp) pear and apple spread
50g (2 oz) oat flakes
50g (2 oz) wholewheat flour

For the topping

100g (4 oz) raisins
150ml (¼ pint) apple juice or water
300g (11 oz) silken tofu
30-45ml (2-3 tbsp) concentrated apple juice (CAJ)
15ml (1 tbsp) brandy
10ml (2 tsp) carob powder

Decoration

grated carob chocolate (optional)

Plumping raisins in fruit juice – so easily done in the microwave – and then puréeing them results in a wonderful sweet sauce with a good dark colour and slightly rough texture. Combined with silken tofu, this makes a light but flavoursome topping.

1 Cream the margarine and the pear and apple spread until smooth and light. Add the oats and flour and mix well.

2 Spread the mixture in a 20cm (8 in) round dish and cover with greaseproof paper and a plate. ▧ FULL for 4 mins. 600W (*3 mins. 700W; 5 mins. 500W*). Uncover and leave to cool.

3 For the topping, put the raisins in a medium dish and pour over the apple juice or water. ▧ FULL for 2 mins. 600W (*1½ mins. 700W; 2½ mins. 500W*). Leave to stand for 15 mins., then drain and liquidize to make a textured purée.

4 Liquidize the tofu, CAJ, brandy and carob powder until smooth. Stir in the raisins. Pour the topping over the base. ▧ MEDIUM-HIGH for 6 mins. 600W (*5 mins. 700W;* ▧ *FULL for 5 mins. 500W*), then ▧ MEDIUM for 2 mins. 600W (*1½ mins. 700W;* ▧ *DEFROST for 3 mins. 500W*).

5 Leave to cool, then chill before serving. Decorate with some grated carob chocolate, if desired.

Preparation:
25 minutes, plus chilling

Cooking time:
14 minutes

Power settings:
FULL,
MEDIUM-HIGH
and MEDIUM

Serves 4

Illustrated on p. 136

Top left: **Carob and raisin chiffon pie** (*see p. 135*); Top right: **Chestnut cheesecake** (*see opposite*);
Bottom: **Stuffed peaches in wine sauce** (*see p. 138*)

Chestnut cheesecake

INGREDIENTS

100g (4 oz) dried chestnuts
600ml (1 pint) boiling water
50g (2 oz) sunflower margarine
25g (1 oz) soft brown sugar
50g (2 oz) oatflakes
For the topping
150ml (¼ pint) skimmed milk
2 eggs, separated
45ml (3 tbsp) honey
400g (14 oz) quark
5ml (1 tsp) finely grated orange rind
5ml (1 tsp) grated fresh root ginger
2.5ml (½ tsp) vanilla essence
Decoration
stem ginger and fresh orange slices

The finished cheesecake is quite delicate, so handle it carefully. You may need to cook it a little longer than recommended here for a firmer texture but be careful not to dry out the mixture as it will continue setting as it cools.

1 Put the chestnuts in a deep dish, pour over the boiling water and leave to soak for 1 hour. Cover and ⊠ FULL for 5 mins. 600W (*4 mins. 700W; 6 mins. 500W*) until boiling, then ⊠ MEDIUM for 15 mins. 600W (*12½ mins. 700W; ⊠ DEFROST for 22 mins. 500W*). Drain and grind.

2 Cream the margarine and sugar together. Add the chestnuts and oatflakes. Mix to a dough. Press into a 20cm (8 in) flan dish and ⊠ FULL for 4 mins. 600W (*3 mins. 700W; 5 mins. 500W*), giving the dish a quarter turn every minute.

3 For the topping, put the milk in a jug and ⊠ FULL for 1 min. 600W (*30 secs. 700W; 1 min. 500W*). Beat in the egg yolks and 15ml (1 tbsp) honey and ⊠ MEDIUM for 2-5 mins. 600W (*1½-4 mins. 700W; ⊠ DEFROST for 5-9 mins. 500W*), stirring once every half minute until the mixture thickens. If the custard starts cooking too quickly, reduce the control setting to LOW and continue cooking until the custard thickens.

4 Whisk the egg whites until stiff. Beat the remaining ingredients into the custard, then fold in the egg whites. Pour on top of the base, then ⊠ FULL for 5-6 mins. 600W (*4-5 mins. 700W; 6-7 mins. 500W*). Cool thoroughly. Decorate with stem ginger and orange slices. Serve chilled.

Preparation:
15 minutes, plus 1 hour soaking and chilling

Cooking time:
32 minutes

Power settings:
FULL and MEDIUM

Serves 4

Dried chestnuts add extra flavour to the base, and are easy to reconstitute in a microwave either by the soaking method given here or from dried (see p. 27).

Illustrated opposite

Stuffed peaches in wine sauce

INGREDIENTS

4 peaches
175g (6 oz) cherries, stoned
25g (1 oz) chopped nuts
300ml (½ pint) rosé wine or apple juice
15ml (1 tbsp) arrowroot
2.5ml (½ tsp) ground cinnamon

It's easy to heat fruit through without losing its colour or texture, to make a distinctive and appetizing dish. Here the peach halves are filled with cherries and nuts and topped with a light wine or fruit-based sauce.

1 Slice the peaches in half, stone and arrange skin-side down around the edge of a large round dish.

2 Chop the cherries very finely, mix with the chopped nuts and spoon this mixture on top of each peach.

3 Pour over the wine or apple juice, cover and ⊠ FULL for 4 mins. 600W (*3 mins. 700W; 5 mins. 500W*), rearranging halfway through the cooking time.

4 Strain off the juice into a jug. Mix the arrowroot with a little of this juice, then stir it back in to the remainder. Add the cinnamon and ⊠ FULL for 3 mins. 600W (*2½ mins. 700W; 3½ mins. 500W*), stirring once or twice.

5 Pour the sauce over the peaches and ⊠ FULL for 1 min.

6 Serve hot or chilled, with cream or ice-cream.

Preparation: 10 minutes

Cooking time: 8 minutes

Power setting: FULL

Serves 4

Other soft summer fruits such as raspberries, redcurrants or blackcurrants could be used in the filling instead of the cherries.

Illustrated on p. 136

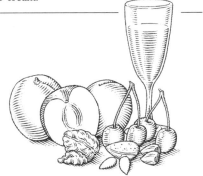

Millet pudding

INGREDIENTS

25g (1 oz) hazelnuts
50g (2 oz) millet
450ml (¾ pint) concentrated soya milk
50g (2 oz) dried apricots, cut into slivers
50g (2 oz) raisins
25g (1 oz) demerara sugar
2.5ml (½ tsp) allspice
1.25ml (¼ tsp) grated nutmeg
To serve
60ml (4 tbsp) concentrated soya milk

Traditional milk puddings, especially rice, really do need the slow cooking of a conventional oven. However, millet is such a creamy grain that this recipe works well in a microwave, especially when using a concentrated soya milk. Any leftovers can be reheated to make a special breakfast cereal.

1 Spread out the hazelnuts on a small plate and 🍚 FULL for 3 mins. 600W *(2½ mins. 700W; 3½ mins. 500W)*, shaking the plate halfway through. Put the nuts in a clean cloth and rub off the skins. Chop the nuts finely and reserve 15ml (1 tbsp) for decorating the pudding.

2 Mix all the other ingredients together in a large dish, adding 150ml (¼ pint) water to dilute the concentrated soya milk.

3 Cover and 🍚 FULL for 5 mins. 600W *(4 mins. 700W; 6 mins. 500W)*, stirring twice, then 🍚 MEDIUM-HIGH for 12 mins. 600W *(10 mins. 700W; 🍚 FULL for 10-12 mins. 500W)*, stirring every 3 mins. Leave to stand for 10 mins. after cooking.

4 Decorate with the chopped nuts and serve with the concentrated soya milk.

⭐ **Preparation:** 10 minutes

🌊 **Cooking time:** 25 minutes

⊘ **Power settings:** FULL and MEDIUM-HIGH

◎ **Serves 4**

⭐ If you can't get hold of any concentrated soya milk, use 500ml (17 fl oz) ordinary soya milk, which doesn't need to be diluted.

Top: **Christmas pudding** (*see opposite*); Bottom: **Mixed fruit compote** (*see opposite*)

Christmas pudding

INGREDIENTS

75g (3 oz) wholewheat flour
5ml (1 tsp) mixed spice
5ml (1 tsp) ground cinnamon
2.5ml (½ tsp) grated nutmeg
finely grated rind and juice of ½ lemon
50g (2 oz) creamed coconut, grated
75g (3 oz) wholewheat breadcrumbs
50g (2 oz) muscovado sugar
100g (4 oz) carrots, grated
1 dessert apple, grated
100g (4 oz) raisins
100g (4 oz) currants
100g (4 oz) sultanas
50g (2 oz) dates
30ml (2 tbsp) molasses
2 eggs
45ml (3 tbsp) brandy
15ml (1 tbsp) cocoa or carob powder (optional)

Microwaving this type of pudding is a great time-saver. As the flavours have less time to develop during cooking, the raw mixture should be left to stand overnight.

1   Mix all the ingredients together in a large bowl, adding the cocoa or carob powder if a darker colour is preferred. The mixture should be moist enough to drop off the spoon – add more brandy or fruit juice if necessary.

2   Cover the bowl with cling film and chill for several hours or overnight so the flavours combine well together.

3   Grease a 1.2 litre (2 pint) basin. Spoon in the mixture, cover and 🍲 FULL for 5 mins. 600W (*4 mins. 700W; 6 mins. 500W*), then let it stand for 5 mins. Repeat this process 3 times to cook the pudding thoroughly.

4   If not serving immediately, store in a cool place wrapped in foil. Unwrap when required and cook, covered, in a basin. Reheat for 5 mins. and stand for 5 mins. Serve with cornmeal custard (see page 154).

⭐ **Preparation:**
15 minutes, plus standing

🍲 **Cooking time:**
20 minutes, plus standing

⌀ **Power setting:**
FULL

▤ **Make in advance**

◎ **Serves 8**

⭐ Remember not to put metal trinkets in the pudding when you cook or reheat it in the microwave.

Illustrated opposite

Mixed fruit compote

INGREDIENTS

350g (12 oz) mixed dried fruit (prunes, peaches, apple rings, apricots, figs)
25g (1 oz) raisins
300ml (½ pint) red wine or red grape juice
6 cardamom pods
6 cloves
5cm (2 in) piece cinnamon stick
honey, to sweeten
Decoration
natural yoghurt

Dried fruits are a good standby to have in the store-cupboard, and with the microwave they come into their own for making emergency puddings or an instant breakfast.

1   Put all the ingredients, except the honey, in a large bowl, and add 150ml (¼ pint) warm water. Cover and 🍲 FULL for 10 mins. 600W (*8½ mins. 700W; 12½ mins. 500W*), stirring once or twice.

2   Leave to stand for 10-30 mins., then sweeten to taste with some honey. Discard the whole spices.

3   🍲 FULL for 1 min. 600W (*30 secs. 700W; 1 min. 500W*) to reheat, then spoon into individual dishes.

4   Serve warm, topped with yogurt.

⭐ **Preparation:**
15-35 minutes

🍲 **Cooking time:**
11 minutes

⌀ **Power setting:**
FULL

▤ **Make in advance**

◎ **Serves 4**

⭐ Try other spices, such as allspice or coriander, and different varieties of fruit juice.

Illustrated opposite

Chocolate or carob pudding

INGREDIENTS

100g (4 oz) margarine or butter
100g (4 oz) barbados sugar
2 eggs
100g (4 oz) wholewheat flour
30ml (2 tbsp) cocoa or carob powder
10ml (2 tsp) baking powder
15-30ml (1-2 tbsp) yogurt

This rich, dark pudding is quick to microwave and the end result is light with a crumbly, spongy texture. Serve the pudding with some yogurt and honey mixed together, a purée of dried or fresh fruit, or a cornmeal custard (see page 154). Carob is an alternative to chocolate for those concerned with their health or waistline.

1 Cream the margarine or butter and sugar together in a medium dish until light and fluffy. ⊠ FULL for 5 secs.

2 Beat the eggs one at a time, blending well into the mixture, then fold in the flour, the cocoa or the carob and the baking powder.

3 Add enough yogurt to give the mixture a soft dropping consistency.

4 Line a 1.2 litre (2 pint) pudding basin with greaseproof paper, then spoon in the pudding mixture. Cover and ⊠ FULL for 5-6 mins. 600W *(4-5 mins. 700W; 6-7½ mins. 500W)*, giving the dish a quarter turn every 1½ mins.

5 Leave to stand for 5 mins. before serving, whilst it is still hot, with the accompaniment you have chosen from those listed above.

Preparation:
10 minutes

Cooking time:
5-6 minutes

Power setting:
FULL

Serves 4

Once the mixture is made up it should be cooked straight away to get the full benefit of the baking powder.

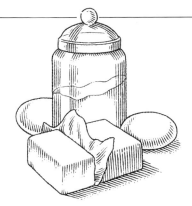

Bread and butter pudding

INGREDIENTS

6 large slices wholewheat bread
50g (2 oz) butter
grated rind of 1 orange
50g (2 oz) sultanas
3 eggs, beaten
30ml (2 tbsp) soft light brown sugar
450ml (¾ pint) milk
few drops of vanilla flavouring
15ml (1 tbsp) demerara sugar

Traditionally, this pudding was made to use up stale bread. It microwaves extremely well; the bread layers, naturally sweetened by the sultanas, soak up the orange-flavoured custard, which sets softly to give a deliciously light pudding.

1 Cut the crusts from the bread, then spread the slices with butter and cut each into 4 triangles.

2 Layer the bread slices, butter-side up with the orange rind and sultanas in a buttered 1.2 litre (2 pint) pie dish.

3 Beat together the eggs and sugar until light and fluffy. Put the milk in a jug and ☵ FULL for 2 mins. 600W (*1½-2½ mins. 700W; 2½-3½ mins. 500W*).

4 Beat the hot milk into the egg mixture, then stir in the vanilla flavouring. Pour over the bread, ☵ FULL for 5 mins. 600W (*4 mins. 700W; 6 mins. 500W*), give the dish a half turn and ☵ MEDIUM for 15 mins. 600W (*12½ mins. 700W; 18 mins. 500W*) until just set, giving the dish a half turn twice.

5 Cover and leave to stand for 5 mins., then sprinkle with demerara sugar and serve the pudding at once.

★ **Preparation:**
15 minutes

☷ **Cooking time:**
20 minutes

⃠ **Power settings:**
FULL and MEDIUM

◎ **Serves 4**

★ For a crispy top, brown the pudding under a conventional grill.

Illustrated on p. 145

Tropical trifle

INGREDIENTS

225g (8 oz) plain sponge cake
425g (15 oz) can pineapple pieces in natural juice
45ml (3 tbsp) custard powder
45ml (3 tbsp) caster sugar
600ml (1 pint) milk
30ml (2 tbsp) rum
300g (11 oz) can satsuma segments, drained
2 bananas, peeled and sliced
200ml (7 fl oz) double cream, whipped

Decoration

25g (1 oz) desiccated coconut, toasted

Smooth custard is so easy to make in the microwave. Use it for this fruity dessert with a blend of tropical flavours that is special enough for a dinner party. Leave out the rum and it is ideal for children as well.

1   Cut the cake into 2.5cm (1 in) cubes and put into a large serving dish. Drain the pineapple, sprinkle the juice over the sponge and leave to soak.

2   Mix the custard powder and sugar with a little of the milk. Pour the rest of the milk into a bowl and ⊠ FULL for 3½-4 mins. 600W (*3 mins. 700W; 4½-5 mins. 500W*), or until almost boiling.

3   Whisk a little of the hot milk into the custard mixture then whisk into the rest of the milk. ⊠ FULL for 4½-5 mins. 600W (*3½-4 mins. 700W; 5½-6 mins. 500W*), until boiling and very thick, whisking every minute.

4   Leave the custard to cool slightly, whisking occasionally, then stir in the rum. Reserve 6 pieces of each of all the fruits for the decoration, mix the rest together and spread over the sponge in an even layer.

5   Pour the custard over the fruit and leave to cool, then chill for at least an hour until set. Spoon the whipped cream over the custard and swirl the surface in a decorative pattern. Decorate with the reserved fruit and sprinkle with the coconut.

Preparation: 25 minutes, plus chilling

Cooking time: 8 minutes

Power setting: FULL

Make in advance

Serves 4

Illustrated opposite

Top left: **Chocolate cheesecake** (*see p. 146*); Middle: **Tropical trifle** (*see opposite*); Bottom: **Bread and butter pudding** (*see p. 143*).

Chocolate cheesecake

INGREDIENTS

65g (2½ oz) butter
200g (7 oz) milk chocolate digestive biscuits, crushed
For the filling
350g (12 oz) cream cheese
350g (12 oz) skimmed milk soft cheese
2 eggs plus 1 egg yolk, beaten
30ml (2 tbsp) cornflour
300g (11 oz) milk chocolate

By using a mixture of cheeses this cheesecake has a wonderful soft texture. Cook it until it just begins to set, then chill thoroughly so that it can set completely.

1 Put the butter in a medium bowl and 🌊 FULL for 1½ mins. 600W (*1 min. 700W; 1½-2 mins. 500W*) to melt. Stir in the biscuit crumbs and mix well. Press into the base of a deep 23cm (9 in) round cake dish.

2 To make the filling: put the cheeses into a large bowl and 🌊 MEDIUM for 2 mins. 600W (*1½ mins. 700W; 2½ mins. 500W*) to soften. Add the beaten egg and cornflour and beat until smooth.

3 Put 250g (9 oz) of the chocolate into a small bowl and 🌊 MEDIUM for 3½-4 mins. 600W (*3 mins. 700W; 4½-5 mins. 500W*) to melt, stirring once. Stir into the cheese mixture, blending well.

4 Pour into the cake dish over the biscuit base and smooth the surface. 🌊 MEDIUM for 20-25 mins. 600W (*17-21 mins. 700W; 25-30 mins. 500W*) or until just set in the centre.

5 Grate the remaining chocolate coarsely and sprinkle over the top. Leave the cheesecake to cool, then chill for at least 2 hours until firm.

Preparation: 20 minutes, plus chilling

Cooking time: 28 minutes

Power settings: FULL and MEDIUM

Make in advance

Serves 8-10

Illustrated on p. 145

SAUCES AND PRESERVES

Spiced tomato and coconut sauce

INGREDIENTS

15ml (1 tbsp) sunflower oil
1 onion, finely chopped
1 clove garlic, crushed
1 small red chilli, deseeded and chopped finely
50g (2 oz) creamed coconut
300ml (½ pint) boiling water
3 cloves, ground
2.5ml (½ tsp) ground allspice
30ml (2 tbsp) tomato purée
150ml (¼ pint) tomato juice or equivalent in fresh tomatoes, puréed
salt

Creamed coconut makes a marvellous addition to sauces, adding a velvet texture and extra rich flavour. Serve this sauce with meat loaves, nut roasts or vegetables.

1 Put the oil in a medium dish and ⊠ FULL for 1 min. 600W (*30 secs. 700W; 1 min. 500W*). Stir in the chopped onion, garlic and chilli and ⊠ FULL for 2 mins. 600W (*1½ mins. 700W; 2½ mins. 500W*).

2 Dissolve the coconut in boiling water, then add to the onion with the remaining ingredients, except the salt. Cover and ⊠ FULL for 7 mins. 600W (*6 mins. 700W; 8½ mins. 500W*), stirring once or twice.

3 Season to taste. Liquidize to make a smooth sauce.

Preparation: 10 minutes

Cooking time: 10 minutes

Power setting: FULL

Good reheated

Freezes well

Makes 600ml (1 pint)

Illustrated on pp. 148-149

Sweet and sour sauce

INGREDIENTS

15g (½ oz) margarine or butter
½ onion, finely chopped
1 clove garlic, crushed
100ml (4 fl oz) water
100ml (4 fl oz) pineapple juice
15ml (1 tbsp) cider vinegar
10ml (2 tsp) honey
5ml (1 tsp) shoyu
2.5ml (½ tsp) grated fresh root ginger
100g (4 oz) plums, chopped
10ml (2 tsp) arrowroot
salt and black pepper

Leaving the plums coarsely chopped gives this sauce a good texture. Take care not to over-thicken with arrowroot or the sauce will become gluey.

1 Put the margarine or butter in a medium dish and ≋ FULL for 30 secs. Stir in the onion and garlic and ≋ FULL for 2 mins. 600W (*1½ mins. 700W; 2½ mins. 500W*).

2 Add the water, fruit juice, vinegar, honey, shoyu, ginger and plums. Cover and ≋ FULL for 5 mins. 600W (*4 mins. 700W; 6 mins. 500W*), stirring once.

3 Dissolve the arrowroot in a little water, then stir into the sauce and ≋ FULL for 2 mins. 600W (*1½ mins. 700W; 2½ mins. 500W*), stirring once.

4 Season to taste with salt and pepper.

★ **Preparation:** 15 minutes

≋ **Cooking time:** 9½ minutes

⊘ **Power setting:** FULL

◎ **Makes 300ml** (½ pint)

Illustrated below

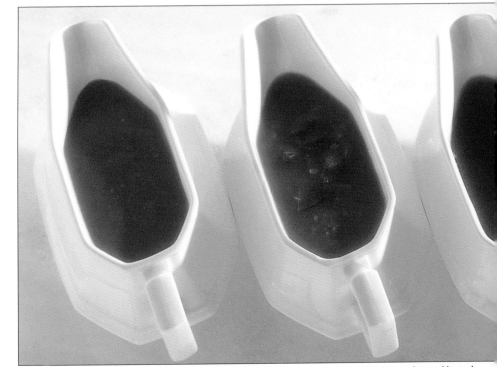

From left to right: **Spiced tomato and coconut sauce** (*see p. 147*); **Sweet and sour sauce** (*see above*); **Concentrated vegetable stock** (*see p. 151*); **White sauce** (*see p. 150*); **Savoury brown sauce** (*see opposite*)

Savoury brown sauce

INGREDIENTS

25g (1 oz) sunflower margarine
2.5ml (½ tsp) celery seeds
1 bay leaf
1 medium onion, finely chopped
1 clove garlic, crushed
25g (1 oz) wholewheat flour
5ml (1 tsp) chopped fresh thyme
15ml (1 tbsp) shoyu
5-10ml (1-2 tsp) miso (see p. 101)
450ml (¾ pint) stock or water
black pepper

This is an easy recipe for a rich gravy which is good served with any savoury bakes or roasts.

1 Put the margarine, celery seeds and bay leaf in a medium dish and ⊠ FULL for 1 min. 600W (*30 secs. 700W; 1 min. 500W*). Stir in the onion and garlic and ⊠ FULL for 2 mins. 600W (*1½ mins. 700W; 2½ mins. 500W*).

2 Stir in the flour and ⊠ FULL for 30 secs. Add the chopped thyme and shoyu.

3 Dissolve the miso in a little of the stock or water and mix into the sauce, then add the rest of the stock.

4 Cover and ⊠ FULL for 5 mins. 600W (*4 mins. 700W; 6 mins. 500W*), stirring once or twice. Season with pepper.

Preparation: 10 minutes

Cooking time: 11 minutes

Power setting: FULL

Freezes well

Makes 450ml (¾ pint)

Shoyu and miso make a good combination, and can make a flavoursome sauce with water.

Illustrated below

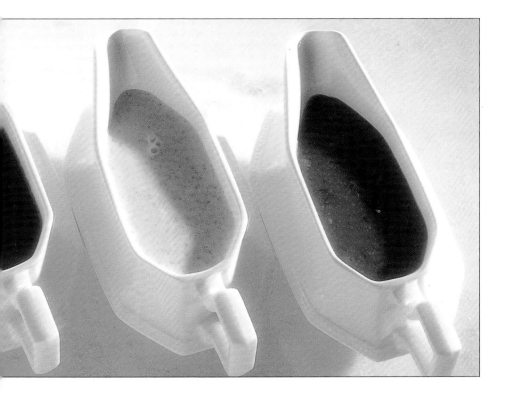

White sauce

INGREDIENTS

300ml (½ pint) milk
½ medium onion
1 bay leaf
6 peppercorns
sprig of parsley or bouquet garni
25g (1 oz) sunflower margarine
25g (1 oz) wholewheat flour
salt and black pepper

Milk-based sauces work particularly well in a microwave as there is little chance of scorching or sticking. Use a container large enough to allow for the liquid's expansion as it heats up.

1 Put the milk, onion, bay leaf, peppercorns, and herbs in a jug. ≋ FULL for 2 mins. 600W (*1½ mins. 700W; 2½ mins. 500W*). Stand for 5 mins., then strain.

2 Put the margarine in a medium bowl and ≋ FULL for 30 secs. Stir in the flour and ≋ FULL for 30 secs.

3 Stir in the milk, blending very well. Season and ≋ FULL for 2-3 mins. 600W (*1½-2½ mins. 700W; 2½-3½ mins. 500W*) until thickened, stirring 2-3 times.

Preparation: 10 minutes

Cooking time: 5 minutes

Power setting: FULL

Makes 300ml (½ pint)

★ For smooth results, stir milk-based sauces once a minute during cooking. You can even leave a wooden spoon in the mixture while it is in the oven.

Illustrated on pp. 148-149

VARIATIONS
Cheese sauce

INGREDIENTS

As for white sauce plus
50g (2 oz) grated cheese
pinch of mustard powder or cayenne pepper

1 Make a white sauce following the method above. Once cooked, add the cheese and spices. Stir well, then cook for 30 secs. or until the cheese is just melted.

Makes 300 ml (½ pint)

Mushroom sauce

INGREDIENTS

As for white sauce plus
100g (4 oz) button mushrooms, thinly sliced
5ml (1 tsp) paprika
pinch of cayenne pepper

1 Infuse the milk as described above, or simply use plain milk and start the sauce by heating the margarine.

2 Put the margarine in a medium dish and ≋ FULL for 30 secs. Stir in the mushrooms, spices and seasoning. Cover and ≋ FULL for 4 mins. 600W (*3 mins. 700W; 5 mins. 500W*), stirring once.

3 Stir in the flour and ≋ FULL for 30 secs.

4 Pour in the milk, stir well, then re-cover. ≋ FULL for 3 mins. 600W (*2½ mins. 700W; 3½ mins. 500W*), stirring regularly.

Makes 300ml (½ pint)

▤ If you don't want to use the sauce immediately, cover the surface with some greaseproof paper to prevent an unsightly skin forming.

Concentrated vegetable stock

INGREDIENTS

15ml (1 tbsp) sunflower oil
½ medium onion, with the skin left on
1 medium carrot, chopped in large chunks
100g (4 oz) leeks, chopped
handful of celery leaves
1.25ml (¼ tsp) celery seeds
sprig of parsley and thyme
salt and black pepper

Make a strongly flavoured stock using less water – anything cooked with a high proportion of water doesn't save much time in the microwave. Dilute the stock to taste when using in soups and sauces.

1 Put the oil in a deep bowl and ⊠ FULL for 1 min. 600W *(30 secs. 700W; 1 min. 500W).*

2 Stir in the vegetables and celery seeds and ⊠ FULL for 3 mins. 600W *(2½ mins. 700W; 3½ mins. 500W),* stirring once or twice.

3 Add 600ml (1 pint) water and herbs. Cover and ⊠ FULL for 12 mins. 600W *(10 mins. 700W; 15 mins. 500W).*

4 Strain, season and dilute as required.

Preparation:
10 minutes

Cooking time:
16 minutes

Power setting:
FULL

Freezes well

Makes 600ml (1 pint)

To make a darker stock add shoyu, miso or tomato purée.

Illustrated on pp. 148-149

Concentrated meat stock

INGREDIENTS

15ml (1 tbsp) sunflower oil
1 small onion, with skin left on, halved
1 carrot, chopped in large chunks
2 celery stalks, quartered
450g (1 lb) cooked meat bones or chicken carcasses broken into small pieces
sprigs of parsley and thyme
1 bay leaf

This is a quick recipe for meat stock, using a mixture of any bones or meat scraps. This concentrated stock has the added advantage of taking up less room in the freezer than conventional stock.

1 Put the oil in a deep bowl and ⊠ FULL for 1 min. 600W *(30 secs. 700W; 1 min. 500W).*

2 Stir in the vegetables and ⊠ FULL for 3 mins. 600W *(2½ mins. 700W; 3½ mins. 500W),* stirring once.

3 Add the bones, 600ml (1 pint) water and herbs. Cover and ⊠ FULL for 30 mins. 600W *(25 mins. 700W; 35 mins. 500W),* stirring two or three times.

4 Strain, season and dilute as required.

Preparation:
10 minutes

Cooking time:
30 minutes

Power setting:
FULL

Freezes well

Makes 600ml (1 pint)

To make a darker stock, brown all the bones in a conventional oven before you start.

Fruit sauce

INGREDIENTS

50g (2 oz) raisins

150ml (¼ pint) orange juice

1 ripe banana

A refreshing, tangy sauce for serving with sponge puddings, baked bananas or ice cream.

1 Put the raisins and orange juice in a jug, cover and ⊠ FULL for 2 mins. 600W (*1½ mins. 700W; 2½ mins. 500W*). Leave for 15-20 mins. until the raisins are plump. Drain, reserving the orange juice.

2 Liquidize the banana with the orange juice until smooth. Add the raisins and liquidize to make a coarse purée.

3 Return the sauce to the jug and ⊠ FULL for 2 mins. 600W (*1½ mins. 700W; 2½ mins. 500W*) to reheat. Stir well, then leave to stand for 2-3 mins. before serving.

★ **Preparation:**
20 minutes

≋ **Cooking time:**
4 minutes

⊘ **Power setting:**
FULL

◎ **Makes 300ml**
(½ pint)

Illustrated opposite

Barbecue sauce

INGREDIENTS

25g (1 oz) butter

75g (3 oz) mushrooms, sliced

150g (5 oz) tomato ketchup

50g (2 oz) soft light brown sugar

10ml (2 tsp) lemon juice

pinch of garlic salt

pinch of ground allspice

pinch of chilli powder

This versatile sauce can either be served as an accompaniment to cooked meats and poultry, or used as a baste to flavour and moisten them during microwaving.

1 Put the butter in a small bowl and ⊠ FULL for 1 min. 600W (*30 secs. 700W; 1 min. 500W*) to melt. Add the mushrooms and ⊠ FULL for 2 mins. 600W (*1½ mins. 700W; 2½ mins. 500W*), stirring once.

2 Stir in the ketchup, sugar, lemon juice, garlic salt and spices. ⊠ FULL for 3-5 mins. 600W (*2½-3 mins. 700W; 3½-5 mins. 500W*) until boiling, stirring two or three times. Serve hot.

★ **Preparation:**
5 minutes

≋ **Cooking time:**
6 minutes

⊘ **Power setting:**
FULL

≋ **Good reheated**

◎ **Serves 4**

Top: **Fruit sauce** (*see opposite*); Centre: **Chocolate or carob sauce** (*see p. 154*); **Cornmeal custard** (*see p. 154*)

Chocolate or carob sauce

INGREDIENTS

25g (1 oz) butter

50g (2 oz) cooking chocolate or sugar-free carob bar, broken into pieces

1 egg yolk, beaten

250ml (8 fl oz) skimmed milk

This versatile and rich sauce can be used as a topping for steamed puddings, served with poached fruit, such as pears, or raw fruit salads, bananas or ice cream.

1 Put the butter and chocolate or carob in a medium bowl and ≋ FULL for 2 mins. 600W *(1½ mins. 700W; 2½ mins. 500W)* until melted. Stir well.

2 Beat in the egg yolk and milk and ≋ FULL for 2½ mins. 600W *(2 mins. 700W; 3 mins. 500W)*, stirring 2-3 times. Leave to stand for 2-3 mins. Serve warm.

★ **Preparation:**
5 minutes

≋ **Cooking time:**
4½ minutes

∅ **Power setting:**
FULL

◎ **Makes 300ml**
(½ pint)

Illustrated on p. 153

Cornmeal custard

INGREDIENTS

300ml (½ pint) skimmed milk or soya milk

45ml (3 tbsp) cornmeal

15-30ml (1-2 tbsp) light brown sugar

2 drops vanilla essence

Custard sauces cook well in the microwave as long as you are careful with the timing and the temperature. Milk can boil over so it is always best to use a large jug or bowl. When not using immediately, cover the surface with greaseproof paper to prevent a skin forming.

1 Put the milk in a jug and ≋ FULL for 1 min. 600W *(30 secs. 700W; 1 min. 500W)*.

2 Mix the cornmeal and sugar together. Beat in a little of the milk to make a smooth paste, then add the remaining milk and the vanilla essence.

3 ≋ FULL for 3½ mins. 600W *(3 mins. 700W; 4-5 mins. 500W)*, stirring or whisking 3-4 times during cooking.

★ **Preparation:**
5 minutes

≋ **Cooking time:**
4½ minutes

∅ **Power setting:**
FULL

◎ **Makes 300ml**
(½ pint)

 Stir in the cornmeal well so that it doesn't all sink to the bottom in a lump. If this does happen, liquidize the mixture for 30 secs. Whisking with a balloon whisk once a minute during cooking should also ensure a smooth mixture.

Illustrated on p. 153

Blackberry and apple purée

INGREDIENTS

450g (1 lb) blackberries

225g (8 oz) dessert apples

25ml (1 fl oz) concentrated apple juice (CAJ)

15ml (1 tbsp) lemon juice

10ml (2 tsp) agar powder (optional)

This thick fruit purée can easily be used as a jam, thinly spread on toast or crispbreads, or as a sauce topping. The purée will keep in the refrigerator for about two weeks.

1 Wash all the fruit carefully. Core and chop the apples. Place all the ingredients in a large bowl and ⊠ FULL for 8 mins. 600W (*6½ mins. 700W; 10 mins. 500W*), stirring twice.

2 If you want a thicker consistency, add the agar powder. Dissolve it in the fruit, then ⊠ FULL for 2-3 mins. 600W (*1½-2½ mins. 700W; 2½-3½ mins. 500W*).

3 Leave to cool, then liquidize and sieve to remove the pips. Store in sterilized jars.

Preparation: 10 minutes

Cooking time: 8 minutes

Power setting: FULL

Freezes well

Makes 450g (1 lb)

Illustrated on p. 157

Tomato relish

INGREDIENTS

100g (4 oz) dried apricots, chopped into slivers

60ml (4 tbsp) cider vinegar

225g (8 oz) tomatoes, skinned and chopped

100g (4 oz) medium onion, diced

1 small green pepper, deseeded and chopped

1.25ml (¼ tsp) salt

1 dried chilli, finely chopped

2.5ml (½ tsp) cumin seeds

2.5ml (½ tsp) mustard seeds

2 bay leaves

8 peppercorns

A colourful, spicy relish that complements all savoury dishes perfectly.

1 Put the apricots and vinegar in a medium dish and ⊠ FULL for 2 mins. 600W (*1½ mins. 700W; 2½ mins. 500W*). Leave to stand for 30 mins.

2 Mix the remaining ingredients with the apricots. Cover and ⊠ FULL for 14 mins. 600W (*11 mins. 700W; 17 mins. 500W*), stirring several times.

3 Leave to cool, then pour into sterilized jars. Store for up to two months.

Preparation: 15 minutes

Cooking time: 16 minutes

Power setting: FULL

Makes 550g (1¼ lb)

 Sterilize clean jars by half-filling with water and bringing to the boil in the microwave. Allow to boil for 1 min., then remove carefully (using oven gloves) and swirl the liquid around each jar before pouring away. Leave jars to dry.

Illustrated on p. 157

Plum and pear jam

INGREDIENTS

450g (1 lb) Victoria plums
1 pear, peeled, cored and chopped
50ml (2 fl oz) concentrated apple juice (CAJ)
15ml (1 tbsp) orange juice
100g (4 oz) soft brown sugar (optional)

This recipe can be used to make a conventional jam or a sugar-free fruit purée, to spread on toast or use as a filling or topping for cakes. Store in the refrigerator, or freeze down in small portions.

1 Chop the flesh of the plums coarsely. Mix with the pear, CAJ and orange juice in a large bowl.

2 Crack the plum stones using a rolling pin, and add to the fruit. Count how many are added so that they can all be taken out afterwards.

3 ▧ FULL for 8 mins. 600W *(6½ mins. 700W; 10 mins. 500W)*, stirring once or twice.

4 Leave to cool, remove the stones, then purée the jam. Stir in sugar, if using, and ▧ FULL for 12 mins. 600W *(10 mins. 700W; 15 mins. 500W)*, stirring every 3 mins. Leave to cool, then bottle.

★ **Preparation:** 25 minutes

▧ **Cooking time:** 20 minutes

⦸ **Power setting:** FULL

◎ **Makes 550g (1¼ lb)**

★ For a sugar-free purée, omit the sugar and refrigerate after liquidizing. The purée will thicken in the refrigerator.

Illustrated opposite

Apple and date chutney

INGREDIENTS

225g (8 oz) dessert apples, peeled, cored and chopped
100g (4 oz) onions, chopped
1 clove garlic, crushed
100g (4 oz) dates
75ml (3 fl oz) cider vinegar
100g (4 oz) raisins
1cm (½ in) fresh root ginger, grated
2.5ml (½ tsp) mixed spice
5ml (1 tsp) mustard seeds
pinch of salt
pinch of cayenne pepper

The smell of vinegar and spices doesn't dominate the kitchen when making chutneys and relishes in the microwave, and you can make them in small quantities.

1 Put the apples, onions, garlic, dates and vinegar in a large bowl. Cover and ▧ FULL for 5 mins. 600W *(4 mins. 700W; 6 mins. 500W)*, stirring once.

2 Add the remaining ingredients and ▧ FULL for 12 mins. 600W *(10 mins. 700W; 15 mins. 500W)*, stirring once or twice.

3 Leave to stand overnight, then pour into sterilized jars and store the chutney for up to three months.

★ **Preparation:** 20 minutes

▧ **Cooking time:** 17 minutes

⦸ **Power setting:** FULL

◎ **Makes 550g (1¼ lb)**

Illustrated opposite

From top to bottom: **Blackberry and apple purée** (*see p. 155*); **Plum and pear jam** (*see opposite*); **Apple and date chutney** (*see opposite*); **Tomato relish** (*see p. 155*)

Red cherry jam

INGREDIENTS

675g (1½ lb) red cherries,
stoned, reserving the stones

30ml (2 tbsp) lemon juice

450g (1 lb) granulated sugar

*Small quantities of jam microwave very
quickly. Make sure the bowl is heatproof and
always use oven gloves as the bowl can get very
hot. Clean jam jars are essential when making
jam (see p. 155).*

1 Put the cherries in a deep, heatproof bowl
with the lemon juice. Tie the cherry stones in
a muslin bag and tuck under the cherries.

2 Cover and ⊠ FULL for 10-12 mins. 600W
(8½-10 mins. 700W; 12½-15 mins. 500W)
until soft, stirring two or three times.

3 Stir the sugar into the cherries and ⊠
FULL for 2-3 mins. 600W *(1½-2½ mins.
700W; 2½-3½ mins. 500W)*, then stir to
dissolve the sugar.

4 Half-cover the bowl and ⊠ FULL for
13-15 mins. 600W *(10½-12½ mins. 700W;
16-18 mins. 500W)*, until setting point is
reached.

5 Leave to settle for 10 mins., then remove
the stones and ladle the jam into clean jam
jars and seal.

Preparation:
15 minutes, plus
cooling

Cooking time:
25 minutes

Power setting:
FULL

**Make in
advance**

**Makes 800g
(1¾ lb)**

To help the sugar
dissolve, warm it
in a conventional oven
at 150C/300F/Gas 2
for 10 minutes.

BREADS, CAKES AND BISCUITS

Wholewheat bread

INGREDIENTS

700g (1½ lb) wholewheat flour
5ml (1 tsp) salt
25g (1 oz) fresh yeast
15ml (1 tbsp) molasses
450ml (¾ pint) tepid water
30ml (2 tbsp) soya flour

A microwave oven makes the actual baking of bread a very speedy process. You can also prove dough in the microwave oven, but the flavour is not as good, the timing is tricky and if you are not careful you can end up with a half-cooked, half-risen loaf!

1 Mix the flour and salt together in a large bowl. Cream the yeast and molasses together. Add 150ml (¼ pint) water and whisk until the yeast is dissolved. Add the soya flour, then leave the mixture in a warm place for 5 mins.

2 Pour the yeast ferment into the flour and add the remaining water. Knead well to form a smooth, pliable dough. It should not be dry at this stage. Place in a clean bowl, cover with cling film and leave to rise for at least 15-30 mins.

3 Knead again briefly, then divide the dough in two. Shape each piece into a loaf and put in a 450g (1 lb) loaf dish. Cover with cling film, prick well and leave to prove for 30 mins.

4 Uncover and bake one loaf at a time. 🔬 FULL for 7 mins. 600W (*6 mins. 700W; 8½ mins. 500W*), giving the dish a half turn every 2-3 mins.

5 Leave to stand, then turn out on to a wire rack and leave to cool. Don't be tempted to eat the bread hot from the oven. It needs to stand and cool to finish cooking.

Preparation: 20 minutes, plus 50-65 minutes rising.

Cooking time: 14 minutes

Power setting: FULL

Good reheated

Makes two 450g (1 lb) loaves

Press the bread with your fingers to see if it is ready – it should spring back when it is. Do not overcook in the oven as the bread continues to cook through during the necessary standing time.

Soda bread

INGREDIENTS

450g (1 lb) wholewheat flour
2.5ml (½ tsp) salt
5ml (1 tsp) bicarbonate of soda
50g (2 oz) butter
225ml (8 fl oz) buttermilk

This type of dough works extremely well in the microwave. It is important to bake the mixture straight away, otherwise the rising effect of the soda will be completely lost.

1 Mix the flour, salt and bicarbonate of soda together, then rub in the butter. Add the buttermilk and mix to a stiff dough.

2 Knead the dough into a cob shape. Place on a small plate or flat dish and make a deep cross on the top.

3 ⊠ FULL for 7 mins. 600W (*6 mins. 700W; 8½ mins. 500W*), giving the plate or dish a half turn every 2-3 mins.

4 Leave to stand and cool on a wire rack.

★ **Preparation:** 15 minutes, plus cooling

⧆ **Cooking time:** 7 minutes

� **Power setting:** FULL

◎ **Makes 700g (1½ lb) loaf**

★ Remember never to put the dough into traditional metal loaf tins, use bakeware specially designed for use in microwave ovens.

Cheese and oat cob

INGREDIENTS

25g (1 oz) fresh yeast
15ml (1 tbsp) molasses
300-450ml (½-¾ pint) tepid water
450g (1 lb) wholewheat flour
225g (8 oz) oat flakes
50g (2 oz) Cheddar cheese, grated
5ml (1 tsp) salt
5ml (1 tsp) paprika
5ml (1 tsp) caraway seeds

This makes a tasty, pleasantly chewy, savoury bread which is delicious served with soups.

1 Mix the yeast with the molasses and 300ml (½ pint) tepid water. Leave for 5 mins.

2 Stir in half the wholewheat flour and ⊠ FULL for 1 min. 600W (*30 secs. 700W; 1 min. 500W*), stirring halfway through.

3 Add the remaining ingredients and knead well, adding a little more water if necessary. Cover with cling film and leave to rise for about 30 mins.

4 Knead again, then divide the dough into two. Shape into cobs or shape each half into five rolls. Cover with cling film and leave to prove for 1 hour.

5 Uncover and bake cobs one at a time on a small plate or flat dish. ⊠ FULL for 7 mins. 600W (*6 mins. 700W; 8½ mins. 500W*), giving the plate or dish a half turn every 2-3 mins. Bake rolls in two batches, arrange in a ring on a dish and ⊠ FULL for 4 mins. 600W (*3 mins. 700W; 5 mins. 500W*), giving the dish a half turn halfway through. Leave to cool on a wire rack.

★ **Preparation:** 25 minutes, plus 1½ hours rising and proving

⧆ **Cooking time:** 15 minutes

⌐ **Power setting:** FULL

◎ **Makes 2 cobs or 10 rolls**

★ The microwave is extremely useful for speeding up the action of the yeast when making bread by the batter method. The batter quickly becomes very light and frothy.

Top: **Savoury scone roll** (*see p. 163*); Bottom right: **Honey and sesame scones** (*see p. 162*); Left: **Orange cake** (*see p. 162*)

Honey and sesame scones

INGREDIENTS

225g (8 oz) self-raising wholewheat flour
pinch of salt
5ml (1 tsp) baking powder
5ml (1 tsp) mixed spice
50g (2 oz) sunflower margarine
25g (1 oz) sesame seeds
30ml (2 tbsp) honey
1 egg, beaten
30-45ml (2-3 tbsp) milk

Scone dough microwaves well and the wholewheat flour gives the scones a good colour. The sesame seeds provide a delicious crunchy quality and the honey adds just enough sweetness.

1   Mix the flour, salt, baking powder and mixed spice together. Rub in the fat, then mix in the sesame seeds.

2   Add the honey, beaten egg and enough milk to make a soft, pliable dough.

3   Quickly pat out the dough to a large round and mark into eight sections. Place on a dish lined with greaseproof paper and ⊗ FULL for 4 mins. 600W (*3 mins. 700W; 5 mins. 500W*), giving the dish a half turn every 2 mins. Leave to stand for 4 mins. Eat while still warm.

Preparation: 15 minutes

Cooking time: 4 minutes

Power setting: FULL

Freezes well

Serves 8

Illustrated on p. 161

Orange cake

INGREDIENTS

1 orange
15ml (1 tbsp) concentrated apple juice (CAJ)
100g (4 oz) sugar
100ml (4 fl oz) sunflower oil
225g (8oz) wholewheat flour
5ml (1 tsp) mixed spice
pinch of salt
5ml (1 tsp) baking powder
Decoration
fresh orange slices
desiccated coconut

This simple cake has a good texture and delicious flavour. The cake can be made with lemon if preferred.

1   Scrub the orange well, and chop into small pieces. Liquidize with 200ml (7 fl oz) water and the CAJ until fairly smooth. Add the sugar and oil and liquidize again.

2   Mix the flour with the spice, salt and baking powder. Stir in the orange mixture and mix until smooth.

3   Line a 1.2 litre (2 pint) ring mould or savarin dish with greaseproof paper. Spoon in the cake mixture and ⊗ FULL for 8 mins. 600W (*6½ mins. 700W; 10 mins. 500W*), giving the dish a quarter turn every 2 mins.

4   Leave to stand for 5-10 mins. before turning out on a wire rack to cool. Remove the paper at the end of the standing time to prevent it sticking to the cake.

5   Decorate with orange slices and desiccated coconut.

Preparation: 10 minutes

Cooking time: 8 minutes

Power setting: FULL

Freezes well

Serves 8

At the end of the cooking time most cakes still look damp on top. Leave to stand for the time specified, then insert a skewer into the centre. If the skewer comes out clean the cake is cooked; if not, cook the cake for a further 1-2 mins., then leave to stand again.

Illustrated on p. 161

Savoury scone roll

INGREDIENTS

225g (8 oz) self-raising wholewheat flour

pinch of salt

5ml (1 tsp) baking powder

pinch of cayenne pepper

50g (2 oz) margarine

1 egg, beaten

45-60ml (3-4 tbsp) milk

For the filling

15ml (1 tbsp) sunflower oil

1 medium onion, finely chopped

1 clove garlic, crushed

15ml (1 tbsp) chutney

15ml (1 tbsp) tomato purée

100g (4 oz) walnuts, chopped

salt and black pepper

This is a useful recipe for a quick snack at home, or for picnics and packed lunches. The filling can be varied by using different nuts and adding extra herbs and vegetables, but be sure that they are all finely chopped.

1 For the filling, put the oil in a medium dish and ❀ FULL for 1 min. 600W *(30 secs. 700W; 1 min. 500W)*. Stir in the chopped onion and garlic and ❀ FULL for 1 min. 600W *(30 secs. 700W; 1 min. 500W)*.

2 Stir in the remaining ingredients for the filling, except the seasoning, and ❀ FULL for 2 mins. *(1½ mins. 700W; 2½ mins. 500W)*. Season well.

3 To make the scone, mix the flour, salt, baking powder and cayenne together. Rub in the fat, then add the beaten egg and enough milk to make a soft dough.

4 Roll out the dough to a 22.5 × 15cm (9 × 6 in) rectangle. Spread over the filling, then roll up the dough carefully from long edge to long edge.

5 Wrap in greaseproof paper and place in a flat dish. ❀ FULL for 4½ mins. 600W *(3½-4 mins. 700W; 5½-6 mins. 500W)*, giving a half turn every 2 mins. Serve hot or cold.

Preparation: 20 minutes

Cooking time: 8½ minutes

Power setting: FULL

Freezes well

Serves 4

Wrapping the roll in greaseproof paper helps retain the moisture and keep the dough soft.

Illustrated on p. 161

Currant biscuits

INGREDIENTS

50g (2 oz) sunflower margarine
50g (2 oz) pear and apple spread
100g (4 oz) wholewheat flour
5ml (1 tsp) orange juice
5ml (1 tsp) orange rind
25g (1 oz) currants

Soft biscuit doughs work well in the microwave, especially if they are a dark colour to begin with, and relatively high in fat and sugar. Although they are less crisp than conventional biscuits, they take only a fraction of the time to cook.

1 Cream the margarine and the pear and apple spread together until smooth. Beat in the flour, orange juice and rind. Work in the currants.

2 Roll out the dough thinly and cut out 12 small biscuits about 5cm (2 in) in diameter.

3 Arrange in a circle on a sheet of greaseproof paper. Cover with absorbent paper and a plate. ▧ FULL for 2½ mins. 600W (*2 mins. 700W; 3 mins, 500W*).

4 Leave to stand for 5 mins., then cool on a wire rack.

★ **Preparation:** 15 minutes

▧ **Cooking time:** 2½ minutes

⊘ **Power setting:** FULL

◎ **Makes 12**

▧ Take care not to overcook. The biscuits should be soft at the end of the cooking time. They will harden as they cool down.

Illustrated opposite

Traditional sponge cake

INGREDIENTS

100g (4 oz) self-raising flour
2.5ml (½ tsp) baking powder
100g (4 oz) caster sugar
100g (4 oz) soft butter
2 eggs, beaten
60ml (4 tbsp) milk
For the filling
150ml (¼ pint) double cream, whipped
icing sugar, to dust

A microwaved sponge cake can be very light and moist, but remember it also cooks while standing.

1 Sift the flour and baking powder into a mixing bowl and add the sugar, butter, eggs and milk. Beat until well blended.

2 Grease and line two 20cm (8 in) sandwich cake dishes with greaseproof paper. Divide the mixture between the dishes and smooth.

3 Cook one cake at a time, ▧ FULL for 3-4 mins. 600W (*2½-3 mins. 700W; 3½-5 mins. 500W*) until springy to the touch and just shrinking from the sides, giving the dish a quarter turn two or three times.

4 Leave to stand for 5 mins., then turn out on to a wire rack to cool. Sandwich with the cream and dust with icing sugar.

5 For a tangy sponge cake, use fruit juice instead of milk and add in 10ml (2 tsp) grated lemon or orange rind to the mix.

★ **Preparation:** 15 minutes

▧ **Cooking time:** 6 minutes

⊘ **Power setting:** FULL

❋ **Freezes well**

◎ **Serves 6**

Clockwise from the top: **Date and chocolate or carob slice** (*see p. 166*); **Flapjacks** (*see p. 166*); **Currant biscuits** (*see opposite*).

Flapjacks

INGREDIENTS

75g (3 oz) margarine
40g (1½ oz) brown sugar
175g (6 oz) oats
15ml (1 tbsp) honey

Flapjacks contain a high proportion of fat and sugar and so work successfully in the microwave. They do tend to soften and become more crumbly during storage so don't leave too long before eating them.

1 Put the margarine in a medium dish and ⧉ FULL for 1 min. 600W (*30 secs. 700W; 1 min. 500W*). Mix in all the remaining ingredients, stirring thoroughly.

2 Press the mixture into a 22.5 × 17.5cm (9 × 7 in) shallow dish and level out the surface. ⧉ FULL for 3 mins. 600W (*2½ mins. 700W; 3½ mins. 500W*).

3 Press down the top with a fork and leave to cool in the dish. While still slightly warm, mark into fingers with a knife.

Preparation:
5 minutes

Cooking time:
4 minutes

Power setting:
FULL

Makes 9

Substitute molasses for the honey to darken the colour of the flapjacks.

Illustrated on p. 165

Date and chocolate or carob slice

INGREDIENTS

100g (4 oz) dried dates, chopped
150ml (¼ pint) boiling water
100g (4 oz) sunflower margarine
1 banana, mashed
100g (4 oz) wholewheat flour
50g (2 oz) soya flour
50g (2 oz) cocoa or carob powder
5ml (1 tsp) baking powder
pinch of salt
50ml (2 fl oz) orange juice
50g (2 oz) blanched, chopped nuts

Cake mixtures with carob or chocolate work well in a microwave because they don't need to brown. The texture of this slice is rather like fudge, and is best when left to cool completely.

1 Put the dates in a small dish and pour over the boiling water. Cover and ⧉ FULL for 3 mins. 600W (*2½ mins. 700W; 3½ mins. 500W*). Cool thoroughly, then beat to a smooth purée by hand or in a food processor.

2 Cream the purée with the margarine until fluffy, then add the banana. Stir in the flour, soya flour, cocoa or carob, baking powder and salt. Add the fruit juice to make a soft mixture. Mix in the chopped nuts.

3 Line a 17.5cm (7 in) shallow dish with greaseproof paper. Spoon in the mixture, then ⧉ FULL for 7 mins. 600W (*6 mins. 700W; 8½ mins. 500W*), giving the dish a quarter turn once every 2 mins.

4 Leave to stand for 5-10 mins., then turn out onto a wire rack to cool. Peel off the greaseproof paper at the end of the standing time to prevent it sticking.

Preparation:
15 minutes, plus cooling

Cooking time:
10 minutes

Power setting:
FULL

Serves 8-10

Drain the cooked dates if necessary, as the purée should be thick and not runny like a sauce.

Illustrated on p. 165

GETTING TO KNOW YOUR MICROWAVE

Buying a microwave might seem a good idea, but with so many different models on the market where do you start? This section tells you what types of microwave are available and describes in non-technical detail how they work, how to clean and maintain them, and what is best to cook in them.

You needn't throw away all your conventional cook books; just follow the details given on how to convert recipes to the microwave style of cooking. A great deal of normal cooking equipment can be used in the microwave, but study the information given on special equipment and materials that work particularly well in the microwave. To make sure all your microwave dishes cook evenly, learn the art of rearranging, turning and stirring food from the different cooking techniques described.

One of the joys of having a microwave is that it can so often save you time, especially with tasks like defrosting food. A comprehensive defrosting and reheating chart is included so that you can see the timings for all types of food at a glance. Helpful hints and tips are also included on other ways the microwave can become an indispensable cooking aid – you will be surprised at just how easy it is to heat up bread rolls, to dry fresh herbs or to toast some nuts.

Converting recipes for the microwave

There is no need to abandon all your favourite conventional recipes when you start to use a microwave oven. Recipes for foods that are naturally moist or cooked by boiling, steaming or poaching can all be adapted quite easily and very successfully for the microwave, usually just by reducing the cooking time and the liquid content. However, it's best not to attempt to adapt recipes until you feel fully familiar with your microwave and understand the different microwave techniques, knowing just when and why they should be employed. The only way to do this is to learn by practice and experimentation.

For the best results when converting a conventional recipe, use an existing microwave recipe with similar ingredients and quantities as a model, refer to pages 8-48 for ingredients' cooking times and techniques, and then just keep to the following guidelines.

■ Preparation is usually the same for microwaved food as for conventionally-cooked food, only it is always far more important that ingredients such as vegetables are cut to a small and uniform size for even cooking in the microwave.

■ Foods that are normally cooked covered should also be covered in the microwave.

■ When cooking a variety of ingredients in a dish, remember to stir thoroughly every few minutes in the microwave.

■ Dishes that cannot be stirred, such as flans, roasts or meat loaves, should be turned every few minutes for even cooking.

■ When cooking separate food items, remember to follow the rules for arrangement (see pp. 198-9) and to rearrange them during the cooking time.

■ As a general guide, reduce the amount of liquid required in a conventional recipe by a quarter or a third. More liquid can always be added during the cooking period if needed.

■ For steamed vegetables, put them in a bowl with 30-45ml (2-3 tbsp) water and they will steam themselves.

■ Cut the cooking time by at least a half, although there is no standard rule on this. Follow the timings used in a comparable existing microwave recipe rather than guessing them.

■ Always underestimate the cooking time and test frequently for readiness. Take particular care when cooking foods like eggs, milk and custards, and foods with a high fat or sugar content, as they cook so quickly.

■ Remember that foods will continue to cook after being removed from the microwave and take this into account. The denser the food, the longer the standing time required.

■ Casseroles and bakes cook very quickly in the microwave but often improve in flavour by being cooked some time in advance and then being reheated so that the flavours really have time to develop and blend together.

■ You may prefer to add more herbs and spices to some dishes than you would when cooking them conventionally as the quick cooking times do not allow their flavours to permeate through a dish in the same way. Test for taste and adjust seasonings to suit your palate.

■ Do not add salt at the beginning of the cooking time as it has a dehydrating effect. Add to taste before serving.

■ Cake and pudding mixtures should be slightly wetter than in conventional recipes. Because they rise so much in the microwave, only half fill containers with the raw mixture. Allow them to finish cooking through by standing for 5 to 10 minutes.

■ Pastry cases must be baked blind before being filled. Cover with absorbent paper and a plate to keep fairly crisp. Allow for shrinkage.

■ Pulses should be presoaked in the normal way.

■ Cook pulses, grains and pasta in the microwave in the usual amount of boiling water. Use slightly larger containers than usual to allow for swelling and prevent the fast-boiling water spilling over.

■ Red kidney beans should be boiled rapidly for the first 10 minutes. Do this conventionally on the hob.

WHICH FOODS WILL WORK IN THE MICROWAVE

A wide range of foods cook extremely well in the microwave, but you must accept that this is a different method of cooking requiring a new approach and yielding cooked foods that may look and taste slightly different to those you are used to.

■ Whole fruits and vegetables cook very successfully in the microwave. The flavours tend to be fresher and the texture slightly different; for example, baked potatoes do not become crisp. Remember when baking whole fruit and vegetables that the skin must be pierced beforehand or steam will build up and cause them to burst during cooking.

■ Ready-prepared sweet and savoury dishes cook well by microwave energy, but the finish may seem pale. These can often be browned under a conventional grill if you prefer a golden look.

■ Nut roasts and grain savouries cook well, provided the raw mixture is well flavoured and quite moist.

■ Casseroles and pulse dishes benefit from being made in advance and then reheated so that their flavours have time to develop.

■ Most cake and bread mixtures bake successfully by microwave, though the raw mixture should be slightly wetter than in conventional recipes. Allow for considerable rising, and see p. 201 for tips on improving their appearance.

■ Fish cooks extremely well and the flesh becomes beautifully moist and flaky. Poached and steamed fish work best, and recipes where the fish is traditionally baked or grilled are also good – the skin of whole fish can be quickly crisped and browned under a hot, conventional grill after microwaving if you wish.

■ Small shellfish such as mussels and clams are very tasty cooked in the microwave, although care must be taken not to overcook them as they have a very short cooking time and can quickly become rather tough and rubbery in texture.

■ All types of poultry microwave very successfully. However, the short cooking times mean that the skin doesn't have time to brown. You can get round this by cooking them in a roasting bag, which helps to promote browning, or you can brush the skin with a browning agent before cooking.

■ Small meaty foods that are usually grilled or fried such as sausages, bacon and chops cook very well in the microwave. They can be done either on a microwave roasting rack, or in a browning dish which helps to brown and seal the food.

■ Meatballs and hamburgers cook very evenly and the smaller sizes can be put in the microwave straight from the freezer, if necessary.

■ Good cuts of meat microwave very well, especially meats with evenly marbled fat. However, large areas of fat attract more microwave energy and as a result the meat cooks unevenly. For this reason, it's best to trim off excess fat from around chops or joints first. Tougher cuts of meat can be cooked in the microwave too, although they need to spend almost as long as in a conventional oven to make them really tender and appetizing.

■ Sauces and custards are cooked in the microwave with amazing ease – there's no direct bottom heat to make them catch or stick so there's no need for continuous stirring. As long as the sauce or custard is stirred two or three times during cooking it will always be smooth and lump-free.

■ Pastry cases work well when cooked blind and covered with absorbent paper and a plate. Do not make their fillings too moist, and never fill a raw pastry case or the pastry will become soggy and unappetizing.

▨ Steamed puddings cook very quickly in the microwave and have a good texture.

▨ Pasta, grains and pulses will cook in the microwave, but be sure to cook them in already boiling water, and do not attempt to do too much at one time. If you want to cook more than 225g (8 oz), it's better to boil conventionally.

▨ Arrowroot, agar agar and stock cubes can all be dissolved in minutes.

▨ Milk can be infused in minutes.

FOODS THAT CANNOT BE COOKED IN THE MICROWAVE OVEN

Some recipes and cooking techniques will not work in a microwave oven and should not be attempted.

● Eggs cannot be hard-boiled. The pressure of steam inside the egg shell would cause it to explode.

● Batters and pancakes cannot be microwaved successfully as they will not become crisp and dry.

● Deep-frying should not be attempted as it is virtually impossible to control the temperature of the oil.

● Double-crust pies rarely work successfully as the fillings tend to cook much faster than the pastry.

● Very large turkeys cook very unevenly so are best cooked conventionally.

● Large shellfish with hard shells like crab and lobster should not be microwaved as they could explode if steam built up inside.

● Smoked bacon joints become very dry because of their high salt content and should not be cooked in the microwave.

Cooking for one

Microwave cookery is a marvellous way to cook for one. It makes it easy to prepare quick, healthy snacks and meals so you can avoid resorting to convenience foods, biscuits and cakes when you want to eat in a hurry. Vegetable dishes can be made in minutes from whatever ingredients you have on hand. Cook them in a little stock or sauce to make a simple casserole, or steam them and enjoy their full, fresh flavours. Garnish the dish by adding a few chopped fresh herbs, toasted nuts or grated cheese for extra nourishment and flavour.

Fish and shellfish are ideal for single portions, especially as they cook so quickly. Chops, steaks and poultry portions are all also microwaved very fast. After taking them out cover them with foil and leave to stand for a few minutes while you cook a few fresh or frozen vegetables. Or to make a more substantial meal, bake a potato while you are preparing the meat or fish, or if you have any leftover cooked grains, pasta or pulses in the refrigerator, they can be reheated in minutes and will taste as if freshly cooked.

Most dishes can be cooked in the dish or container you want to serve them in, which means that you save on messy washing up. The microwave also allows you to cook small portions without any worry of them burning as they often do on the hob. Nor do you have the cost of heating up a conventional oven just to cook one portion of food. You can cook small quantities of any of the recipes in this book. Remember to reduce the cooking time accordingly: for half the quantity, cook for approximately two-thirds of the original time; for a quarter of the quantity, cook for aproximately one-third of the original time.

If you have a freezer too, cooking for one with a microwave becomes even more economical. You can take advantage of seasonal gluts and bargains, and blanch vegetables in the microwave (see pp. 210-11). They can then be stored in the freezer until you are ready to use them. You can bake extra portions or even several dishes at a time when you are in a cooking mood, and then freeze them for future use. Read in particular the notes on blanching, freezing and defrosting on pp. 204-11.

◆

Menu-planning

When you want to combine several dishes into a meal, you'll need to plan the order in which you cook them because the timing factor is so important and varies from food to food. Take your time at the planning stage and read through the recipes carefully, taking note if some dishes are marked as being better cooked in advance and served after being reheated.

Many food items can be reheated as required. One of the major benefits of the microwave is that most dishes that are reheated remain moist and taste freshly cooked. However, vegetables are less flexible because they cook so quickly and although reheating is possible, they can easily become overcooked.

The fact that denser foods require standing times means that you can microwave any accompanying vegetables after the main dish has been removed from the oven. On the other hand, the more dense vegetables like baked potatoes, corn-on-the-cob and stuffed vegetables will retain their heat for about 20 minutes once cooked if you wrap them in some foil immediately after removing them from the microwave.

Recipes containing egg or cheese do not usually reheat well; they cook so quickly it is very easy to overcook them, so dishes that include these as ingredients are usually better cooked just before serving. Dishes that have cheese as a garnish can always be cooked in advance without the cheese, and then the cheese can be added for reheating.

Grains, pulses and pasta all reheat well by microwave. You may even prefer to cook them conventionally and just use the microwave to reheat them before serving.

Cook foods in the dishes you plan to serve them in whenever possible as this helps to retain their heat. Single portions can be served onto a plate for any latecomers and then simply covered and reheated in the microwave when required.

◆

Microwave troubleshooting guide

Some common questions and problems answered and explained

Q I notice that dish size is always specified in microwave recipes. Is the size more important than in conventional recipes?

A Dish size can make all the difference to a microwave recipe. If the dish is too large the food will spread out and may overcook at the edges before the centre is done. On the other hand, if it is too small or narrow, the food may bubble over the top or be squeezed into a dense mass that may not cook through to the centre. Always use the dish size recommended.

Q I thought that dishes stayed cool in the microwave, yet I find that I frequently need to use oven gloves when taking cooked items out of the oven. Does this mean that I am using the wrong kind of dishes?

A Dishes frequently do become hot from the food conducting heat to them. As long as the food in the dishes is cooking in the times specified in the recipes, it simply means that the hot food is heating the dish. If food is taking much longer than the recipes state, then test the dish to make sure it is suitable, following the instructions on p. 191.

Q I have heard that it is a good idea to keep a cup of water in the microwave oven when it is not in use. Why is this?

A This is a good safety precaution in case the oven is accidentally switched on, and it is a particularly good idea when there are children in the house. If the oven is switched on and there is nothing to absorb the microwaves they will bounce off the walls and floor and may damage the oven. A cup of water will absorb the microwaves, preventing them from causing any damage.

Q Is cooking in the microwave a cheaper method than using a conventional oven?

A Microwave ovens are much more economical than conventional ones. They cook very quickly, there is no need for preheating and part of the cooking process takes place after microwaving during standing time – using no power at all!

Q How do you convert the cooking times in recipes that do not give alternative timings for machines with other wattages?

A As a general guide, if recipes have been tested on a 600 watt machine on Full power, then reduce the cooking time by 10 seconds per minute if you have a 700 watt machine. If you have a 500 watt machine, increase the times by 15 seconds per minute, checking frequently to make sure the food does not overcook.

Q If you can sear and brown foods in a special browning dish, why can't you fry foods in them?

A It is impossible to control the temperature of oil in a microwave and this could be dangerous, particularly if deep-frying when a large quantity of oil is used. The only frying that should be done in the microwave is "stir-fry style" using a very small amount of oil. This method produces beautifully crunchy, tender vegetables.

Q Is microwaving a healthier way of cooking vegetables?

A It is the perfect way to cook vegetables as it keeps vitamin loss to a minimum. Water-soluble vitamins, such as vitamin C, are easily lost in cooking water, but because so little water is needed for microwave cooking this loss is kept to a minimum. It can be reduced still further by using the cooking water for stock or soup.

The very fast cooking times also mean that vegetables keep their bright colours and natural crunchy textures. Try to prepare vegetables just before you want to cook them, and serve them as soon as possible after cooking; if they are kept warm for a long time more vitamins will be lost.

Foods can also be cooked with less fat and, because vegetables retain more flavour, very little salt is needed – and fats and salt are two of the things that nutritionists are urging us to cut down on for good health.

Q If the microwaves can pass straight through glass, what stops them coming through the glass door of the oven?

A The glass panel on a microwave door is covered with a very fine metal mesh screen that is specially designed to prevent the microwaves passing through it, but still allows you to see into the oven during the cooking process.

Q How safe are microwave ovens?

A All microwave ovens are designed with a safety mechanism that ensures the oven cannot operate unless the door is shut and the Start button has been operated. Opening the oven door immediately stops the generation of microwaves which cannot re-start until the door is shut and the Start control operated again.

When buying a microwave oven, check that the model you wish to purchase is approved by a national electrical safety agency. This means that it has been subjected to stringent tests for safety and microwave leakage, including opening and closing the door 100,000 times – which represents many years of normal wear.

Microwave cooking is also safer as the sides of the oven do not become hot like a conventional oven, though the floor of the cooker may become warm by conduction.

Q If my microwave has a Defrost button, do I still need to leave foods to stand during defrosting?

A It depends on the food. For many items the Defrost power level is low enough to ensure gentle defrosting without switching off the machine during the defrosting time, but with a dense quantity of food, such as a cooked moussaka or lasagne, it is better to allow some standing time during defrosting. This enables the centre to defrost without the edges overheating.

Q Why is salt added before cooking in some recipes, while others recommend adding it afterwards?

A Vegetables are usually cooked in very tiny amounts of water, and if salt is sprinkled on the vegetables it will cause dehydration of the surface of the vegetables. If food is cooked in a larger quantity of water and the salt can be completely dissolved, then it can be added before cooking in the microwave. The texture of pork rind, for example, is improved if it is rubbed with salt before cooking, but you should avoid salting the surface of other meats or fish. You can, however, season inside meat or fish before cooking if you like.

Q Why is it possible to use aluminium foil to shield food inside the oven when you cannot use metal dishes for cooking?

A Foil is used in very small quantities for shielding. The amount of food unshielded must be greater than the amount covered with foil, so that there is plenty of food to absorb all the microwave energy. This is not the case when metal dishes are used as the microwave energy does not even reach the food.

Q **What should you do if you suddenly realize you've put a metal trimmed dish in the microwave and it starts sparking?**

A Switch off the microwave immediately and the sparking will stop. As long as you turn off immediately, you are unlikely to do any harm to the oven, but if sparking is allowed to continue the walls of the cooker may become pitted, and this will distort the microwave pattern. In extreme cases, sparking may even damage the magnetron. If in doubt, have your microwave checked by a qualified engineer – never try and repair or dismantle your microwave yourself.

Q **Why do some sauces and hot drinks bubble over the rim of the container once they have been stirred?**

A When you microwave liquids in a confined space, particularly those with a high milk content, the temperature gets much higher below the surface than on the surface. When you stir it, the gases produced by the heating process escape and spill over the edge. To overcome this problem, never allow liquid to fill a container more than three-quarters and stir at least halfway through the cooking time.

Q **Why was my cake hard and dried by the time it had cooled?**

A This is the result of overcooking. The cake should still look moist when removed from the microwave as it will cook through during the standing time. Always aim to undercook rather than overcook in the microwave and remember not to expect items to look cooked until after their standing times. A cake is ready to come out of the oven when the sides come away from the edge and a wooden cocktail stick inserted in the centre comes out clean.

Q **What does it mean when recipes talk about heat equalizing?**

A Microwaves only penetrate food to a depth of about 5cm (2 in), and this area becomes very hot while the centre of the food is still quite cool. During standing time, heat is conducted through to the centre of the food and the two areas become equally hot.

Q **Why do some cakes rise well in the microwave and then sink after being removed?**

A This is due to overbeating when mixing the cake. Too much air is trapped in the mixture causing it to rise well in the oven, but then the cake sinks as air is released during cooling.

Q **Why do I have to extend the cooking time when I am cooking a larger quantity of food than that specified in a recipe?**

A When microwaves enter the food they have to spread themselves through the total quantity for the food to cook. On the whole, microwave ovens should only be used to cook moderate quantities – up to four to six portions at a time.

Q **Is there any way of rescuing overcooked foods?**

A Because food cooks so quickly in the microwave, it's always better to undercook and then return food to the oven for another minute or so if necessary. Once overcooked, there is no way of restoring texture and flavour to vegetables. They can, however, be liquidized to make soups or sauces. Overcooked fruits can also be liquidized, then sieved if necessary, to make purées or sauces. Overcooked sponge cakes can be used for trifles, and plain biscuits for making biscuit-crumb bases for sweet flans and cheesecakes.

Overcooked fish dries out, but can be

rescued by flaking it into a flavoursome sauce. Overcooked shellfish are more of a problem because they become tough and inedible. However, if you catch them quickly enough – before they are too overdone – stop them cooking immediately by plunging them into cold water.

Q | **Can I heat up plates in the microwave?**

A | Yes, so long as they are microwave proof and don't contain any metal. Stack up to six plates, putting a little water between each one and sprinkling some water on the top one. ⊠ FULL for up to 1 minute. Remember to wear oven gloves when removing them and dry off any excess water before serving the food.

Q | **If chicken and meats don't brown, how can I tell that they are ready?**

A | If you insert a knife into the thickest, fleshiest part of poultry, pork or another well-done meat the juices should run clear. They should still be slightly pink for rare and medium lamb and beef.

Q | **Duck always seems to take much longer to cook than the recommended time; what could I be doing wrong?**

A | During the cooking process duck releases a great deal of fat and juice, which collects in the roasting dish. This liquid absorbs some of the microwave energy, leaving less for the duck – so it cooks more slowly. You should always remember to pour off the juices several times during cooking.

Q | **Why is it necessary for joints of meat to stand for such a long time – surely the meat will be cold when it is carved?**

A | Because meat and poultry are so dense, they benefit from a long standing time. After microwaving, as long as the meat is wrapped in foil, the internal temperature actually continues to rise for about an hour. Initially the outside is much more cooked than the centre, but on standing the heat travels to the centre, cooking that too. At the same time, the juices are re-absorbed by the meat and the fibres 'settle' so the meat carves more easily and stays very moist.

Q | **My meat thermometer seems to be very inaccurate – the temperature sometimes goes down rather than up after more cooking. Why is this?**

A | The thermometer is probably working very well. It must be pushed into the fleshiest and thickest part of the joint each time you check or you will always get different readings. The thickest part is likely to be last to cook so gives the lowest reading. If the thermometer tip presses against bone instead of flesh or if it is pushed in too far (or not far enough) the reading will be much higher.

Choosing a microwave oven

When it comes to buying a microwave oven, there appears to be a bewildering range to choose from. They can be portable or built-in; they have different capacities, wattages and systems of power control; they may offer a choice of additional features as shown on page 178; or even combine microwave power with conventional cooking facilities. Your choice will depend upon such factors as size, price, availability and how you plan to use the microwave power. Consider your present and your future needs: how many people will be using the oven; what other cooking facilities you have, etc. After examining different models for their facilities, do check that your final choice complies with national safety standards and that it also has good servicing arrangements.

TYPES OF MICROWAVE OVEN

There are four basic categories of microwave oven, which are described and illustrated below.

Portable ovens
These come in various sizes and wattages. The larger the oven, the higher the output has to be. Installation is straightforward. They simply require a firm work surface, table or trolley to stand on and a nearby electrical socket. Some models can be built into your kitchen units so long as you ensure that there is sufficient space between the machine's air vent and any neighbouring surfaces so that air can circulate freely and steam can escape. If the vents are at the back of the machine, don't push or fit it

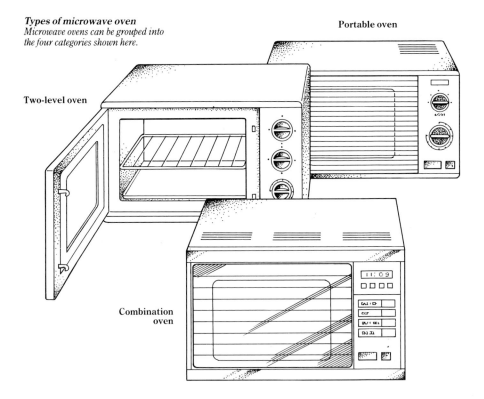

Types of microwave oven
Microwave ovens can be grouped into the four categories shown here.

Portable oven

Two-level oven

Combination oven

against a wall; if they're on top, don't put the machine directly under a shelf or cupboard.

Two-level microwave ovens

Some microwave ovens are fitted with a shelf which allows cooking on two levels. In this type of oven, the microwave energy usually enters the oven cavity through the sides rather than the top. About 60 percent of the energy is fed to the upper section of the oven and 40 percent to the bottom part. Foods which require more microwave energy for thorough cooking can be placed on the shelf, while those needing slower, gentler cooking can be put on the floor of the oven. This type of microwave gives greater flexibility, especially if you want to cook a whole meal at one time or if you regularly cook for a number of people, but it does need a certain amount of planning and calculation. Also, with more food in the oven, cooking times will be longer than in other types of microwave oven. Shelves

cannot be added to other models, they can only be used in microwave ovens that have been designed to take them.

Double-oven units

Double units consist of a conventional oven and a microwave oven. The cooking operations are quite separate, but the two are situated conveniently close together. Food can be microwaved for speed, then browned in the conventional oven or under the grill. You can, however, use a portable model with an existing conventional oven in much the same way.

Combination ovens

Combination ovens provide microwave and conventional cooking facilities in the same oven cavity. They are particularly good for roasting and baking, as you can combine fast cooking in the microwave with conventional browning. A whole meal can be produced in a very short time, but with all the look of traditionally baked food. The microwave and conventional cooking facilities may be used simultaneously or in sequence, depending upon the model. You can also use them separately. The microwave oven's maximum output, however, is usually lower than in portable or double-oven models.

ADDITIONAL FEATURES ASSESSED AND EXPLAINED

Most microwave ovens, whatever category they come under, also incorporate some or all of the following features. Consider these carefully when making your choice and select those that will suit your needs: for example, if you frequently use frozen foods, a separate Defrost button is an advantage. You should also consider the design of the controls and make sure you understand how to operate them. Some of the more technologically advanced systems may seem rather daunting.

Timing control

In microwave cookery, control is by time rather than by temperature and most microwave ovens incorporate some means of time control. This may be set by a touch pad, push buttons or a dial. Some controls

Double oven

Microwave oven

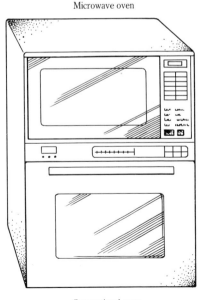

Conventional oven

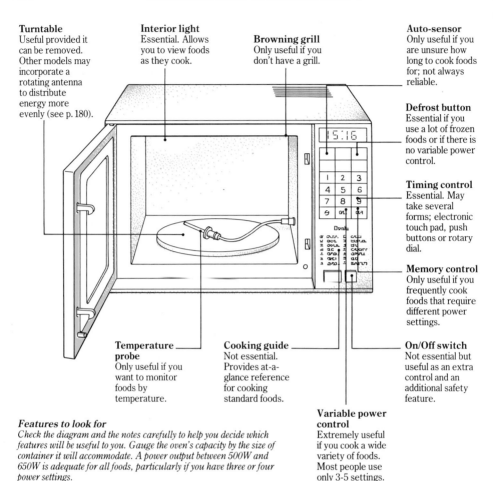

Turntable
Useful provided it can be removed. Other models may incorporate a rotating antenna to distribute energy more evenly (see p. 180).

Interior light
Essential. Allows you to view foods as they cook.

Browning grill
Only useful if you don't have a grill.

Auto-sensor
Only useful if you are unsure how long to cook foods for; not always reliable.

Defrost button
Essential if you use a lot of frozen foods or if there is no variable power control.

Timing control
Essential. May take several forms; electronic touch pad, push buttons or rotary dial.

Memory control
Only useful if you frequently cook foods that require different power settings.

Temperature probe
Only useful if you want to monitor foods by temperature.

Cooking guide
Not essential. Provides at-a-glance reference for cooking standard foods.

On/Off switch
Not essential but useful as an extra control and an additional safety feature.

Variable power control
Extremely useful if you cook a wide variety of foods. Most people use only 3-5 settings.

Features to look for
Check the diagram and the notes carefully to help you decide which features will be useful to you. Gauge the oven's capacity by the size of container it will accommodate. A power output between 500W and 650W is adequate for all foods, particularly if you have three or four power settings.

can be set very accurately to as little as one second, others are programmed in minutes. Once the cooking time is set, the timer works back to 0 and a bell, buzzer or pinger will alert you when the cooking time is completed. The timer will also turn off the microwave energy automatically at the end of the cooking period. If you find you frequently require cooking timings in seconds and your oven cannot set them, invest in a mechanical cooking timer that registers seconds.

Interior light
This lights up the cooking chamber once the machine is turned on and enables you

to keep an eye on foods as they cook. It normally goes off automatically when the cooking time is completed and the oven has turned itself off.

Defrost button
Most microwave ovens have a separate Defrost facility. This lowers the microwave energy emitted either by pulsing it on and off in a regular pattern, or by reducing the overall wattage. Less energy is necessary to ensure that frozen foods are completely thawed rather than just thawed on the surface, and to prevent them from starting to cook at the edges before the centre has thawed. On models that do not offer variable

power control, the Defrost setting can also be used to cook and reheat foods at a more gentle speed.

On/Off switch

Some models require a power On button to be operated separately once the cooking and timing controls have been selected, the food placed in the cavity and the oven door closed. This often turns on the interior light and a cooling fan, which prevents the electrical components becoming overheated and helps to disperse steam. The Off switch turns the power off during cooking if desired. It is really supplementary to the Door Release button, which cuts off all circuits before the door can be opened, but it acts as an additional safety control.

Memory control

A few models have a memory control panel which can store instructions for cooking at a particular power level for a specified amount of time. Other models incorporate memory

VARIABLE POWER CONTROL

Many microwave ovens offer a choice of anything up to ten different power settings. These provide you with far greater control of cooking and allow you to cook foods at a slower rate when this is necessary. However, power levels in different models have not been standardized and settings may be indicated in numerals, percentages, wattages or by various cooking descriptions. On most models, you can reduce or increase the cooking power by adjusting the control at any time during the cooking programme.

10 100% Full **600W**		**1** 10% Low **60W**
9 90% Sauté **550W**		**2** 20% Warm **120W**
8 80-85% Reheat **500W**		**3** 30-35% Defrost **200W**
7 70% Roast **450W**		**4** 40% Braise **250W**
6 60% Bake **400W**	**5** 50-55% Simmer **300W**	

Comparative power settings
The dial shows the different systems commonly used by manufacturers.
The most accurate guide is by wattage.

controls that allow you to select a series of cooking times at different power levels; the oven will start with one then move onto the next. These models also offer a delayed start so that you can leave foods to cook while you are doing other things. Check that such controls are not too complicated.

Auto-sensor
An auto-sensor microwave is controlled in a slightly different way from other microwave cookers. You indicate on the control panel the type of food that is going to be cooked. The machine calculates the required cooking time by measuring air temperature and the amount of steam released during cooking, and switches itself off automatically when the food is done.

Cooking guide
The oven fascia may have a display guide showing the different power settings available and the types of cooking they are most often used for.

Temperature probe
Some ovens incorporate a temperature probe which has a flexible connection to a socket inside the cooking cavity. The probe is usually used for cooking meat, but can be used with other foods. The point of the probe is inserted into the food and is left in position throughout the cooking process. The degree of cooking is selected and when the required temperature is reached, the microwave either turns off automatically or reduces the power setting to the right level to keep the food warm.

Browning grill
Some models have a browning grill element fitted into the roof of the oven cavity. Although this is less powerful than a conventional grill, it can be used for browning foods before or after cooking. When using this facility, however, you should take care to use a suitable container.

Turntable
Many ovens incorporate a revolving turntable on the floor of the oven. This may be instead of or as well as a stirrer fan to aid the even distribution of microwaves through the cooking cavity. Turntables are usually made of toughened ceramic glass and can be removed for cleaning, or if you want to use a large or awkwardly-shaped container. You should never put a dish on the turntable if it is going to knock against the oven's walls as it rotates during cooking. Check in the manufacturer's instruction guide that the turntable is removable and that the oven operates effectively without it.

Rotating antenna
This is a slatted metal disc which may be concealed below the oven floor or above the ceiling. It rotates, driven by air from the cooling system, and helps to distribute the microwaves more evenly around the complete cooking cavity.

Removable floor
Some microwave ovens without a turntable have a ceramic glass tray on the floor of the oven. Usually this is sited just above the oven's base to allow microwaves to be reflected. This type of floor acts as a spillage tray and can be removed and thoroughly washed when necessary.

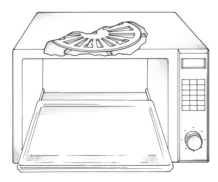

Rotating antenna and removable floor
Microwave ovens that don't have a turntable may incorporate a rotating antenna and a removable floor instead. The antenna is another device designed to aid the distribution of microwaves.

Understanding microwave ovens

The microwave oven is a revolutionary electrical appliance that can cook, defrost and reheat foods with incredible speed and efficiency. But despite its increased popularity, it is probably the least understood of all kitchen appliances. Its mechanics and facilities are explained in more detail on the following pages but, basically, instead of generating heat like a conventional oven, it generates microwaves. These agitate the molecules in foods at such an incredibly high speed that they create instantaneous heat and start the cooking process, as shown on page 182.

Microwaves themselves are high-frequency electromagnetic waves of energy present in the atmosphere, similar to those that convey radio, television and radar signals. They are invisible and non-accumulative, unlike X-rays, gamma rays and ultra-violet rays, which can build up and cause irreversible damage to cellular and chemical structures in our bodies. But because microwave ovens are so different from conventional ovens, they are often regarded with unnecessary wariness. In fact, cooking by microwave is far safer than traditional methods that involve direct heat.

The basic microwave oven
All microwave ovens consist of the same basic unit. This may incorporate some of the additional facilities described on page 178. When the machine is turned on, the microwaves are produced by the magnetron. They travel along the wave guide and enter the oven, as shown here. The stirrer fan distributes them evenly throughout the metal cooking cavity. The specially designed safety door prevents any microwave leakage while the oven is in operation. The air vent allows any steam to escape during cooking.

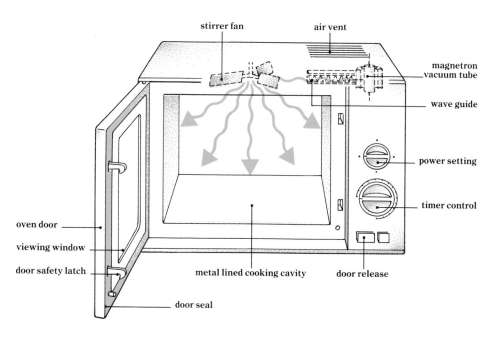

stirrer fan

air vent

magnetron vacuum tube

wave guide

power setting

timer control

oven door

viewing window

door safety latch

metal lined cooking cavity

door release

door seal

HOW MICROWAVE OVENS WORK

The mechanics of a microwave oven are really very simple. The machine is plugged into the regular domestic electricity supply but converts the electrical energy emitted to electromagnetic waves by passing it through a magnetron vacuum tube. The high frequency microwaves produced are directed into the oven cavity by a wave guide. The oven cavity is made of metal, a material which reflects microwaves without absorbing them. So once the door is closed and the machine is turned on, all the microwave energy produced is safely contained within the cooker. The microwaves bounce off and across the oven's metal walls in a regular pattern and are distributed evenly throughout the cavity by a stirrer fan.

The three diagrams below show how microwaves react to different materials in the cooking cavity. They can be reflected, transmitted or absorbed according to the composition of the items they come into contact with. Microwave cookery exploits these properties in order to cook food safely and efficiently, as explained opposite.

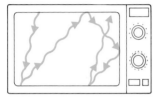

Reflection
Microwaves are reflected by metal; they cannot pass through it. Microwaves bounce off the metal surfaces (walls, ceiling and floor) of the oven cavity in a regular pattern.

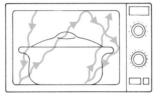

Transmission
Microwaves are transmitted by other materials, such as glass, ceramics, paper and some plastics. Microwaves can pass through these substances without heating them up.

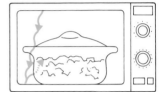

Absorption
Microwaves are absorbed by the moisture molecules in foods. The microwaves can only penetrate to about 5cm (2 in) but the food then heats through by conduction.

HOW MICROWAVES COOK FOOD

The unique properties of microwaves allow them to cook foods directly without heating up the cooking cavity. Microwaves are absorbed by the moisture molecules – water, fat and sugar – contained in foods. They make the molecules vibrate at an intense rate, millions of times per second, which causes friction and generates heat as shown below. The heat spreads rapidly through the food from the microwaves' initial point of penetration, which is all over the surface to a depth of about 5cm (2 in), with one layer heating up the next by conduction. Those microwaves that do not hit the food

How microwaves affect food molecules

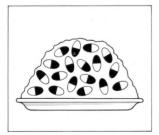

1 All foods are composed of thousands of molecules; in particular, water, fat and sugar molecules which all attract microwave energy.

2 A pulse of microwave energy is absorbed by a piece of food and has the effect of aligning all the molecules in one direction.

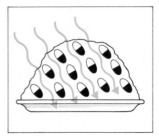

3 The next pulse of microwave energy reverses their direction. This happens millions of times per second, producing instant frictional heat.

initially continue being reflected to and from the oven's metal walls until they do penetrate the food.

Microwave energy is absorbed at different rates depending upon a food's density and composition. Foods which contain a lot of air, moisture, sugar or fat cook faster by microwave energy than foods that have a dense molecular structure, which takes longer to penetrate and heat through (see p. 194).

Microwaves pass through certain materials, such as glass, china, paper, and some plastics, without being reflected or absorbed by them. Items made from these materials make suitable utensils for microwave cookery as they do not use up any of the microwave energy produced, allowing it all to pass through to the food. Consequently, containers made from these materials remain comparatively cool, although they may heat up through conduction by being in contact with hot food.

Items made from or containing metals should never be used in microwave ovens. The fact that metals reflect microwaves means that they do not allow the energy to reach food but reflect it away. This can cause sparking in the oven cavity, disturb the carefully balanced electromagnetic field and the magnetron, and thus seriously damage the oven.

ARE MICROWAVE OVENS SAFE?

A microwave oven is one of the safest kitchen appliances you can have. Unlike a conventional cooker, it has no hot surfaces either inside or outside the machine; there are no naked flames and items are safely contained within the cooking cavity. The microwave oven's exterior casing is designed to be sturdy and stable so you cannot accidentally tip the oven over.

Tests, standards and maintenance

All microwave ovens undergo stringent tests at the manufacturers for both electrical safety and microwave leakage (the most common anxiety). These include opening and closing the door 100,000 times to simulate many years of usage. Tests are carried out after every 10,000 such operations to check that there is no deterioration in the machine's safety level.

Those models designed for domestic use that comply with national electrical safety standards will also have been independently tested and approved by the relevant government agency. All such microwave ovens have many special safety features. They have a series of door locks and switches that make it impossible to operate the oven unless the door is properly shut. Special tests are carried out on each of these locking devices. In particular, to check that if one interlock fails, the magnetron will immediately stop producing microwaves. Microwave oven doors are constructed to precise specifications to ensure that once they are shut, the cooking cavity is completely sealed against energy leakage, and when opened, the machine's generation of microwaves immediately ceases.

Provided you comply with the manufacturer's recommendations for installation, usage and maintenance (see pp. 184-5), your microwave should remain safe to use for many years. If your microwave oven becomes damaged in any way, do not use it until it has been repaired and checked by one of the manufacturer's qualified service technicians. Never attempt to repair it yourself.

Cleaning and maintaining your microwave oven

When you first buy a new microwave oven, inspect it for damage and check that all the components you expect are there. Pay particular attention to the oven door, seal and hinges, and to the oven interior, which should not be dented or scratched in any way. Do not attempt to repair any damage yourself. Always contact the manufacturer or dealer if you have any worries or problems. Follow the manufacturer's recommendations for installation, then read the instructions.

Cleaning a microwave oven

Clean the exterior occasionally by wiping with a damp cloth. Take care not to splash water onto or into the vents. The interior walls do not heat up so any splashing or spilling of foods that occurs during cooking does not get baked onto the surface and can be quickly wiped off. It is important to keep the oven cavity clean as any foods that do get spilled inside will absorb microwave energy and start to slow down the normal cooking process.

How to clean your microwave

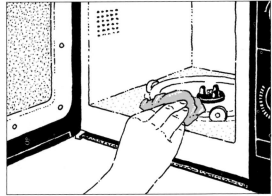

The cooking cavity
Clean the cooking cavity frequently with a cloth soaked in warm, soapy water. Take out and clean any removable parts.

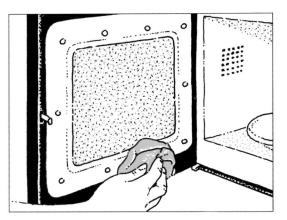

The door seals
Keep the door seals spotlessly clean. Use a mild detergent, rinse and wipe dry. Never use abrasive materials.

How to clean your microwave

Removing stains
*Stubborn stains
should be loosened by
bringing a bowl of water
to the boil in
the oven. Then clean
in the normal way.*

Follow these cleaning guidelines:

■ First, make sure the electrical supply to the machine is turned off.

■ Use a damp cloth to wipe over all the interior surfaces and the door after each use. Do not use cleansing agents unless the manufacturer recommends any.

■ Take out and clean any removable parts such as turntable, ceramic tray, shelves, at regular intervals.

■ If a stain proves difficult to remove, heat a bowl of water in the oven to boiling point. The steam produced should loosen the food particles. Wipe off with a damp cloth. Use a cloth soaked in warm, soapy water to wipe off greasy stains. Then wipe the area with a rinsed cloth.

■ Pay particular attention to the oven door seal area. This should be kept spotlessly clean by wiping with a cloth soaked in warm, soapy water, then with a rinsed cloth and finally with a dry cloth.

■ To remove lingering smells from the oven, place a bowl containing three parts water to one part lemon juice in the oven cavity and heat on 🕱 FULL for about 5 minutes. Wipe thoroughly and dry the oven surfaces afterwards.

■ Never use a knife, scouring pad or any type of abrasive cleaner in the microwave as these will scratch the surfaces and thus damage the oven by distorting the set wave patterns of the microwaves.

IMPORTANT POINTS TO REMEMBER

● Never turn the oven on when it is empty. Always put a mug of water in the oven cavity when it is empty if there is any chance that the oven may be switched on inadvertently.

● Never use the oven cavity as a storage cupboard.

● Never use a microwave oven to dry or heat clothes, papers or any items other than food.

● Never put any undue strain upon the door; for example, by hanging towels from it.

● Never attempt to close the oven door when there is an object between it and the oven or the door seal may become damaged.

● If the door seals or latches look damaged, do not use the oven until a service engineer has checked and replaced them.

● Do not tamper with the machine in any way, either with its casing or with the controls.

● Only use qualified microwave technicians when the machine is in need of repair or servicing.

Microwave tools and equipment

O ne of the great advantages of a
microwave oven is the wide range of
utensils and containers you can use in it. In
many cases, foods can even be cooked in the
same dishes you wish to serve them in.
Although a growing range of specialist
microwave equipment is available in the
shops, on most occasions you should be able
to manage with equipment you already have
in your kitchen cupboards.

CHOOSING EQUIPMENT FOR THE MICROWAVE

When deciding which container to use, your
first consideration should always be whether
it will allow the microwaves to pass through
it onto the food. Suitable equipment is made
from glass and ceramic, natural substances
such as paper, straw and cotton, and certain
plastics. It should not contain any materials
that will reflect or absorb microwaves.
Metal dishes should never be used as metal
reflects microwaves and so prevents the
food from heating up. More importantly, the
introduction of metal into a microwave oven
will cause sparking (arcing) which can
damage the oven walls and cause pitting.
Pitting will alter the pattern of the
microwaves and so affect the oven's
performance. In some cases, severe
sparking may even damage the magnetron.
Select items from those shown here and on
the following pages.

Pottery and china
Containers made of sturdy china or pottery
are suitable for microwave cookery.
Ordinary china cups and plates can be used
as long as they do not have any metal
trimmings, such as a gold or silver pattern.
When using china crockery, check that there
isn't any gold lettering on the underside or
metal screws in the handles. Do not use fine
porcelain as this could be damaged in the
microwave. Fully glazed earthenware and
stoneware can be used, but food in these

china cup

china plate

china mug

dishes may take slightly longer to cook as
these materials are often slightly absorbent.
Avoid using unglazed earthenware as this is
porous and will absorb microwaves,
becoming extremely hot and slowing up the
cooking process.

Ceramic baking beans
These grey beans look like small opaque
marbles and can be used in place of
traditional baking beans – which can't be
used because they absorb microwave
energy. Ceramic beans are excellent for
keeping pastry crisp and flat. Just spread a
layer on top of a sheet of absorbent paper
inside the raw pastry case and leave them
there for two-thirds of the cooking time,
then remove the beans and paper and cook
without them for the last third.

Glassware
Glass dishes are ideal for microwave
cookery. They transmit microwaves and

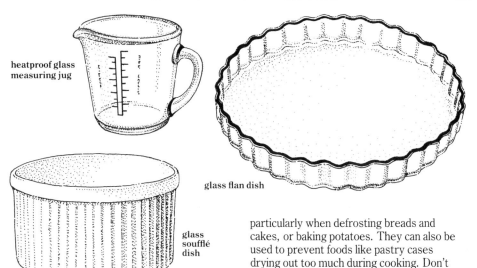

heatproof glass measuring jug

glass flan dish

glass soufflé dish

allow you to keep an eye on foods as they cook. When cooking foods with a high fat or sugar content, use heatproof glass as these foods can reach such high temperatures in the microwave oven. Heatproof glass measuring jugs, soufflé dishes, basins and flan cases are all particularly suitable. Never put delicate lead crystal in the microwave for obvious reasons.

Paper and cardboard
Absorbent kitchen paper and plain white paper napkins are very useful for soaking up excess moisture while microwaving foods,

particularly when defrosting breads and cakes, or baking potatoes. They can also be used to prevent foods like pastry cases drying out too much during cooking. Don't use patterned or coloured absorbent papers as the dyes can transfer to foods or the oven base during the heating process. Grease-proof paper is good for lining loaf and cake

greaseproof paper

absorbent kitchen paper

paper cake cases

(use double thickness in the microwave)

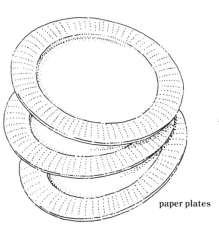

paper plates

dishes, and also for covering foods.
Cardboard containers can be used in the
microwave, although those with waxed
linings should only be used for defrosting as
the heat emitted by foods as they cook may
melt the wax.

Wood, straw and linen

Equipment made from wood or straw can be
used in the microwave oven for reheating
foods such as bread rolls, but should not be
used for long periods of cooking or they will
dry out and eventually split. Wooden spoons
may be left in the microwave for short
periods of time when making sauces,
although the handles start to get hot after
about 2 minutes. Pure linen cloths and
napkins may be used to line bread baskets or
to wrap foods for short periods. Check that
they do not contain synthetic fibres.

Plastics

Rigid plastic containers and utensils that are
labelled dishwasher-safe are usually
designed to withstand high temperatures
and can be used in the microwave too.
Articles made from polypropylene and
polysulfone are made in a range of shapes
and sizes and these are suitable for freezer-
to-microwave cookery. There is also a wide
choice of specialized microwave cookware
made from plastic, as shown overleaf.
Lightweight plastic containers, such as
yogurt or margarine tubs, can be used for
defrosting but are unsuitable for cooking
foods as they are likely to distort and may
melt when the food becomes hot. Plastic
microwave boiling bags and roasting bags
make good containers, although they should
always be pierced or fastened loosely so
steam can escape during cooking. Be sure to
secure the bags with plastic tags *not* metal
ones, or use rubber bands. Ordinary plastic
bags are not suitable for cooking.

Roasting bags are especially good for
cooking meat and poultry because they also
help to promote browning. You will still need
to raise the joint or bird out of the cooking
juices, so make sure you place the
microwave rack inside the bag and not
underneath it. If the bag is too small, slash it
along one side and make a tent over the top.
Tuck the ends underneath.

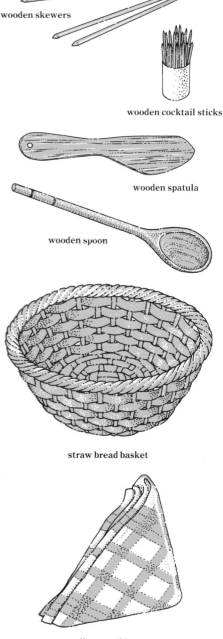

wooden skewers

wooden cocktail sticks

wooden spatula

wooden spoon

straw bread basket

linen napkin
(ensure cloth napkins contain no man-made fibres)

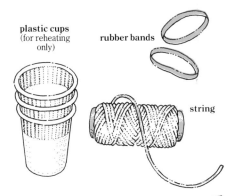

plastic cups (for reheating only)

rubber bands

string

roasting bags and boiling bags

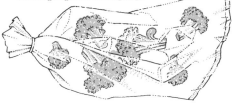

The use of **plastic cling film** in the microwave is a contentious subject at the moment. There has been increasing concern about this product and it is currently undergoing stringent tests and investigation. It has been noted that some of the plasticizer di-2-ethyhexyladipate (DEHA) used to soften plasticized polyvinyl chloride film (commonly known as cling film) can migrate into closely wrapped foods, and the level of migration is markedly higher as foods increase in temperature. As a result of these findings, many authorities now recommend that ordinary cling film should not be used in the microwave oven. Manufacturers are now producing a microwave-safe polythene film which does not contain these additives. Look for the label saying: 'suitable for the microwave' when buying cling film. Alternatively, another option is to make use

polythene cooking wrap

of boiling bags, paper, casserole lids and plates when you want to cover foods.

Microwave thermometers

These specially designed plastic thermometers are used to determine the internal temperature of meats so you can tell more accurately how the meat is cooking. They can be inserted into the meat about halfway through the cooking time. As the meat cooks, you can check the temperature from time to time, through the glass door. Conventional meat thermometers must not be left in the meat during microwaving, but can be used to check the temperature after the joint or bird is removed from the cooker.

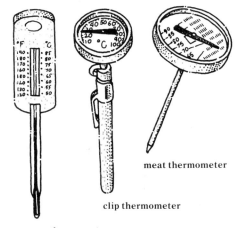

meat thermometer

clip thermometer

mercury thermometer

Specially designed microwave cookware

A large and varied range of microwave cookware made from glass, ceramic or thermoplastic materials is now available. It includes a wide selection of containers, such as cake, loaf and ramekin dishes, baking moulds, pudding basins, and stacking rings for reheating foods. Many of these cookware items are microwave and freezer safe, so foods can be cooked in the microwave, frozen, then defrosted and reheated all in the same dish.

The microwave cookware includes special browning dishes. These are the only dishes that can be put into the microwave when empty. They have a special coating on the base which absorbs microwave energy and

Special microwave cooking equipment
A wide range of containers made from thermoplastics and glass-ceramics have been designed specifically for microwave cookery.

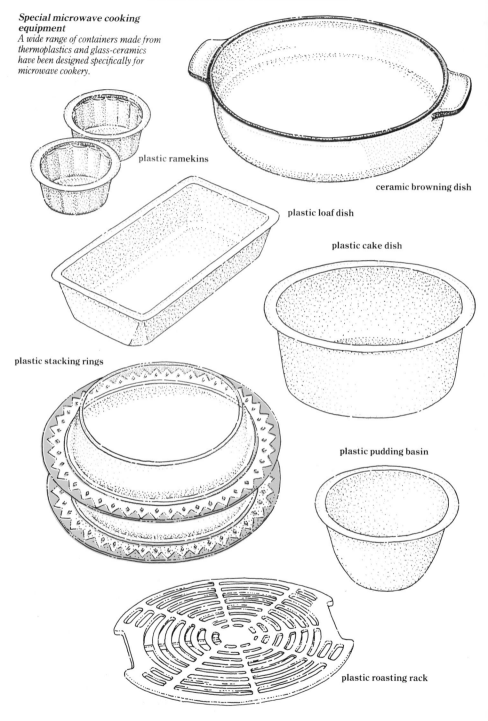

plastic ramekins

ceramic browning dish

plastic loaf dish

plastic cake dish

plastic stacking rings

plastic pudding basin

plastic roasting rack

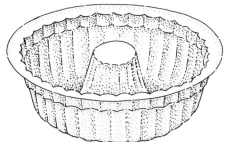

plastic savarin
ring mould

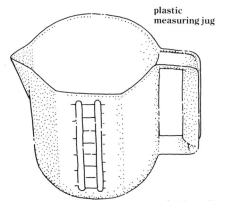

plastic
measuring jug

becomes very hot. Food can be browned on one side on the hot surface, then turned over and browned on the other. The side done first is usually the browner. Microwave cooking can then continue in the same dish. Once food is added to the dish, the microwaves are attracted to the food rather than the coating. Do not cover food in a hot browning dish with absorbent paper as it may scorch.

Microwave roasting racks made from a ceramic or rigid plastic material are also available. They are specially designed for cooking meats and poultry as they raise them out of their cooking juices. Some racks come with an integral roasting dish underneath, otherwise put a shallow dish under the rack to catch the cooking juices. Racks are also effective for baking cakes, breads, and meat and vegetable loaves, in fact anything that benefits from all-round microwave energy.

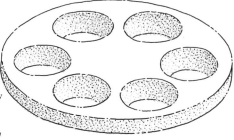

plastic muffin tray

microwave
cooking bags

plastic spatula

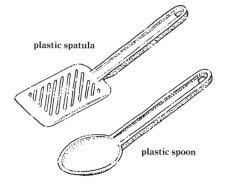

plastic spoon

HOW TO TEST WHETHER A CONTAINER SHOULD BE USED IN THE MICROWAVE

If you are not sure about using a dish in the microwave oven, you can carry out a simple test to check its suitability and efficiency. Place the dish in the microwave, then put a glass jug containing about 300ml (½ pint) water in the dish and ☒ FULL for 1-2 minutes. At the end of the cooking time, if the dish is cool and the water in the jug is hot, the dish is suitable. If the dish is hot and the water is still cool, the dish should not be used as it contains moisture which is attracting some of the microwave energy and preventing it reaching the food.

CONTAINER SHAPES

The speed that foods cook at will be affected by the type of container and its shape. China and pottery, for instance, are slower cookers than special microwave plastic dishes. Round dishes give better results than rectangular ones in which food tends to overcook in the corners, where it receives more microwave energy. Ring moulds are extremely effective in microwave cookery as they provide even heat distribution and allow microwave energy to reach foods on all sides and in the centre. You can easily improvise this shape by standing a plain glass tumbler in the centre of a round dish. Hold the glass in position while you surround it with food.

Choose deep bowls or dishes when cooking foods that require a large quantity of fast boiling water, for example, pasta, pulses or rice, otherwise the water may boil over. Allow space for foods to swell or rise during cooking. Pasta, pulses and grains all expand as they cook, and milk-based sauces swell as they heat up. When cooking these items, they should only take up half to two-thirds the volume of a container. For other foods, make sure that the dish is not too large or the food will spread out thinly and overcook at the edges before the centre has been cooked. A medium-sized shallow dish is suitable for many of the recipes in this book. Avoid using narrow-necked containers when heating liquids as the steam produced may not be able to escape fast enough and the container may explode due to the build-up of pressure. Do not use tall, narrow dishes for heating food either as it will be packed into too dense a mass to cook evenly.

WHAT NOT TO USE IN THE MICROWAVE

Never use the following equipment in a microwave oven:

● Metal dishes, such as baking trays, loaf tins and foil trays, or dishes with metal trims. Anything metal will reflect the microwaves and cause harmful sparking. Use only special microproof bakeware instead.

● Unglazed pottery and earthenware. These attract the microwave energy, becoming very hot, and will slow down the cooking of food.

● Melamine containers. These attract microwave energy and may melt or become charred.

● Dishes that have been repaired with glue or that have glued handles as the glue may absorb microwave energy and begin to melt.

● Tall, narrow-necked containers which may trap steam and cause it to build up dangerously.

● Wire fasteners on paper or plastic bags. The metal in the fastener becomes hot and could spark off a fire.

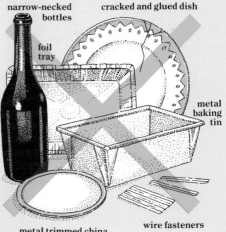

narrow-necked bottles

cracked and glued dish

foil tray

metal baking tin

metal trimmed china

wire fasteners

Factors that affect microwave cooking

Many factors affect the length of cooking time required by different foods in the microwave oven: the machine itself; the nature of the food and the quantity: the container used and the recipe method. All these factors have to be taken into consideration for a recipe to work successfully in your microwave oven.

The microwave oven itself

Microwave ovens have yet to have their power levels standardized, so one machine can vary from another in power output, even if both have the same wattage and are made by the same manufacturer. Machines offering variable power control also use different systems to describe their various power levels (see p. 179). Whenever you consult microwave recipes, check how the power levels recommended in them compare with those of your own oven and make necessary adjustments. The recipes in this book use three different power levels as shown on the chart on p. 50. Compare these levels to the wattages offered on your microwave oven and select the nearest appropriate setting. In the recipes and cooking instructions provided, the alternative times given in brackets for 700W and 500W machines are the lowest times recommended to avoid any possibility of overcooking. You can always extend the cooking time but you can't rescue overcooked foods.

Although most microwave ovens now have stirrer fans, turntables or rotating antennae to help distribute the microwave energy evenly, models may still have individual hot spots – areas in the oven where food will cook faster. To check if your oven has hot spots, put equal amounts of water in nine cups, mugs or other small containers, all made of the same material. Space them out over the base of the oven as shown below, then turn on to full power. Watch carefully to see which container comes to the boil first and note that this is

the hottest spot in the oven. Techniques like turning the dish, stirring or rearranging the food during cooking (see pp. 198-9) are designed to ensure that all food cooks evenly, despite the existence of any hot spots in the oven.

Testing for hot spots
By heating up nine identical cups with equal amounts of water, as described opposite, you can find out your oven's hot spots and then arrange foods accordingly.

Starting temperature of food

The higher the starting temperature of food, the faster it will heat up and cook in the microwave. Foods taken out of the refrigerator and put straight into the microwave will take longer to cook than foods that are allowed to come to room temperature first. You may even find that the same foods take slightly longer to cook on cold days than on hot ones. It is important always to follow the instructions for temperatures of ingredients in recipes, for example, when the addition of boiling stock

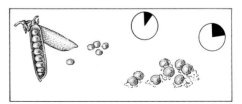

Food temperature
The colder a food is, the longer it will take to cook. Frozen peas need a minute or so more than fresh.

is recommended, do use boiling stock. Adding cold stock will slow down the cooking process and affect all the recommended cooking times in the recipe.

Composition of food

Different components in the food also affect the cooking time. Foods with a high fat and sugar content will reach higher temperatures and cook at a faster rate than other foods because fats and sugars absorb microwave energy more quickly. Consequently, items with a sweetened fruit filling will cook more quickly than similar-sized ones with a low-fat savoury filling. Note that particular care is needed when reheating and serving foods with jam-type fillings as the jam will heat up much faster and become scalding hot while the outside remains quite cool.

Foods that have a high liquid content, such as soups, take longer to cook than foods that cook by their own moisture content. Always add the minimum amount of water when cooking vegetables, whether fresh or frozen, as the more water you add, the slower the cooking time will be, and the more vitamins and minerals you will lose in the cooking water.

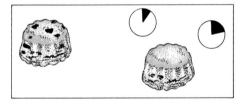

Food composition
A sweetened scone heats up slightly faster than a plain scone because of its higher sugar content.

Density of food

Density is the most important factor in determining the cooking time of food in the microwave. Dense foods take longer to cook than foods identical in size that have a loose, airy structure; for example, fibrous root vegetables take longer to cook than bread rolls. The dense nature of the food slows down heat conduction. When you are cooking a mixture of dense and light-structured foods, try to arrange the denser

foods around the edge of the dish where they will receive more microwave energy. Place light-structured foods in the centre so that they don't cook too quickly.

When you are microwaving a dense quantity of food, such as a lasagne or meat loaf, the centre is always the slowest part to cook through because the microwave energy only penetrates the surface to a depth of 5cm (2 in). If possible, use a round, shallow dish or a ring mould for such foods. Alternatively, place the dish on an upturned plate or a microwave roasting rack so that more microwave energy can reach the centre from underneath.

The density of the container used will also affect the cooking time: foods take longer to cook in heavy china than in a glass dish or special microwave plastic container.

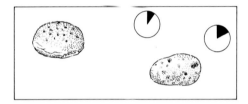

Food density
A light and airy bread roll needs less time to heat up than a potato, which is denser.

Size and shape of food

Always cut food into uniform shapes and sizes for even cooking in the microwave. Small or thin pieces cook faster than large, thick pieces. If cooking irregular shapes, such as broccoli, fish, or chicken portions place the thinner or less solid area towards the centre of the dish and the thick parts to the outer edge of the dish. The same principle applies to delicate foods, such as

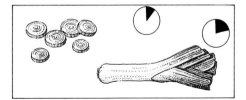

Food size
Vegetables sliced to a similar size cook faster and more evenly than whole vegetables.

Food shape
Thick areas of food take longer to cook than thin areas. Put thicker parts around the edge of the dish.

asparagus tips, which would overcook and spoil if exposed to too much microwave energy. With these foods, you may wish to shield the delicate areas from the microwaves for part of the total cooking time (see p. 199).

Quantity of food

In microwave cookery, the cooking time is dependent on the amount of food in the oven, unlike a conventional oven which will take the same length of time to cook eight potatoes as it does one. This is because the same amount of microwave energy has to be absorbed by fewer or more items.

Most of the recipes in this book are intended to serve four people, but you can reduce the amounts successfully for one or

two people by following certain guidelines given below. As a general rule, when reducing the quantity, use a smaller dish so that the food does not spread out any more than in the original recipe.

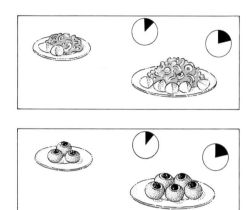

Food quantity
The larger the amount, the longer it will take to cook by microwave power.

Remember that when the amount of food is reduced the microwaving time will have to be reduced too, though not in direct proportion. If halving a recipe, cook for approximately two-thirds of the original time; if quartering it, cook for approximately one-third of the original time. Always test the food a minute or two before the estimated time is up, to avoid overcooking it. Cover, stir and rearrange the food exactly as directed in the original recipe.

Microwave cooking techniques

Most of the techniques employed in microwave cookery are similar to those used in conventional cookery. They are designed to promote even cooking, to speed up cooking processes, to accelerate or lessen evaporation and to improve the finish of the cooked item. For the best results, use them whenever a recipe recommends and they'll soon become second nature.

Covering

Covering foods in the microwave reduces the cooking time, helps to retain moisture and prevents spattering of the oven walls. As a general guide, food that is usually covered for conventional cooking is likely to be covered in the microwave too. Dishes such as vegetables and meat stews are best cooked covered, but items that are meant to have a dry finish, such as biscuits or bread, are better left uncovered. Casserole dishes with lids made of suitable (non-metallic) materials are ideal for microwave cookery. If your dish doesn't have a lid, put a plate or a saucer over it. Alternatively, use a microwave bag as a cover.

Some foods that are best cooked without a firm lid or cling film, such as chops, bacon or hamburgers, need to be covered instead with absorbent kitchen paper. The paper doesn't really affect the food, but it does prevent it spattering the inside of the cooker as it cooks. Make sure you remove the paper from bacon as soon as it is cooked as the paper has a tendency to stick.

Always take great care when removing a lid or cover at the end of the cooking time as you will release a cloud of scalding steam. Lift it away from you, using oven gloves, to avoid any burns to your face or arms.

Instead of cooking vegetables in a covered dish, you can place them in a boiling or roasting bag. Remember to pierce the bag in a few places first, or tie it loosely at the neck so that steam can escape. This is a particularly good method for cooking whole vegetables such as cauliflower.

Uncovering foods
Lift covers away from you to avoid scalding steam.

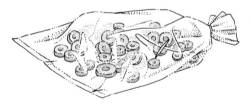

Boiling bags
These are excellent for cooking vegetables.

Greaseproof paper can also be used for covering foods during cooking, but make sure that it doesn't become loose and flap around, particularly if the oven has a strong fan. You can secure the paper with wooden cocktail sticks if necessary.

Whole fish and fish steaks can be wrapped in greaseproof paper before cooking. Lay the fish on a large round or square of paper, and tuck in a few sprigs of herbs and a lemon wedge. Fold the paper in half, then fold the edges over once or twice to seal completely. Place the parcel in a shallow dish to catch any juices. This is an excellent way to cook fish because the moisture and delicious flavours become trapped inside the parcel.

Pastry flan cases cook more successfully when covered with absorbent paper and a plate. This produces comparatively dry results without the pastry becoming unpleasantly hard.

Piercing

A considerable build-up of steam can occur during microwaving, so any food items with a tight-fitting skin or membrane, such as whole fruit, vegetables, fish, kidneys, chicken livers or raw egg yolk, must be pierced before being cooked in the microwave to prevent them exploding. Fruit and vegetables can be pierced with a fork or the tip of a sharp knife; egg yolks are best pierced with a cocktail stick. Rather than piercing whole fish, slash on both sides at the thickest part; this also helps them to cook more evenly.

As stated above, boiling bags and cooking wrap must either be pierced or secured loosely so some steam can escape.

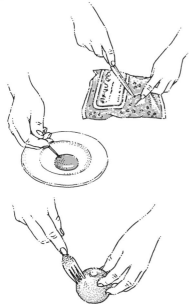

Piercing
Always pierce foods that have skins and membranes.

Wrapping

The microwave process brings out the moisture content of foods, drawing it to the surface. As a result, items that you want to cook with a dry surface, such as baked potatoes, benefit from being wrapped in absorbent paper while they cook. This soaks up most of the excess moisture produced and helps to spread the heat more evenly over the food. Always remove the paper once you've taken the food out of the oven or it may stick.

For a dinner party, line a basket with cotton or paper napkins before adding the rolls. They can be warmed in the basket, and the napkin will help keep the crusts from becoming soggy.

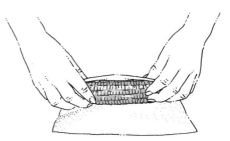

Wrapping
Wrap foods in absorbent paper to soak up excess moisture.

Lining dishes

Cake dishes should be lined with greaseproof paper as specified in the recipe. Remove the lining paper after the standing time has been completed to prevent it sticking to the cake. Do not grease cake dishes or coat them with flour as this results in an unpleasant film being left on the cake.

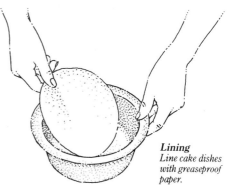

Lining
Line cake dishes with greaseproof paper.

Stirring

Stirring is one of the most important techniques in microwave cookery. As microwaves only penetrate food to a depth of about 5cm (2 in), the food at the edges of the dish may cook before food in the centre, especially if the food is dense in structure. To prevent food at the edges overcooking before the centre is ready, dishes should be stirred at frequent intervals or as directed in recipes. Stirring should be from the outside edges inwards, so that the heat is distributed equally to the centre. Stirring sauces in this way also prevents lumps forming, although continuous stirring is not necessary in microwave cookery.

If you are cooking something that requires stirring several times during cooking, one method is to divide the total amount of cooking time and set the timer at regular intervals so that you will be reminded to stir enough times.

Even if your microwave has a turntable, it is still a good idea to stir foods when advised to do so.

Stirring
Stir from the edges to the centre for even cooking as directed in recipes. Stirring is equally important when reheating and defrosting foods.

Turning or rotating

To ensure even cooking, foods that cannot be stirred, such as lasagne, moussaka, savoury loaves and cakes, need to be given a half or quarter turn at intervals throughout the cooking time as specified in the recipes. This is usually unnecessary if your oven features a turntable.

Turning
Turn cakes, pies, and whole dishes at regular intervals.

Arranging

In microwave cookery, food has to be arranged carefully to ensure even cooking. Always place denser, thicker items at the edge of the dish so they receive more microwave energy. When cooking several items of the same food, arrange them in a circle around the edge of a plate or in a round dish. Space them out evenly so that the microwave energy reaches all sides. Leave the centre of the dish empty as this area receives less microwave energy while the edges receive equal amounts. Make sure that the food is an even depth in the dish, and spread it out in a shallow dish rather than piling it up in a deep container. Denser items such as vegetable loaves and pâtés often benefit from being cooked in a ring mould so that microwaves can penetrate directly from the centre as well as from the edges.

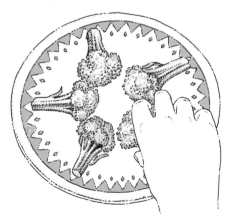

Arranging
Arrange foods in circles, not rows. Place denser areas at the edge and more delicate areas in the centre.

When reheating an individual meal on a plate, arrange the food so that it is evenly spread out with denser foods on the outside and more delicate items in the centre.

Any small items like cup cakes, biscuits, hamburgers, meatballs or individual dishes of food cook much more evenly when arranged in a circle. Remember to rotate individual items a half turn at least once during cooking.

Arrange unevenly shaped foods with the thicker parts to the outside. For instance, arrange chicken portions with thin bony parts to the centre, or lay fish fillets in a round dish like the spokes of a wheel, overlapping the thin tail ends in the centre where they will cook more slowly. When cooking only two fish at a time, arrange them head to tail and tuck the tails underneath the head of the other fish to protect them from getting burnt.

Turning over

Large solid items, such as baked potatoes, roasts, whole fish or chops or whole cauliflowers, should be turned over halfway through the cooking time unless otherwise specified in the recipe to promote even cooking. This allows all sides and surfaces to receive even exposure to the microwaves.

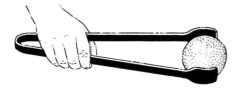

Turning over
Turn over large, whole items for even cooking.

Rearranging

To ensure that no food stays in a hot spot in the oven for the whole of the cooking time, you need to rearrange foods that cannot be stirred. Baked potatoes, hamburgers, sausages and shellfish can be moved around in the dish or on the base of the oven at the same time as turning them over. Move items from the edge to the centre, from the back to the front, etc, so that nothing remains in the same position throughout the cooking time.

Rearranging
Move foods from the edges to the centre.

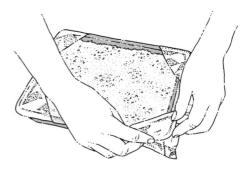

Shielding
Use strips of foil to prevent corners burning.

Shielding

Delicate or thin areas of food that are in danger of overcooking before the rest of the food is ready, can be shielded from the microwaves for part of the cooking time with small, smooth strips of aluminium foil. This is the only time that foil should be used in the microwave, but you should check your manufacturer's instructions before using it. The amount of food left uncovered must be much greater than the area shielded by foil.

You can add the foil at the beginning of the cooking time and remove it halfway through, or it can be added to areas once they are cooked.

Bony ends of large joints such as leg of lamb and the tails and heads of large fish should be covered for the first half of cooking time. Also, parts of large birds, such as the wing tips, which are cooking too quickly can be covered with small pieces of foil as necessary. However, if you make sure that poultry is trussed into a neat shape before microwaving, wing tips and drumstick ends shouldn't overcook. But the top of the breast may still need to be shielded before the end of the cooking time.

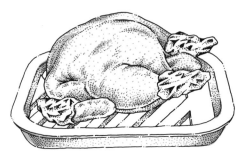

Shielding
Use pieces of foil to prevent poultry wing tips and drumsticks burning.

Shielding can be useful when you are using a square or rectangular container, to prevent the corners from overcooking. Arrange the foil as illustrated.

The foil strips must always be secured firmly. Wooden cocktail sticks are good devices to use. Do not use plastic ones as they could melt from being in contact with the hot food. The foil must never be allowed to touch the sides of the oven cavity or it could cause sparking. If any piece of foil becomes loose, switch off the microwave power immediately and remove it.

Standing time

Standing time is an essential part of microwave cookery as food continues to cook by conduction of heat after it has been removed from the microwave or the microwave power has been turned off. Some foods, such as cakes, may still look uncooked when they come out of the microwave, but will firm up and dry out as they finish cooking through during the standing time. Removing food while it is still slightly undercooked or underthawed and allowing it to finish by standing prevents the edges becoming overcooked by being exposed to further microwave energy before the centre has cooked through.

Standing times vary considerably and depend upon the density and volume of different foods. Vegetables need very little standing time; cakes usually need between 5 and 10 minutes. As a rule, the denser the food, the longer the standing time required.

Joints of meat and whole birds need quite a long standing time – half an hour or more

for very large birds. This is because the time includes a resting time, just like conventional roasts. If you attempt to carve meat or poultry too soon, you will find that the flesh is difficult to slice and that the cooking juices start to run out of the meat. After a long standing time they are absorbed into the meat so it stays moist and juicy and is rather easier to carve.

Large fish need 5-10 minutes standing time, whereas small fish, fish steaks and small meat items may only need 3 minutes. Recipes will state when standing times are necessary so follow their recommendations and don't judge a food until after it has completed its standing time. When further cooking is required in the microwave, there is usually no need to repeat the specified standing time.

Tenting

Foods, such as roasts, whole birds and large fish, that require a long standing time to complete the cooking process, should be covered with a tent of foil to maintain their temperature. Smaller items of food such as baked potatoes, stuffed peppers and corn-on-the-cob, can be wrapped in foil, shiny side inwards so it reflects the heat, and they will stay hot for at least 20 minutes while

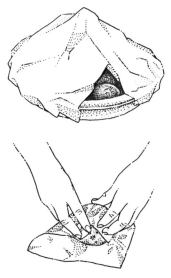

Tenting
Enveloping foods in foil helps to retain their heat once they have been removed from the oven.

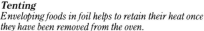

other dishes are prepared. The foil must obviously be removed if they are returned to the microwave oven.

Don't wrap meat or poultry too tightly in foil, because this makes them steam, changing the texture and taste of the flesh. They also tend to shrink less if they are just loosely covered.

Browning

Because foods cook so quickly by microwave energy, the surfaces are not exposed to heat changes in the normal way so they do not dry out and brown as they would in a conventional oven.

Most meats and poultry, especially small items like chops, hamburgers and chicken or duck portions don't brown in the microwave, so can look quite unpalatable. Cakes and breads may also look paler and unappetizing compared to traditionally baked products, even though their flavour is just as good.

Fortunately, you can improve the appearance of such foods in several ways:

■ Microwave browning dishes, which have a special coating that enables the base of the dish to become very hot, can be used for browning joints of meat and small meaty items such as steaks, chops, sausages, poultry portions, whole fish, and fish steaks and fillets. These dishes can even be used to shallow fry eggs and omelettes, and to brown microwave 'toasted' sandwiches.

■ Cook joints of meat and whole birds in roasting bags to help them brown.

■ Sprinkle poultry skin and meat fat with special microwave browning seasonings – or just use mild paprika pepper – to give a golden appearance.

■ Brush chops or poultry portions with a brown sauce such as Worcestershire or soy before cooking.

■ Sprinkle fish fillets or steaks with toasted breadcrumbs before cooking.

■ Brown and crisp whole fish, chops, sausages and poultry portions under a conventional, preheated grill after they have been microwaved.

■ Use wholewheat flour in cakes, pastry and bread. These are all items that remain

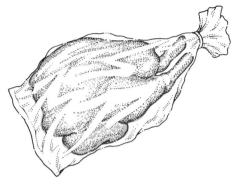

Browning
A roasting bag will brown meat and poultry while cooking in the microwave.

very pale when cooked in the microwave. Using wholewheat flour immediately gives them a better colour as well as more flavour and nutritional value.

■ Add dried fruit, such as apricots or dates, or chopped nuts and seeds, to breads and cakes for extra colour.

■ Decorate pale cakes with slices of fresh fruit or a colourful topping using natural fruit juice and not artificial food colouring.

■ Sprinkle loaves and scones with poppy seeds, toasted sesame seeds, cracked wheat or oatmeal before baking.

■ Sprinkle cakes or biscuits with chopped nuts, toasted desiccated coconut, ground cinnamon or poppy seeds.

■ Add carob powder, cocoa, or ground cinnamon to cake and biscuit mixtures with the flour to make them darker.

■ Put gratin-style dishes with a grated cheese topping under a preheated conventional grill to brown. Deduct this grilling time from the standing time.

Testing

When testing food to see if it is cooked, it is important to remember that it continues to cook for some time after it has been taken out of the microwave oven. If it is not cooked enough for your liking after completion of the recommended standing time, return it to the microwave oven for

REHEATING FOOD

Cooked food reheats extremely well by a low level of microwave energy. Flavour, colour and texture remain as if freshly cooked, and the fast reheating times ensure that fewer vitamins are lost than when food is reheated in a conventional oven. The techniques and procedures used for cooking foods in the microwave also apply when reheating them.

Meat casseroles, fish, poultry or vegetables in a sauce reheat better than foods on their own. Do not put them into too large a dish or the sauce will spread and dry out at the edges. Any foods in a sauce should be loosely covered during reheating. Dry foods with a crisper finish can be reheated covered in absorbent paper.

Soups are easy to reheat in individual portions, either in a mug or a bowl, and take only a few minutes depending on the thickness of the soup. Stir the soup when it starts bubbling up at the edge of the container, then cook for another minute or so to allow it to heat through to the centre.

Small containers such as mugs or jugs don't need a lid as reheating is so fast, but larger casseroles should be covered to keep in the moisture and speed up the process. Meat and vegetable casseroles reheat more quickly in a shallow dish as long as they are spread in an even layer.

Fish cooked by a moist method or covered in a sauce reheats very well on a low power. Make sure that the fish is covered with a lid before microwaving.

Cover slices or small pieces of meat or poultry with gravy or a sauce before reheating – remember to arrange the narrow parts to the centre.

Always take care when reheating anything with a jam or other high-sugar filling, such as a pie, as the filling will become very hot very quickly while the outside may still feel cool.

When reheating plates of food, make sure that the food is evenly distributed on the plate, with the thicker items on the outside edges. Up to three plates of food can be heated at a time in an average sized oven. Position them one on top of the other using special microwave stacking rings. Alternatively, cover the first plate with another upturned plate or large soup bowl and place the next plate on top of this. Avoid positioning the plates so that the same items of food are directly above one another. Give the plates a half turn every few minutes in the same way as you would for other cooking. The food is reheated when the bottom of the plate feels warm.

Stacking rings
Three separate plates of food during reheating.

another minute or two. Use the following guidelines when deciding if items are completely cooked:

■ Microwaved meats and poultry can be tested by piercing the thickest part with a skewer or the point of a sharp knife. The juices will run clear if the meat is well done; slightly pink with a hint of brown if medium; and quite pink if rare. To test more accurately, try using a proper meat thermometer (see p. 189).

■ Fish becomes opaque as it cooks and will flake easily. Check the flesh nearest the bone of whole fish, as this is the last to cook, remembering that it will still continue to cook during standing time.

■ Microwave vegetables until they are just tender when pierced with a fork. If you cook them until they are soft, they will have overcooked by the time they are served.

■ Cakes, particularly sponges, look unpleasantly wet on top at the end of the recommended cooking time. By the end of the standing time they should look dry and be thoroughly cooked. Test them at the end of the time by inserting a wooden cocktail

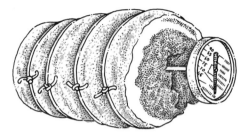

Testing the temperature
Use a meat thermometer to check accurately the temperature of roasting meat.

stick or fine skewer into the centre. If it comes out clean, the cake is cooked. If it is slightly coated, put the cake back in the microwave for a few minutes more, stand for 5 minutes then test again.

■ Pastry flan cases are cooked when the pastry looks opaque. If cooking in a glass dish, you can double check by seeing if the base looks dry from underneath.

■ Quiche fillings may look soft and wet on top after the recommended cooking time, but they soon dry out after a few minutes standing time.

The microwave and the freezer

The microwave and the freezer are perfect partners. Both help to keep flavour, texture and vitamin loss in foods to a minimum and both are great time-savers as well as being economical. The great advantage of using a microwave oven in combination with a freezer is that it can defrost food in a matter of minutes, eliminating the need to pre-plan and take foods out of the freezer hours before they are required in order for them to defrost. Some foods, particularly vegetables, can even be defrosted and reheated in one action. You can also blanch small quantities of fresh vegetables in the microwave in minutes for storage in the freezer as described on pp. 210-11.

The recipes in this book that freeze well are marked with a blue symbol. Make sure that all dishes are thoroughly chilled before freezing. Use rigid containers for soups and sauces and allow room for expansion. Seal all items tightly and label. Test for flavour during reheating and add more seasoning if necessary. Seasoning flavours can diminish during freezing.

Defrosting and reheating foods

Most microwave ovens have a Defrost control which allows food to defrost slowly and evenly without danger of it drying out or cooking at the edges. If your microwave oven doesn't have a special Defrost or comparably low setting, you can simulate the Defrost control by turning the oven on to Full power for 30 seconds and then off for 1½ minutes. Repeat this process until the food is almost defrosted and allow it to thaw completely by standing. Even with a Defrost control, you'll find that certain, denser foods need additional resting times to prevent the edges cooking while the centre still needs to thaw out fully.

Follow the defrosting guidelines below and you should always have perfect results.

■ Defrost food in a container the same size as the block of food. If the food has too much room it will spread out as it melts and the edges will start to cook.

■ Loosen containers, but leave the food covered.

■ Break up food blocks as they start to defrost to bring frozen parts to the edges.

■ Stir suitable foods from the edge to the centre as they start to thaw.

■ Foods that cannot be stirred should be separated out, turned over and rearranged to ensure even defrosting.

■ Pies and cakes should be given a quarter turn every minute or so during defrosting.

■ When defrosting food in a bag, pierce or slit the bag to prevent it bursting.

■ Flex bags during defrosting to rearrange the food inside and speed up the process.

■ Shield any delicate areas with small pieces of foil to prevent them cooking while denser parts are still thawing.

■ When defrosting frozen foods that you do not want to cook or reheat, such as soft fruit, use only the Defrost setting. If the food starts to feel warm, leave it to stand for a few minutes then continue defrosting.

■ Place breads, cakes, biscuits or pastry on a double layer of absorbent kitchen paper, so that any excess moisture is absorbed and the food does not become soggy.

■ Vegetables can be cooked directly from the freezer without being defrosted.

■ As the defrosting process continues after foods have been removed from the oven, do not wait until foods are completely defrosted before removing them or the outer edges may start to cook.

■ Always remove food from foil containers and remove any metal ties from plastic bags before putting in the microwave to defrost.

Defrosting chart

FOOD	QUANTITY	MICROWAVING TIME	METHOD
Butter	225g (8 oz)	❊ DEFROST for 1½ mins. 600W (*1-1½ mins. 700W; 2-2½ mins. 500W*). Leave to stand for 5 mins.	Remove any foil wrappers. Give a half turn and turn over halfway through.
Biscuits	225g (8 oz)	❊ DEFROST for 1 min. 600W (*30-60 secs. 700W; 1½ mins. 500W*). Leave to stand for 5 mins.	Turn over halfway through. Remove any wrappings.
Bread, large unsliced loaf	1	❊ DEFROST for 7-9 mins. 600W (*5-7 mins. 700W; 10-14 mins. 500W*). Leave to stand for 5-10 mins.	Stand on absorbent kitchen paper, turn over and rearrange twice.
Larged sliced loaf	1	❊ DEFROST for 11-12 mins. 600W (*9-10 mins. 700W; 15-18 mins. 500W*). Leave to stand for 10-15 mins.	Stand on absorbent kitchen paper, turn over and give loaf a half turn several times.
Bread rolls	2	❊ DEFROST for 30-60 secs. Leave to stand for 2-3 mins.	Place on absorbent kitchen paper.
	4	❊ DEFROST for 1½-3 mins. Leave to stand for 2-3 mins.	Place on absorbent kitchen paper. Rearrange halfway through.
Fruit cake	1	❊ DEFROST for 5 mins. 600W (*4 mins. 700W; 7 mins. 500W*). Leave to stand for 10 mins.	Give a half turn halfway through defrosting time.
Scones	2	❊ DEFROST for 1-2 mins. Leave to stand for 1-2 mins.	Place on absorbent kitchen paper. Turn over and rearrange once.
Fruit (soft fruit, eg raspberries, etc.)	225g (8 oz)	❊ DEFROST for 3-5 mins. 600W (*2-4 mins. 700W; 4-7 mins. 500W*).	Stir gently once or twice. Leave to stand until completely thawed.
	450g (1 lb)	❊ DEFROST for 6-8 mins. 600W (*5-7 mins. 700W; 7-10 mins. 500W*).	As above.
Fruit juice concentrate	1 can 200ml (7 fl oz)	❊ DEFROST for 2-3 mins. 600W (*2 mins. 700W; 3-4 mins. 500W*).	Remove from can if made of metal. Allow to stand for 3-5 mins.
Fruit purée	600ml (1 pint)	❊ DEFROST for 10 mins. 600W (*8 mins. 700W; 12 mins. 500W*).	Stir several times. Allow to stand for about 10 mins.

FISH

Fish fillets	225g (8 oz)	❊ DEFROST for 5 mins. 600W (*4 mins. 700W; 6 mins. 500W*). Stand for 10 mins.	Place in a shallow dish and cover. Turn over and rearrange thin parts to the centre halfway through.

FOOD	QUANTITY	MICROWAVING TIME	METHOD
Fish steaks and cutlets	225g (8 oz)	❄ DEFROST for 5 mins. 600W *(4 mins. 700W; 6 mins. 500W)*. Stand for 10 mins.	Place in a shallow dish and cover. Turn over and rearrange thin parts to the centre halfway through.
	450g (1 lb)	❄ DEFROST for 8 mins. 600W *(6½ mins. 700W; 10 mins. 500W)*. Stand for 10 mins.	
Whole fish	per 450g (1 lb)	❄ DEFROST for 7-9 mins. 600W *(6-8 mins. 700W; 8-11 mins. 500W)*. Stand for 15-20 mins.	Cover, turn over halfway through and shield tails with small pieces of foil, if necessary.
Scallops and mussels, raw, shelled	225g (8 oz)	❄ DEFROST for 3-5 mins. 600W *(2-4 mins. 700W; 4-6 mins. 500W)*. Stand for 3 mins	Cover, break blocks carefully and spread into a single layer, as soon as possible. Stir two or three times.
Prawns, cooked	100g (4 oz)	❄ DEFROST for 1½-2 mins. 600W *(1-1½ mins. 700W; 1-2 mins. 500W)*. Stand for 3 mins.	Spread out on a plate and cover. Stir once or twice.
	225g (8 oz)	❄ DEFROST for 3-4 mins. 600W *(2½-3 mins. 700W; 3½-5 mins. 500W)*.	

POULTRY AND GAME

Chicken thighs and drumsticks	4 × 100g (4 oz)	❄ DEFROST for 8 mins. 600W *(6½ mins. 700W; 10 mins. 500W)*. Stand for 5 mins.	Arrange thin ends to the centre. Cover and turn over halfway through.
Chicken or turkey boned breasts	2 × 175g (6 oz)	❄ DEFROST for 6-8 mins. 600W *(5-6½ mins. 700W; 7-10 mins. 500W)*. Stand for 5 mins.	Cover, separate as soon as possible. Arrange thin ends to the centre. Turn over and rearrange halfway through.
	4 × 175g (6 oz)	❄ DEFROST for 13-15 mins. 600W *(10-12 mins. 700W; 16-18 mins. 500W)*. Stand for 5 mins.	
Chicken and duck quarters	2	❄ DEFROST for 7-10 mins. 600W *(6-8½ mins. 700W; 10-12½ mins. 500W)*. Stand for 10 mins.	Arrange in a dish with thin ends to the centre. Cover. Turn over and rearrange halfway through.
Rabbit and hare joints	per 450g (1 lb)	❄ DEFROST for 11-12 mins. 600W *(9-10 mins. 700W; 13½-15 mins. 500W)*. Stand for 10 mins.	Arrange in a shallow dish, thin ends to the centre. Cover. Turn over and rearrange halfway through.
Cubed meats, freeflow	450g (1 lb)	❄ DEFROST for 5-6 mins. 600W *(4-5 mins. 700W; 6-7 mins. 500W)*. Stand for 5 mins.	Spread out on a shallow dish and cover. Stir two or three times.
	900g (2 lb)	❄ DEFROST for 5-6 mins. 600W *(4-5 mins. 700W; 6-7 mins. 500W)*. Stand for 10 mins.	

FOOD	QUANTITY	MICROWAVING TIME	METHOD
Whole birds	under 1.75kg (4 lb)	≋ DEFROST for 8-10 mins. 600W (*6½-8½ mins. 700W; 10-11 mins. 500W*). Stand for 30-45 mins.	Remove any metal ties, place in a bowl. Leave in wrapper or cover. Rotate and rearrange every 5 mins. Remove giblets as soon as possible.
	over 2kg (4 lb)	≋ DEFROST for 8-10 mins. 600W (*6½-8½ mins. 700W; 10-11 mins. 500W*). Stand for 30-45 mins.	Defrost as above, but take bird out and stand for 5 mins. several times during cooking.

MEAT

FOOD	QUANTITY	MICROWAVING TIME	METHOD
Steaks and chops	2 × 175g-225g (6-8 oz)	≋ DEFROST for 7-8 mins. 600W (*6 mins. 700W; 8½-10 mins. 500W*). Stand for 10 mins.	Separate and arrange in a shallow dish. Arrange thin ends to the centre. Cover, turn over halfway through.
	4 × 175g-225g (6-8 oz)	≋ DEFROST for 9-11 mins. 600W (*7-9 mins. 700W; 11½-13½ mins. 500W*). Stand for 10 mins.	
Cubed meat, freeflow	225g (8 oz)	≋ DEFROST for 6 mins. 600W (*5 mins. 700W; 7 mins. 500W*). Stand for 10 mins.	Spread out in a shallow dish and cover. Stir two or three times.
	450g (1 lb)	≋ DEFROST for 9 mins. 600W (*7 mins. 700W; 11½ mins. 500W*). Stand for 10 mins.	
	900g (2 lb)	≋ DEFROST for 15 mins. 600W (*11 mins. 700W; 18 mins. 500W*). Stand for 10 mins.	
Minced meat, freeflow	per 450g (1 lb)	≋ DEFROST for 3½-4 mins. 600W (*3 mins. 700W; 4½-5 mins. 500W*). Stand for 10 mins.	Spread out in a shallow dish and cover. Stir two or three times.
Minced meat, block	per 450g (1 lb)	≋ DEFROST for 6-8 mins. 600W (*5-6 mins. 700W; 7-10 mins. 500W*). Stand for 10 mins.	Place in a shallow dish. Cover. Scrape off soft meat and break up as soon as possible. Stir several times.
Joints	900g (2 lb)	≋ DEFROST for 18 mins. 600W (*15 mins. 700W; 21 mins. 500W*). Stand for 10 mins.	Place in a large dish. Cover. Turn over and rotate every 5 mins. Shield bony ends and thin parts with foil for half the cooking time.
	1.5kg (3 lb)	≋ DEFROST for 25 mins. 600W (*20 mins. 700W; 30 mins. 500W*). Stand for 15 mins.	
	2kg (4 lb)	≋ DEFROST for 32 mins. 600W (*27 mins. 700W; 37 mins. 500W*). Stand for 20 mins.	
Sausage-meat, block	per 450g (1 lb)	≋ DEFROST for 3½-4 mins. 600W (*3 mins. 700W; 4½-10 mins. 500W*). Stand for 10 mins.	Place in a shallow dish. Cover. Scrape off soft meat and break up as soon as possible. Stir several times.

Reheating from frozen chart

FOOD	QUANTITY	MICROWAVING TIME	METHOD
Vegetable casseroles	4 portions	▨ FULL for 15-16 mins. 600W (*12-13 mins. 700W; 18-19 mins. 500W*).	Place in a shallow dish and cover. Give the dish a half turn every minute until defrosted enough to stir gently to break up then stir once or twice until hot.
Moussaka, lasagne	4-portion size	▨ DEFROST for 8 mins. 600W (*6½ mins. 700W; 12 mins. 500W*). Leave to stand for 6 mins. then ▨ DEFROST for 5 mins. 600W (*4 mins. 700W; 7 mins. 500W*), then ▨ FULL for 9 mins. 600W (*7½ mins. 700W; 11 mins. 500W*).	Place in a shallow dish and cover. Give the dish a half turn every 2 mins. until the food is heated through.
Vegetable, meat loaves and bakes	450g (1 lb) 4 portion size	▨ FULL for 5-8 mins. 600W (*4-7 mins. 700W; 6-10 mins. 500W*).	Place in a dish that fits and cover. Give the dish a half turn every 2 mins. until hot.
Plated meal	1 portion	▨ DEFROST for 4 mins. 600W (*3-4 mins. 700W; 6 mins. 500W*). Leave to stand for 4 mins. then ▨ DEFROST for 4 mins. 600W (*3-4 mins. 700W; 6 mins. 500W*).	Cover with an upturned plate. Test by feeling the base of the plate; when it feels hot the food should be ready.
Rice, cooked	100g (4 oz)	▨ FULL for 1½-2 mins. 600W (*1-1½ mins. 700W; 1½-2½ mins. 500W*).	Place in a shallow dish and cover. Break up with a fork halfway through the time. Stir at the end of the reheating time.
Pasta, cooked	300g (10 oz)	▨ DEFROST for 10-12 mins. 600W (*7-10 mins. 700W; 15-18 mins. 500W*).	Place in a shallow dish and cover. Stir 2-3 times until hot.
Soup	300ml (½ pint)	▨ FULL for 4-6 mins. 600W (*3-4 mins. 700W; 5-7½ mins. 500W*).	Place in a serving dish, allowing room for bubbling. Break up and stir the soup 2-3 times.
	600ml (1 pint)	▨ FULL for 7-10 mins. 600W (*5-8 mins. 700W; 8-12 mins. 500W*).	
Sauces	300ml (½ pint)	▨ FULL for 5-6 mins. 600W (*4-5 mins. 700W; 6-7½ mins. 500W*).	Place in a dish that fits, allowing room for bubbling. Break up and stir the sauce 2-3 times.
	600ml (1 pint)	▨ FULL for 10-12 mins. 600W (*8-10 mins. 700W; 12-15 mins. 500W*).	
Fish cakes	2 × 175g (6 oz)	▨ FULL for 4-5 mins. 600W (*3-4 mins. 700W; 5-6 mins. 500W*). Stand for 2-3 mins.	Place fish cakes on a microwave roasting rack. Turn them over halfway through.
	4 × 175g (6 oz)	▨ FULL for 6-8 mins. 600W (*5-6½ mins. 700W; 7-10 mins. 500W*).	

FOOD	QUANTITY	MICROWAVING TIME	METHOD
Beefburgers	2	▨ FULL for 2-3½ mins. 600W (*1½-3 mins. 700W; 2½-4½ mins. 500W*). Stand for 5 mins.	Preheat a browning dish as manufacturer's instructions, add burgers and press down well. Turn over halfway through.
	4	▨ FULL for 3-4½ mins. 600W (*2½-3½ mins. 700W; 3½-5½ mins. 500W*).	
	6	▨ FULL for 3½-5 mins. 600W (*3-4 mins. 700W; 4½-6 mins. 500W*).	
Chicken breasts in breadcrumbs	2 × 100g (4 oz)	▨ FULL for 4½-5 mins. 600W (*3½-4 mins. 700W; 5½-6 mins. 500W*).	Preheat a browning dish as manufacturer's instructions, press breasts onto dish. Cook for one-third of the time then turn over.
Fish fingers	4	▨ FULL for 2 mins. 600W (*1½ mins. 700W; 2½ mins. 500W*). Stand for 2 mins.	Preheat a browning dish as manufacturer's instructions. Add fish fingers, press down well. Turn over halfway through.
	6	▨ FULL for 3 mins. 600W (*2½ mins. 700W; 3½ mins. 500W*). Stand for 3 mins.	

READY-MADE MEALS

Sliced meat in gravy		▨ FULL for 4-6 mins. 600W (*3-5 mins. 700W; 5-7 mins. 500W*). Stand for 3 mins.	Pierce bag, place on plate, or place in a dish and cover. Turn over and rotate or rearrange two or three times until hot.
Meat casseroles	1 portion	▨ FULL for 4-5 mins. 600W (*3-4 mins. 700W; 5-6 mins. 500W*). Stand for 2 mins.	Pierce bag, place on plate or place in a shallow bowl and cover. Turn over bag or stir casserole halfway through.
	2 portions	▨ FULL for 7-10 mins. 600W (*6-8½ mins. 700W; 8½-12½ mins. 500W*). Stand for 3 mins.	
Spareribs in sauce	2 portions	▨ FULL for 5-6 mins. 600W (*4-5 mins. 700W; 6-7 mins. 500W*). Stand for 2 mins.	Pierce bag, place on a plate or place in a shallow bowl and cover. Turn over bag or stir halfway through.
Roast chicken in gravy	2 portions	▨ FULL for 5-7 mins. 600W (*4-6 mins. 700W; 6-8½ mins. 500W*). Stand for 2 mins.	Pierce bag, place on plate or place in shallow bowl and cover. Turn over bag or stir halfway through.
Dry spicy chicken	2-3 portions 450g (1 lb)	▨ FULL for 6-8 mins. 600W (*5-6½ mins. 700W; 7-10 mins. 500W*). Stand for 2 mins.	Arrange on a plate, narrow ends to the centre. Turn over and rearrange halfway through.

FOOD	QUANTITY	MICROWAVING TIME	METHOD
Chicken Kiev, raw	2 portions	≋ FULL for 8-10 mins. 600W *(6½-8½ mins. 700W; 10-12½ mins. 500W)*. Stand for 2 mins.	Preheat browning dish as manufacturer's instructions; add 10ml (2 tsp) oil. Press down chicken pieces. Turn over after one-third of the cooking time.
Liver and kidneys in gravy	1 portion	≋ FULL for 4-5 mins. 600W *(3-4 mins. 700W; 5-6 mins. 500W)*. Stand for 2 mins.	Pierce bag, place in plate or transfer to dish, cover. Rotate and turn over or rearrange halfway through.
Smoked fish fillet with butter	1 portion	≋ FULL for 3 mins. 600W *(2½ mins. 700W; 3½ mins. 500W)*. Stand for 2 mins.	Pierce bag, place in shallow dish. Turn the fish over and rotate halfway through.
Prawn curry	1 portion	≋ FULL for 5 mins. 600W *(4 mins. 700W; 6 mins. 500W)*. Stand for 2 mins.	Place in dish and cover, stir two or three times. Or pierce bag and place in dish. Turn the curry over and rotate halfway through.

Blanching fruit and vegetables for the freezer

A microwave oven takes much of the effort out of blanching vegetables and is a boon to people who grow their own produce. Vegetables can be picked at the peak of perfection and then blanched in small quantities in the microwave. When blanching large amounts, it is usually better to use conventional methods.

Blanching is necessary to stop enzyme activity in vegetables and fruits which would otherwise continue even at freezer temperature, causing loss of flavour and texture. Deterioration is noticeable in some produce after only a few days. Others will last longer but the eating quality will also start to deteriorate.

Before blanching, clean, trim and slice the vegetables to a uniform size. To blanch 450g (1 lb) vegetables, place in a casserole dish or bowl with 45ml (3 tbsp) water. Cover and cook on FULL for the time specified on the chart. Stir once halfway through the blanching time.

Drain then plunge into iced water to prevent further cooking. Once chilled, drain well and pack into freezer bags, or boiling bags if you want to reheat them in the microwave. For smaller amounts, put the prepared vegetables into a boiling bag. Do not add any water. Secure the bag loosely with a non-metallic fastener and cook on FULL for the appropriate time, turning the bag over halfway through. After the blanching time, put the bag into iced water. Keep the top of the bag above the surface and leave open to allow steam to escape. Once the vegetables have chilled, secure the bag tightly, wipe dry and freeze as normal.

Most blanched produce will keep for up to a year in the freezer. Do not thaw before cooking or more vitamin content will be lost and the texture will be poor.

Blanching vegetables by microwave

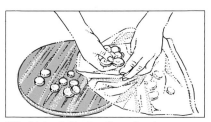

1 Clean, trim and slice vegetables evenly into 5cm (2 in) pieces.

2 Pack into a boiling bag. Secure loosely. Cook on FULL as detailed on chart.

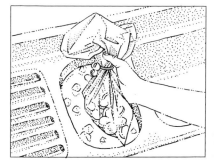

3 Chill thoroughly in iced water. Secure bag tightly, label and freeze.

Blanching chart

VEGETABLE/FRUIT 450g (1 lb)	MICROWAVING TIME on FULL
Broad beans	3 mins. 600W (2½ mins. 700W; 3½ mins. 500W)
Green beans, *whole*	3 mins. 600W (2½ mins. 700W; 3½ mins. 500W)
sliced	2 mins. 600W (1½ mins. 700W; 2½ mins. 500W)
Broccoli florets	2½-4 mins. 600W (2-3 mins. 700W; 3-5 mins. 500W)
Peas	2 mins. 600W (1½ mins. 700W; 3-5 mins. 500W)
Carrots	3½ mins. 600W (3 mins. 700W; 4 mins. 500W)
Corn-on-the-cob (2)	7 mins. 600W (6 mins. 700W; 8½ mins. 500W)
Courgettes	3 mins. 600W (2½ mins. 700W; 3½ mins. 500W)
Cauliflower florets	3 mins. 600W (2½ mins. 700W; 3½ mins. 500W)
Brussels sprouts	5 mins. 600W (4 mins. 700W; 6 mins. 500W)
Leeks, *sliced*	2-2½ mins. 600W (1½-2 mins. 700W; 2½-3 mins. 500W)
Sweetcorn	3 mins. 600W (2½ mins. 700W; 3½ mins. 500W)
Asparagus	4 mins. 600W (3 mins. 700W; 5 mins. 500W)
Spinach	2 mins. 600W (1½ mins. 700W; 2½ mins. 500W)
Beetroot, *small*	5 mins. 600W (4 mins. 700W; 6 mins. 500W)
Parsnips	3 mins. 600W (2½ mins. 700W; 3½ mins. 500W)
Peppers, *sliced*	3 mins. 600W (2½ mins. 700W; 3½ mins. 500W)
Onions, *sliced*	2 mins. 600W (1½ mins. 700W; 2½ mins. 500W)
Apples	3-4 mins. 600W (2-3 mins. 700W; 3-5 mins. 500W)
Pears	3-4 mins. 600W (2-3 mins. 700W; 3-5 mins. 500W)
Rhubarb	3-4 mins. 600W (2-3 mins. 700W; 3-5 mins. 500W)

Hints and tips

BUTTER AND MARGARINE

◼ Use the microwave for softening butter and margarine. For 225g (8 oz) heat on DEFROST for 30-60 seconds. This will speed up the creaming process when preparing cake mixtures.

◼ To melt 100g (4 oz) butter or margarine, place in a small dish and ⊠ MEDIUM for 1-2 minutes.

BREADS

◼ Heat up rolls and bread before serving with a meal; you can even heat them in their serving basket. Put them in the oven just before you want to serve them as they soon begin to cool down again, and ⊠ FULL for 1-2 minutes.

◼ You can freshen bread that has gone slightly stale by heating it on ⊠ FULL for about 15 seconds.

◼ Make dry breadcrumbs for coating foods by heating a slice of bread on ⊠ FULL for 2-3 minutes. Then crush with a rolling pin or in a blender and store the crumbs in an airtight container.

◼ You can defrost a single slice of bread in 10-15 seconds. Place it on absorbent paper.

MEAT AND POULTRY

◼ Always bring meat to room temperature before cooking to achieve the best results.

◼ If you like a crispy finish to your roast, try cooking it for half the time in the microwave and the remainder of the time in a conventional oven.

◼ Allow 5 minutes additional cooking time if cooking a bird with stuffing.

◼ If cooking poultry portions in a sauce, try skinning them first as this allows the sauce to penetrate right through the flesh.

◼ Chicken, which has been cooked without any additional browning, is particularly suitable for use in salads and sandwiches.

FISH

◼ Some fish have a strong odour which can often linger after cooking. To get rid of this, boil some water and lemon juice in a jug in the microwave for 3-4 minutes. Cooking with wine, vinegar or lemon juice also helps to minimize cooking odour.

FRUIT

◼ Soften dried dates to make chopping easier by heating on ⊠ DEFROST for 30-40 seconds.

◼ Microwave citrus fruit on ⊠ FULL for 15-20 seconds to make peeling the rind easier. Prick the skin first.

Drying citrus peel

◼ Dry large pieces of peel from citrus fruit to use as a flavouring in teas, cakes and sauces. Orange, tangerine and grapefruit are particularly good. First, make sure that the peel is scrubbed well to remove any traces of chemical pesticides. Lay the pieces out on absorbent paper and ⊠ FULL for about 1 minute, until dried and crisp. Rearrange and turn over halfway through the cooking time. Store the dried and cooled peel in an airtight container.

◼ To dry grated peel, place in a bowl and ⊠ FULL for 30-60 seconds, or until dry. Stir once.

◼ To extract more juice from citrus fruit, prick the skin in several different places. For each fruit, ⊠ FULL for about 30 seconds before squeezing.

■ Speed up the process of reconstituting dried fruit in the microwave. For 100g (4 oz), place in a bowl with 600ml (1 pint) boiling water. Cover and ⊠ FULL for 6-10 minutes. Stir, then leave to stand for 10-30 minutes.

HONEY

■ To restore smooth, runny texture to honey that has crystallized in the jar, place in the microwave (after removing the lid) and ⊠ FULL for 1-2 minutes.

SEEDS

■ Bring out the full flavour of seeds by toasting them in the microwave. For 50g (2 oz) spread on a dish and ⊠ FULL for about 2 mins. Stir frequently during this time to prevent scorching.

NUTS

■ Toast desiccated coconut by spreading 75g (3 oz) over a 22cm (9 in) plate. ⊠ FULL for 1-2 minutes or until golden brown. Stir at least once.

■ To roast whole nuts, spread 100g (4 oz) over a medium-sized plate. ⊠ FULL for 3-4 minutes and stir at least twice.

DESSERTS

■ Soften ice cream before serving by warming on ⊠ DEFROST for between 30 and 60 seconds. This timing should also enable you to loosen jellies and mousses from their moulds.

SAUCES

■ Save on washing up by making sauces in the jug you wish to serve them in. Select a jug large enough to allow for any bubbling and liquid expansion.

■ To prevent sauces cooking unevenly and lumps forming, watch for the mixture thickening around the edge of the bowl or jug. As this happens, open the door and stir the sauce briskly.

■ Bring starch-thickened sauces to the boil and remove from the microwave as soon as they have thickened. Overcooking will destroy the thickening agent and the sauce will start to thin.

TOMATOES

■ To make skinning tomatoes easier, put them into a bowl, cover with boiling water and ⊠ FULL for about 30 seconds. Drain and then skin.

PASTRY

■ Bake pastry blind by covering with absorbent paper and a plate. This helps to keep the pastry crisp and dry. Avoid adding very moist fillings or the pastry will absorb the moisture and become soggy.

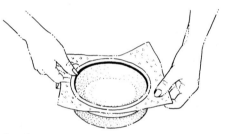

Covering pastry

EGGS AND CHEESE

■ Always pay special attention when cooking eggs in the microwave as timings will vary according to the size, composition and freshness of the eggs. It is better to take them out of the oven slightly undercooked, then they can finish cooking in the standing time.

■ To soften curd or cream cheese for easier spreading or mixing, just ⊠ DEFROST for 30-60 seconds.

CAKE-MAKING

■ Tap the sides of cake dishes during the standing time to help loosen the cake and bring it away from the edges.

■ The inside diameter of a cake container should not exceed 20cm (8 in), or the centre will probably not cook through. Use a ring mould for larger cakes.

■ To melt down chocolate or carob bars, put 50g (2 oz) in a dish and ▨ MEDIUM for 2-3 minutes.

■ When baking cakes in the microwave, only half fill the container as the mixture will rise considerably in the oven and cause a mess if it overflows.

DRYING HERBS

■ Fresh herbs can be dried effectively in the microwave for use all the year round. Dry about 15g (½ oz) at a time. Remove the stalks from the leafy herbs. Rinse the leaves carefully, then pat dry with absorbent paper. Place the herbs between two sheets of absorbent paper on the floor of the oven. Add a small bowl of water as a safety measure: the moisture content in this small amount of herbs is very low and the water will prevent the absorbent paper scorching. ▨ FULL for 4-6 minutes, depending on the type of herbs, until they lose their bright colour and become brittle to touch. Rearrange the herbs several times and watch them carefully throughout the cooking time. Leave them to cool, then run through a sieve. Store in an airtight jar in a cool, dark place.

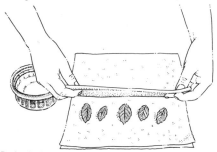

Drying herbs

JAM-MAKING

■ Sterilize jars by half filling with water and heating in the microwave until they reach boiling point. Swirl the water around the whole of the inside of the jar then drain and dry well before filling.

■ To test if a jam has reached setting point,

place a small amount onto a cold saucer and leave until cool. Push the surface of the jam and if it wrinkles, it's ready.

JARS

■ To scrape the last of the contents from preserves and jams in jars, remove lids and ▨ DEFROST for 30 seconds.

■ To heat baby foods in the jar. Remove the lid and ▨ MEDIUM for 40-60 seconds. Always test the temperature before serving.

WINE

■ To bring red wine to room temperature, pour into a suitable jug, and ▨ FULL for 10 seconds. Do not leave in the bottle.

FROZEN FOODS

■ Cook frozen vegetables in their own bags. Simply pierce the bag first and rest it on a plate.

■ Freeze foods in small or individual portions for speedier defrosting.

■ When freezing a casserole, it is a good idea to insert an empty paper cup in the centre so food isn't concentrated there and the defrosting process takes less time.

REHEATING PASTA, GRAINS AND PULSES

■ With the microwave you can reheat pasta, grains and pulses so that they keep their texture and flavour in full. For one or two servings, place in a dish, toss in a little oil, cover and ▨ FULL for 1-2 minutes.

IMPROVISING CONTAINERS

■ To make your own ring mould for cooking cakes and grain dishes, stand a glass tumbler in the centre of a round dish. Hold in position when adding food.

■ Unusually-shaped cardboard boxes can be used to make interesting cake containers. Line the box with greaseproof paper first. Do not use boxes with wax coatings or any metal trimmings.

GLOSSARY

Arcing
Small sparks that occur in the oven cavity during cooking when an electric discharge is conducted from one surface or electrode to another. This may be caused by metal being introduced into the oven either as foil, a utensil or a container. Never use metal utensils in a microwave. Also, be careful to use only foil in small amounts as advised in the manufacturer's instruction manual, and never let it come near to or in contact with the oven walls.

Arcing may also be the result of scratches or indentations on the oven cavity's surfaces; care must be taken when cleaning the oven interior. Always wipe or soak off spilt foods (see pp. 184-5) as carbonization can cause sparking.

Audible reminder
A bell, buzzer or pinger that sounds to let you know when the cooking time set has been completed.

Blanching
Process of boiling vegetables or fruit for a brief period to halt enzyme activity before freezing. See pp. 210-11 for detailed instructions on blanching vegetables in the microwave.

Browning dish
A special dish with a tin-oxide coating on its base designed to brown or crisp foods in the microwave oven. The coating absorbs microwave energy and becomes very hot when preheated in the oven. These dishes come in a variety of shapes and sizes and can be used with a lid for sautéing and simmering. Each type of dish is supplied with a set of instructions which should be followed when using.

Browning grill
Some microwave ovens incorporate a radiant electric grill which is usually sited in the roof of the cooking cavity. This can be used to crisp or brown foods after cooking or, in some of the more advanced models, during cooking.

Combination oven
As the name suggests, combination ovens incorporate microwave power with conventional cooking facilities. Depending upon the model, these can be operated either separately, in sequence or at the same time, combining the speed of microwave energy with the browning and crisping qualities of conventional cooking by heat.

Conduction
The way heat spreads from one layer to the next. This is an important part of the microwave cooking process and is how foods continue to cook after being removed from the microwave. It is also the reason why microwave-proof plates get hot in the microwave oven – it's not the plate that is being heated up by the microwaves but the food it contains, and the heat generated by the hot food heats up the plate.

Defrosting
The process by which ice crystals revert to moisture as food thaws. As the pattern of ice crystals in foods is not uniform, thawing is often uneven. For even thawing, set the microwave on Defrost. This pulses out energy at regular intervals so the temperature of the food evens out between bursts.

Density
The density of different foods affects the length of time they need to cook, defrost and reheat. The denser the food, the longer the cooking time it will require. Similarly, the density of containers also affects cooking times.

Door seals
Although microwave ovens vary in design, all have door seals which run around the perimeter of the door's interior. The seal consists of a metal channel filled with absorbent material to reduce the risk of any microwaves escaping while the oven is in use.

Freeflow
A term used by many retailers to describe food frozen in small chunks (such as meat) or individually (such as peas) to make using small quantities easier.

Hot spots
Although modern microwave ovens incorporate at least one device to help distribute the microwave energy evenly throughout the cooking cavity, hot spots may still exist. Find out where your oven's hot spots are by following the test on p. 193. The existence of hot spots necessitates food being turned, stirred and rearranged for even results.

Magnetron
A high-frequency radar tube that converts electrical energy into microwave energy.

Microwave thermometer
A thermometer specially designed for use in the microwave. Traditional thermometers cannot be used because the mercury is affected by microwaves.

Piercing
Any item covered by a membrane or skin must be pierced before

being microwaved. This is to allow steam to escape during cooking and to prevent anything bursting from the pressure. Any boiling bags used in the oven should first be pierced to prevent too much steam building up inside.

Rearranging
Some items need rearranging in the microwave oven in order to cook evenly (see p. 199).

Shielding
A technique used to protect delicate areas of food from receiving too much microwave energy during cooking, by covering them with smooth strips of foil. Always follow your oven's manufacturer's guidelines when employing this technique and only use the minimum amount of foil.

Splash guard
Some wave stirrers are protected from food spatterings by a splash guard. This should be cleaned regularly according to the manufacturer's instructions.

Stacking
Plates of food being reheated should be stacked one above the other using microwave-proof stacking rings or upturned plates as separators (see p. 202).

Standing time
This is an essential part of microwave cookery and allows food to continue cooking by conduction after the microwave energy has been turned off.

Stirring
A most important technique used in microwave cookery to distribute heat and help foods, particularly liquids, cook evenly. Always stir from the edges of the container to the centre (see p. 198).

Tenting
This is the method of covering foods with foil once they have been removed from the oven so that they keep their heat during their standing time.

Variable power
A setting control that offers a range of energy outputs for different functions. The different powers available may be expressed in numerals, words, or percentages (see p. 179). The lower powers are usually achieved by pulsing the energy on and off for varying lengths of time.

Wave guide
A metal duct that directs microwave energy produced by the magnetron into the cavity of the oven.

Wave stirrer
A device sited close to the wave guide outlet, designed to distribute the emerging microwaves evenly throughout the cooking cavity.

INDEX

Page numbers in *italic* refer to illustrations

A

absorbent paper 187, *187*, 196, 197, *197*, 213
absorption 182-3, *182*
aduki beans 28
air vents 176-7, *181*, 185
aluminium foil 173-4, 199-200, *199-200*
antennae, rotating 180
apples 23
    apple and date chutney 156, *157*
    blackberry and apple purée 155, *157*
    blanching for freezing 211
    dried apple slices 26
apricots 25
    apricot petit pots 131, *132-3*
    braised fennel in tomato and apricot sauce 123
    dried 26
    hunza 26
arame 29
    oriental mushroom soup 55, *57*
arcing (sparking) 174, 183, 186, 192, 200
arrangement of food 194-5, 198-9, *198*
artichokes
    green bean, mushroom and artichoke medley 116, *117*
asparagus 11
    blanching for freezing 211
aubergines 14
    aubergine dip 64, *65*
    aurbergine layer *108*, 110
    ratatouille *120*, 121
auto-sensors *178*, 180
avocados
    hot green salad 130
    stuffed avocados 63

B

baby beetroots with orange sauce *120*, 121
bacon steaks with orange and raisin sauce *88*, 89
baked pears with mango sauce 134
baked potatoes 124, *125*, 197, *197*, 199, *199*
    fillings *125*, 126
baking beans, ceramic 186
bananas 25
    date and chocolate or carob slice *165*, 166
    dried 26

fruit sauce 152, *153*
plum and banana crumble 132, *132*
tropical trifle 144, *145*
barbecue-style baked potatoes 124, *125*
barley 30
    stuffed cabbage leaves 100, *101*
bass
    lemony sea bass 80
beansprouts
    saffron rice with mangetout 106
beef 38-9
    beef and bean soup 59, *60*
    beefburgers 39
    blade bone 39
    brisket 39
    chili con carne 84, *85*
    chuck 39
    entrecote steak 38
    fillet steak 39
    forerib 39
    minced 39
    rib 39
    rump steak 38
    silverside 38
    sirloin 38
    steak 38
    steak and kidney pudding 86
    top rib 39
    top rump 38
    topside 38
beetroots 20
    baby beetroots with orange sauce *120*, 121
    blanching for freezing 211
    borsch 56, *57*
biscuits
    currant biscuits 164, *165*
    defrosting 205
    flapjacks 166
blackberries 23
    blackberry and apple purée 155, *157*
blackcurrants 23
    summer compote 133, *133*
black-eye beans
    beef and bean soup 59, *60*
    blanching 210, *211*
    chart 211
blind baking of pastry 168, 169, 186, 203, 213
blueberries 23
bobby beans 18
boiling bags 188, *189*, 196-7
borlotti bean casserole 107, *108*
borsch 56, *57*

brains 47
braised fennel in tomato and apricot sauce 123
braised red cabbage 128, *129*
brassicas 8-10
bread 212
    bread and butter pudding 143, *145*
    cheese and oat cob 160
    defrosting 205
    heating before meal 212
    soda bread 160
    wholewheat bread 159
brill 32
broad beans 18
    blanching 211
broccoli 9
    blanching 211
    broccoli with olives and garlic 127, *129*
    marinated tofu with vegetables 111, *113*
browning 201
    dishes 189, *190*, 191, 201
    grills *178*, 180
brown rice 30
brown sauce, savoury 149, *149*
brussels sprouts 8
    blanching 211
bubbling over 174
buckwheat 30
bulbs 11-13
bulgar wheat 30
butter, softening and melting 212

C

cabbage 10
    braised red cabbage 128, *129*
    stuffed cabbage leaves 100, *101*
cakes 168-9
    browning 201
    date and chocolate or carob slice *165*, 166
    defrosting 205
    lining containers 197, *197*
    orange cake *161*, 162
    standing time 200
    testing 174, 203
    traditional sponge cake 164
    turning and arranging 198, *198*
cardboard containers 188
carob
    carob and raisin chiffon pie 135, *136*
    carob pudding 142
    carob sauce *153*, 154
carp 35

carrots 21
  carrot and parsnip bake 127, *129*
casseroles
  borlotti bean casserole 107, *108*
cauliflower 8
  leek and cauliflower cobbler 104, *105*
  spiced cauliflower *117*, 118
celeriac 22
celery 12
  aubergine layer *108*, 110
  braised red cabbage 128, *129*
ceramic baking beans 186
cereals 30
cheese
  aubergine layer *108*, 110
  cheese and oat cob 160
  cheese and potato layer 122
  cheese filling *125*, 126
  cheese sauce 150
  chestnut cheesecake *136*, 137
  spinach cream 119, *120*
cheesecake, chestnut *136*, 137
cherries
  red cherry jam 158
  stuffed peaches in wine sauce *136*, 138
chestnuts 27
  chestnut and tomato soup 51, *53*
  chestnut cheesecake *136*, 137
chicken 44
  checking cooked 175
  chicken korma 95
  chicken liver pâté 68, *69*
  roast chicken with redcurrants *93*, 94
chicory 11
chilli con carne 84, *85*
china containers 186, *186*
Chinese leaves 9
chocolate
  chocolate cheesecake *145*, 146
  chocolate or carob pudding 142
  chocolate sauce *153*, 154
  date and chocolate or carob slice *165*, 166
choosing a microwave oven 176-80
Christmas pudding *140*, 141
chunky chowder 58, *60*
chutney, apple and date 156, *157*
cider and onion soup 52, *53*
citrus fruit 212-13, *212*
clams 37
cleaning microwave ovens 184-5, *184-5*
cling film 189, *189*
cobbler, leek and cauliflower 104, *105*
coconut
  lentil and coconut pâté 62, *65*
  prawn and coconut curry *76*, 77
  spiced tomato and coconut sauce 147, *148-9*
cod 35
  cod steaks Niçoise *81*, 83
  seafood shells 66
combination microwave ovens *176*, 177
comparative power outputs 50, 193
composition of food 194, *194*

compotes
  mixed fruit compote *140*, 141
  summer compote 133, *133*
concentrated meat stock 151
concentrated vegetable stock *148-9*, 151
conduction 182
containers 186-92, *186-91*
  shapes 192
  testing for suitability 191
converting recipes for the microwave 168-9
cooking for one 170-1
cooking guides *178*, 180
cooking techniques 196-203, *196-203*
cooking times: conversion 172
  extension 174
cookware, microwave 189, *190-1*, 191
coriander ramekins 62, *65*
cornmeal custard *153*, 154
corn-on-the-cob 19
cost of cooking by microwave 172
cottage cheese: spinach cream 119, *120*
courgettes 15
  blanching 211
  borlotti bean casserole 107, *108*
  ratatouille *120*, 121
covering food 196-7, *196*
crab and prawn cocktail 67, *69*
crayfish 37
cream of garlic soup 54
cream of lettuce soup 54, *57*
creamy carrot and parsnip bake 127, *129*
creamy onion flan 114
crunchy Chinese vegetables 99
currant biscuits 164, *165*
curry, prawn and coconut *76*, 77

D
dab 33
dates
  apple and date chutney 156, *157*
  date and chocolate or carob slice *165*, 166
  dried 26
  softening 212
defrosting 173, 204-7
  buttons 178-9, *178*
  charts 205-7
density of food 194, *194*
desserts
  apricot petit pots 131, *132-3*
  baked pears with mango sauce 134
  bread and butter pudding 143, *145*
  carob and raisin chiffon pie 135, *136*
  chestnut cheesecake *136*, 137
  chocolate cheesecake *145*, 146
  chocolate or carob pudding 142
  Christmas pudding *140*, 141
  millet pudding 139
  mixed fruit compote *140*, 141
  plum and banana crumble 132, *132*
  stuffed peaches in wine sauce *136*, 138
  summer compote 133, *133*

  tropical trifle 144, *145*
dish size 172 heating 172
door seals 173, 183, *184*, 185
double-oven units 177, *177*
dover sole 33
dried apple slices 26
dried fruit 26
drying herbs 213
Dublin Bay prawns 37
duck 44, 175
  duck with cherry sauce 92, *93*
dulse 29

E
eggs 170, 214
  apricot petit pots 131, *132-3*
  coriander ramekins 62, *65*
  egg and spinach noodles 31
equipment 186-92, *186-91*
  testing 191
escalopes (veal) 48

F
factors affecting microwave cookery 193-5
fennel 13
  blanching 211
  braised fennel in tomato and apricot sauce 123
  braised red cabbage 128, *129*
figs (dried) 26
fish lasagne 75, *76*
flans
  creamy onion flan 114
flapjacks *165*, 166
flat fish 32-3
floors, removable 180
flounder 32
food and cooking times 193-5, *193-5*
foods that cannot be cooked in the microwave 170
foods which will work in the microwave 169-70
freezers 204
freezing 204
French beans 18
fruit 23-6
  sauce 152, *153*
  summer compote 133, *133*
  vegetables 14-16
fruity spare ribs 70
frying 172

G
gado gado, vegetable 112, *113*
game 44-5
gammon 41
garden peas 17
garlic
  cream of garlic soup 54
glassware 186-7, *187*
globe artichoke 13
glue 192, *192*
goose 45
grains and cereals 30
greaseproof paper 196-7, *197*, 214

green beans 18
  beef and bean soup 59, *60*
  blanching 211
  green bean, mushroom and artichoke
    medley 116, *117*
  vegetable gado gado 112, *113*
greengages 24
green peas (whole, dried) 28
grey mullet 34
guinea fowl 45

H
haddock 36
  chunky chowder 58, *60*
hake 35
halibut 33
hare 44
hazelnuts 27
  hazelnut roast 102
hearts 46
heat equalizing 174
herbs, drying 213
herrings 35
hints 212-14
honey 213
  honey and sesame scones *161*, 162
horseradish and leek filling for baked
  potatoes *125*, 126
hot green salad 130
hot spots 193, *193*
Hungarian marrow 115, *117*

I
icecream, softening 213
interior lights 178, *178*

J
jams 214
  blackberry and apple purée 155, *157*
  plum and pear jam 156, *157*
  red cherry jam 158

K
key to symbols 50
kidney 46
  kidneys in cream sauce *85*, 87
  steak and kidney pudding 86
kidney beans
  chilli con carne 84, *85*
King prawns 37
kipper 35
kohlrabi 11
kombu 29

L
lamb 42-3
  best end of neck 42
  breast 43
  chump chops 43
  leg 43
  lemony lamb kebabs *88*, 90
  loin 43
  loin chops 42
  middle neck 42
  neck cutlets 42
  noisettes 43

riblets 42
scrag end of neck 43
shoulder 42
lasagne 31
  fish lasagne 75, *76*
lead crystal 187
leeks 12
  blanching 211
  leek and cauliflower cobbler 104, *105*
  leek and horseradish filling *125*, 126
  leek vinaigrette 64
  marinated tofu with vegetables 111,
    113
lemon sole 33
lemony lamb kebabs *88*, 90
lemony sea bass 80
lentils 28
  lentil and coconut pâté 62, *65*
  lentil and vegetable loaf *108*, 109
lettuce
  cream of lettuce soup 54, *57*
  hot green salad 130
linen 188, *188*
lining dishes 197, *197*
liquids 174
liver 46

M
macaroni 31
mackerel 36
magnetrons 181, *181*
main course dishes:
(1) fish and shellfish
  cod steaks Niçoise *81*, 83
  fish lasagne 75, *76*
  lemony sea bass 80
  moules marinière 72, *73*
  orange and parsley monkfish kebabs
    81, 82
  prawn and coconut curry 76, *77*
  salmon with tarragon sauce *73*, 74
  seafood paella *76*, 78
  sole véronique 71
  stuffed trout with fennel sauce 79, *81*
(2) meat, poultry and game
  bacon steaks with orange and raisin
    sauce *88*, 89
  chicken korma 95
  chilli con carne 84, *85*
  duck with cherry sauce 92, *93*
  kidneys in cream sauce *85*, 87
  lemony lamb kebabs *88*, 90
  roast chicken with redcurrants *93*, 94
  roast pheasant with port and lemon
    sauce *96*, 98
  steak and kidney pudding 86
  sweet and sour pork *88*, 91
  turkey tetrazzini *96*, 97
(3) vegetable dishes
  aubergine layer *108*, 110
  borlotti bean casserole 107, *108*
  creamy onion flan 114
  crunchy Chinese vegetables 99
  hazelnut roast 102
  leek and cauliflower cobbler 104,
    105

lentil and vegetable loaf *108*, 109
marinated tofu with vegetables 111,
  113
saffron rice with mangetout 106
spicy layered mango pilaff 103, *105*
stuffed cabbage leaves 100, *101*
stuffed tomatoes 101, *101*
vegetable gado gado 112, *113*
maintenance of microwave ovens
  184-5, *184-5*
mangetout 18
  crunchy Chinese vegetables 99
  saffron rice with mangetout 106
  vegetable gado gado 112, *113*
mango
  baked pears with mango sauce 134
  spicy layered mango pilaff 103, *105*
margarine, softening and melting 212
marinated beef tomatoes 122
marinated peppers 128
marinated tofu with vegetables 111, *113*
marrow 16
  Hungarian marrow 115, *117*
meat; checking cooked 175
melamine 192
memory controls *178*, 179-80
menu planning 171
metals 174, 183, 186, 192, *192*
microwave cooking
  factors affecting 193-5
  mechanics 182, *182*
  oven types 176-7, *176-7*
microwave ovens 167-211
  additional features 177-80, *178*, *180*
  choosing 176-80, *176-80*
  cleaning 184-5, *184-5*
  controls 177-80, *178-9*
  converting recipes for 168-9
  cooking for one 170-1
  cooking techniques 196-203,
    196-203
  equipment for 186-9, 191, *186-91*
  factors affecting cooking 192-5,
    193-5
  food that will work in 169-70
  foods that won't work in 170
  freezer and 204-11, *211*
  maintaining 184-5, *184-5*
  menu planning 171
  power levels 50, 193
  safety 172, 173, 174, 183, 185, 186,
    189, 192
  troubleshooting guide 172-5
  types 176-7, *176-7*
  working of 181-3, *181-2*
microwaves 181
millet 30
  millet pudding 139
minced beef 39
mixed fruit
  Christmas pudding *140*, 141
  fruit sauce 152, *153*
  mixed fruit compote *140*, 141
  tropical trifle 144, *145*
mixed vegetables
  aubergine layer *108*, 110

concentrated vegetable stock *148-9*, 151
crunchy Chinese vegetables 99
hot green salad 130
lentil and vegetable loaf *108*, 109
marinated tofu with vegetables 111, *113*
ratatouille *120*, 121
saffron rice with mangetout 106
spicy layered mango pilaff 103, *105*
tomato relish 155, *157*
vegetable gado gado 112, 113
monkfish 36
   orange and parsley monkfish kebabs *81*, 82
mooli (white radish)
   crunchy Chinese vegetables 99
   vegetable gado gado 112
moules marinière 72, *73*
mullet 34
mung beans 28
mushrooms 29
   green bean, mushroom and artichoke medley 116, *117*
   mushroom sauce 150
   mushrooms stuffed with garlic vegetables 61, *65*
   oriental mushroom soup 55, *57*
   stuffed cabbage leaves 100, *101*
mussels 37
   moules marinière 72, *73*
   seafood paella *76*, 78

N

napkins 187, 188, *188*, 197
nectarines 24
noisettes of lamb 43
nuts 27, 213

O

oats 30
   cheese and oat cob 160
   flapjacks *165*, 166
offal 46-7
okra 19
olives
   broccoli with olives and garlic 127, *129*
onions 13
   blanching 211
   cheese and potato layer 122
   creamy onion flan 114
   onion and cider soup 52, *53*
on/off switches *178*, 179
oranges
   baby beetroots with orange sauce *120*, 121
   fruit sauce 152, *153*
   orange and parsley monkfish kebabs *81*, 82
   orange cake *161*, 162
   peel, drying 212
   tropical trifle 144, *145*
oriental mushroom soup 55, *57*
overcooked foods 174-5
oxtail 47

P

paper 187-8, *187*
parsnips 21
   blanching 211
   cream of garlic soup 54
   creamy carrot and parsnip bake 127, *129*
   yellow split pea and parsnip soup 56
pasta 31
pastry 168, 169, 186, 203, 213
pâtés
   chicken liver 68, *69*
   lentil and coconut 62, *65*
peaches 24
   dried 26
   stuffed peaches in wine sauce *136*, 138
peanuts 27
   peanut and yogurt filling *125*, 126
   vegetable gado gado 112, *113*
pears 25
   baked pears with mango sauce 134
   blanching 211
   dried 26
   plum and pear jam 156, *157*
peas 17-18
   blanching 211
   saffron rice with mangetout 106
   vegetable gado gado 112, *113*
   yellow split pea and parsnip soup 56
peppers 15
   aubergine layer *108*, 110
   blanching 211
   marinated peppers 128
   ratatouille *120*, 121
   vegetable gado gado 112, *113*
petit pois 17
pheasant 45
   roast pheasant with port and lemon sauce *96*, 98
piercing 197, *197*
pilaffs
   spicy layered mango pilaff 103, *105*
pineapple
   crunchy Chinese vegetables 99
   sweet and sour pork *88*, 91
   tropical trifle 144, *145*
pinto beans
   barbecue-style baked potatoes 124, *125*
pitting 174, 186
plaice 32
plastic
   cling film 189, *189*
   containers 188-9, 191, *189-91*
plates, heating 172, 175
plums 24
   plum and banana crumble 132, *132*
   plum and pear jam 156, *157*
   sweet and sour sauce 148, *148-9*
pods and seeds 17-19
polenta 30
porcelain 186
pork 40-1
   bacon steaks 41
   blade 40

chops 40
fillet 41
fruity spare ribs 70
gammon 41
hand and spring 41
leg 41
loin 40
loin chops 40
sausages 41
spare rib 40
spare rib chops 40
sweet and sour pork *88*, 91
tenderloin 41
portable microwave ovens 176, *176*
potatoes 20
   aubergine layer *108*, 110
   barbecue-style baked potatoes 124, *125*
   cheese and potato layer 122
   cheese filling *125*, 126
   leek and horseradish filling *125*, 126
   peanut and yogurt filling *125*, 126
pot barley *see* barley
pottery containers 186, *186*
poultry 44-5
power outputs, comparative 50, 193
prawns 37
   crab and prawn cocktail 67, *69*
   prawn and coconut curry *76*, 77
preserves 155-6, *157*, 158
   apple and date chutney 156, *157*
   blackberry and apple purée 155, *157*
   plum and pear jam 156, *157*
   tomato relish 155, *157*
   red cherry jam 158
prunes 26
pulses 28
pumpkin 16

Q

quantity of food 195, *195*
quark
   chestnut cheesecake *136*; 137

R

rabbit 44
radishes, white *see* mooli
raisins
   apple and date chutney 156, *157*
   carob and raisin chiffon pie 135, *136*
   fruit sauce 152, *153*
ratatouille *120*, 121
ready-made-meals
   charts 209-10
rearranging food 199, *199*
recipe conversion for the microwave 168-9
red bream 36
red cabbage, braised 128, *129*
red cherry jam 158
redcurrants 24
   summer compote 133, *133*
red lentils 28
red mullet 34
reflection 182-3, *182*
reheating 171, 202, *202*

from frozen (charts) 208-9
relish, tomato 155, *157*
removable floors to microwave ovens 180
rhubarb 25
  blanching 211
rice
  hazelnut roast 102
  saffron rice with mangetout 106
  seafood paella *76*, 78
  spicy layered mango pilaff 103, *105*
roast chicken with redcurrants *93*, 94
roasting bags 188, *189*
roasting racks *190*, 191
roast pheasant with port and lemon sauce *96*, 98
roots and tubers 20-2
rotating 198, *198*
  antennae 180
round fish 34-6
runner beans 17
  runner beans with walnut sauce 119, *120*

S

safety 172, 173, 174, 183, 185, 186, 189, 192
saffron rice with mangetout 106
salads
  hot green salad 130
salmon 34
  salmon with tarragon sauce *73*, 74
salmon trout 35
salt 173
sardine 36
sauces
  blackberry and apple 155, *157*
  cheese 150
  chocolate or carob *153*, 154
  cornmeal custard *153*, 154
  fruit 152, *153*
  mushroom 150
  savoury brown *148-9*, 149
  spiced tomato and coconut 147, *148-9*
  sweet and sour 148, *148-9*
  white *148-9*, 150
sausages (pork) 41
savoury brown sauce *148-9*, 149
savoury scone roll *161*, 163
scallops 37
  seafood shells 66
scones
  honey and sesame *161*, 162
  savoury scone roll *161*, 163
seafood
  paella *76*, 78
  shells 66
seaweeds 29
seeds 27
  toasting 213
shapes of containers 192
shellfish 37
shielding 199-200, *199*
shitake (dried mushrooms) 29
  oriental mushroom soup 55, *57*
shoots 11-13

shrimp 37
silken tofu
  carob and raisin chiffon pie 135, *136*
size and shape of food 194-5, *194-5*
skate 33
smells, removal of 185, 212
soda bread 160
sole véronique 71
soups
  beef and bean 59, *60*
  borsch 56, *57*
  chestnut and tomato 51, *53*
  chunky chowder 58, *60*
  cream of garlic 54
  cream of lettuce 54, *57*
  onion and cider 52, *53*
  oriental mushroom 55, *57*
  yellow split pea and parsnip 56
spaghetti 31
sparking (arcing) 174, 183, 186, 192, 200
spiced cauliflower *117*, 118
spiced tomato and coconut sauce 147, *148-9*
spicy layered mango pilaff 103, *105*
spinach 10
  blanching 211
  spinach cream 119, *120*
split peas 28
squid 37
stacking rings 189, *190*, 202
stains, removing 184-5, *184-5*
standing time 168, 171, 175, 200
starters
  aubergine dip 64, *65*
  chicken liver pâté 68, *69*
  coriander ramekins 62, *65*
  crab and prawn cocktail 67, *69*
  fruity spare ribs 70
  hot green salad 130
  leek vinaigrette 64
  lentil and coconut pâté 62, *65*
  mushrooms stuffed with garlic vegetables 61, *65*
  seafood shells 66
  stuffed avocados 63
starting temperatures 193-4, *193*
steak (beef) 38
steak and kidney pudding 86
stirrer fan *181*
stirring 198, *198*
stock, concentrated
  meat 151
  vegetable *148-9*, 151
straw containers 188, *188*
string *189*
stuffed avocados 63
stuffed cabbage leaves 100, *101*
stuffed peaches in wine sauce *136*, 138
stuffed tomatoes 101, *101*
stuffed trout with fennel sauce 79, *81*
summer compote 133, *133*
swede 22
sweet and sour pork *88*, 91
sweet and sour sauce 148, *148-9*

sweetbreads 47
sweetcorn 19
  blanching 211
  chunky chowder 58, *60*
sweet potatoes 20
symbols: key 50

T

techniques of cooking 196-203, *196-203*
temperatures probes 175, *178*, 180
tenting 200-1, *200*
testing 201, 203, *203*
  containers 191
thawing *see* defrosting
thermometers, meat 175, 189
timing controls 177-8, *178*
tips 212-14
tofu
  marinated tofu with vegetables 111, *113*
tomatoes 14
  aubergine layer *108*, 110
  borlotti bean casserole 107, *108*
  braised fennel in tomato and apricot sauce 123
  chestnut and tomato soup 51, *53*
  chilli con carne 84, *85*
  marinated beef tomatoes 122
  ratatouille *120*, 121
  skinning 213
  spiced tomato and coconut sauce 147, *148-9*
  stuffed tomatoes 101, *101*
  tomato relish 155, *157*
tongue 47
tools and equipment 186-92, *186-91*
  testing 191
traditional sponge cake 164
transmission 182-3, *182*
tropical trifle 144, *145*
troubleshooting guide 172-5
trout 34
  fish lasagne 75, *76*
  stuffed trout with fennel sauce 79, *81*
turbot 32
turkey 45
  turkey tetrazzini *96*, 97
turning 198, *198*
turning over 199, *199*
turnips 21
  blanching 211
  crunchy Chinese vegetables 99
  marinated tofu with vegetables 111, *113*
turntables *178*, 180
two-level microwave ovens *176*, 177

U

utensils 186-92, *186-91*
  testing 191

V

variable power controls 179, *179*
veal 48
  best end neck cutlets 48
  escalopes 48

knuckle or shin 48
loin 48
loin chops 48
pie veal 48
vegetable accompaniments
baby beetroots with orange sauce 120, 121
barbecue-style baked potatoes 124, 125
braised fennel in tomato and apricot sauce 123
braised red cabbage 128, 129
broccoli with olives and garlic 127, 129
cheese and potato layer 122
cheese filling 125, 126
creamy carrot and parsnip bake 127, 129
hot green salad 130
Hungarian marrow 115, 117

leek and horseradish filling 125, 126
marinated beef tomatoes 122
marinated peppers 128
peanut and yogurt filling 125, 126
ratatouille 120, 121
runner beans with walnut sauce 119, 120
spinach cream 119, 120
spiced cauliflower 117, 118
vegetable cooking and health 173
vegetable gado gado 112, 113
vegetable stock, 148-9, 151
venison 45
vinaigrette, leek 64

W
wakame (dried seaweed) 29
wave guides 181
wave stirrers 181, 182
white fish

seafood paella 76, 78
white sauce 148-9, 150
whiting 36
fish lasagne 75, 76
wholewheat 30
bread 159
wine 214
mixed fruit compote 140, 141
stuffed peaches in wine sauce 136, 138
wire fasteners 192, 192
wooden utensils 188, 188
wrapping 197, 197

Y
yellow split pea and parsnip soup 56
yogurt
coriander ramekins 62, 65
yogurt and peanut filling for baked potatoes 125, 126

Acknowledgments

Dorling Kindersley would like to thank the staff who worked on the original title **Sarah Brown's Vegetarian Microwave Cookbook:** Carolyn Ryden, Felicity Jackson and Anita Ruddel.

Designer: Mick Keates
Editor: Mary Lambert

Photographer: Clive Streeter
Home economist: Linda Fraser
Stylist: Sue Russell
Illustrator: John Woodcock
Studio: Del & Co
Typesetter: Bournetype, Bournemouth
Reproduction: Colourscan, Singapore